GAY SIGNS

GAY
SIGNS

An Astrological Approach
to Homosexuality

J.E. Kneeland

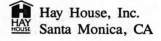
Hay House, Inc.
Santa Monica, CA

First Hay House edition published 1988.

ISBN 0-937611-31-X

Library of Congress Catalog No. 87-082492

10 9 8 7 6 5 4 3 2 1

To
Florence, who taught me the basics
of Astrology,
to
Christopher, who taught me further
by becoming my student,
and to
Warren, who encouraged me
to put what I knew on paper.

CONTENTS

FOREWORD

BY LOUISE L. HAY, D.D.

In the beginning of recorded history, the only science that was practiced was astrology. All the wise men (in those days) were astrologers. We remember the wise men who searched for the Christ Child were astrologers. They followed a star to find Jesus. In the present time, we have many other sciences and methods of exploring life; and still we read the stars to find our own personal meaning.

It seems to me that we all seek deeper understanding of ourselves, and of life. Where did we come from? Where are we going? Why are we here? Who are we? Why are we like we are? These are the questions so many ask. It is part of our spiritual challenge to seek out answers that will help us to change and to grow. *Gay Signs*, by J.E. Kneeland, assists us in opening our minds to another level. It touches an intuitive place within each of us, whether we are gay men, parents, lovers, siblings, or friends or associates.

For me, astrology is another way of describing the extraordinary process of life. I believe it to be an excellent tool to help us understand more about ourselves and why we choose certain experiences in different lifetimes. J. E. Kneeland has expressed here a great depth of astrological knowledge, and he shows a wonderful ability and style in sharing his understanding with us. *Gay Signs* is the first book to help the male homosexual of our culture to see a cosmic view of his life.

There are so many of us who are willing to go beyond stereotyped condemnations of homosexuals, but still we have wondered why there are gay people on this planet. What is their purpose? What have they come to fulfill? (We also can ask why are gay men so connected with the dread disease AIDS at this time, on this planet?) Questions few of us even begin to have the answers for. Yet we know that everything in this universe has to be in perfect Divine Right Order. There is a rhyme and a reason for everything and everyone, even if we do not yet understand. *Gay Signs* revealed to me insights I had not thought of before. I am certainly willing to consider Mr. Kneeland's concepts and ideas, and I hope you will also.

Astrology also confirms what I have long believed, that yes, we indeed do choose our parents, our sexuality, our time and place of birth, and of course our lessons for this incarnation. I have always felt that prejudice was a silly waste of time, for if you haven't been something in one lifetime, you will in another. We all get to experience every condition, and how we treat someone in this lifetime has a lot to do with how we will be treated in the next life.

I do not believe in good or bad, or right or wrong. There is only the experience of the moment, which just is. Whoever we are, wherever we are, whatever we are doing is perfect for us at this moment. It all contributes to our opportunities for our spiritual growth. All choices of sexuality are perfect. The soul has no sexuality and can choose before it enters the physical whatever is the best for this lifetime. So let us all feel safe and secure in our sexuality and rejoice in all our choices.

Some of us are young souls, and our experiences on the planet are like going to kindergarten, relatively easy and simple. Some of us are very old souls, and our experiences are like going to graduate school, much more difficult. Gay men are like graduate students; they have chosen some of the harder lessons of life. Yet we are all equipped to handle what we have chosen. Our biggest lesson is always love. To love ourselves first of all. Then to give and receive unconditional love in spite of what our parents or the neighbors may say or do. When we leave the planet each time, the only thing we take with us is our capacity to love.

In the past, unenlightened astrologers used to talk of good planets and bad planets, or malefic planets. Now we have come to realize that all planets and their configurations are but choices to help us with our growth. What used to be considered adversities are now considered, in Mr. Kneeland's thesis, challenges that we can work through. Our astrological chart is but a map of the choices we have made for this lifetime.

Gay Signs is surely to be a forerunner for future studies on this aspect of astrological knowledge and interpretation in years to come. This is a great book to increase our awareness. Bravo, Mr. Kneeland!

PREFACE

Gay Signs began as nothing more than idle curiosity. Being a Sagittarius, I tend to be eclectic in my interests, and having Virgo Rising, I tend to want to analyze everything. In the beginning, it did not matter whether I believed in astrology or not; it was merely a subject to be pursued in leisure moments, along with many other subjects—acquiring knowledge for its own sake.

In 1977, a friend taught me the basics of erecting horoscopes, and as I did more and more charts of friends and acquaintances, I began to accept that there was some validity to the subject. There were definite patterns in charts. I began to buy books on the subject and to read, searching for more detailed knowledge. As I did so, I began to wonder about how homosexuality would appear in an individual's chart. Few books touched upon the subject, and those that did treated it rather vaguely, and usually unsympathetically, as an abstraction.

I felt that, if there was indeed validity to astrology, there would have to be some consistent pattern in the charts of gays, because sexuality plays such an important part in their lives. I also felt that it had to appear as a perfectly normal process of the planets that would occur with regularity, involving aspects that would not necessarily be negative in nature.

I began to collect gay charts and to analyze them, keeping statistics on Sun signs, Rising signs, and placement of planets. By 1981, I had approximately sixty charts, and a distinct pattern had begun to emerge. It seemed to confirm the view of one book I had read—*Sex and the Outer Planets*, by Barbara H. Watters (Valhalla Paperbacks, Ltd., 1971). However, that work treated homosexuality as a sickness, and referred to the Uranus–Moon relationship as an "affliction."

My own research indicated that it resulted from any relationship between Uranus and the Moon, making no distinction between those that were considered "positive" and those that were considered "negative." If anything, the majority of charts involved positive relationships—conjunctions, sextiles, and trines.

I continued to collect charts and data, thinking, "Someday, when I have enough material, maybe I'll write a book on the subject." Writing is my profession, but most books I've done have been by assignment rather than choice. Occasionally, I would mention this to friends when the subject of astrology would come up. Several friends began to help me collect birth data. The most helpful in this regard was Ray Locke, who would give me information without telling me whether the individual was gay or not, until after the chart had been erected and interpretation done.

In 1986, Warren Bayless, editorial director of Hay House, suggested I finally put the book together. (I had casually mentioned the idea to him two years before.)

At first, I hesitated. I didn't think I had enough data. I didn't think my writing schedule would permit. I was a writer and editor, not a professional astrologer, so who would listen to me? Warren would not accept excuses. I had done his chart, as well as charts for a number of mutual friends, and he was impressed with the accuracy of my interpretations. He considered my lack of professional standing in astrology a moot point. I was a professional writer, and that, combined with my research, qualified me to do this book. So I agreed.

In looking over my collection of data, I realized I did indeed have a "random" sampling, however casually it might have been collected, and it was far larger than the minimum required for statistical analysis. Almost every age group over adolescence was included, along with the widest array of professions—writers, editors, accountants, real estate salesmen, stage actors, film actors, directors, models, construction workers, marketing analysts, secretaries, receptionists, artists, advertising executives, students, teachers, prison guards, hair stylists, pharmacists, policemen, servicemen, insurance salesmen, street hustlers, porno stars, photographers, landscape architects, athletes, doctors, lawyers, restaurant managers, waiters, cooks, bankers, mail room clerks, hotel managers, maintenance men, set designers, dancers, house painters, carpenters, computer programmers, musicians, and the chronically unemployed.

Also, the sampling was not limited to persons born in the United States, though they represented the largest segment. There were persons born in Canada, Mexico, England, France, Ireland, Germany, Russia, and Japan. However, there were only a few born in the southern hemisphere, and all were from South American countries. Racially, the sampling included whites, blacks, Hispanics, and orientals.

Because of the current concern about AIDS, especially for homosexuals and bisexuals, I felt it was important to cover the subject astrologically. I had a theory, but it was unconfirmed by actual data, for none of the sampling I had gathered included persons who had at the time been diagnosed with AIDS or ARC or even as seropositive.

I turned to Warren Bayless to help me acquire a sampling. I am grateful to him, to Louise Hay, to Ron Tillinghast, and the staff of Hay House and the Hay Foundation for helping me to acquire this information. I am especially grateful to those persons who had been diagnosed as being HIV positive or having AIDS or ARC who were willing to share their birth data with me. Their contribution to this research has been invaluable.

In order to complete this work in a timely fashion, the total sampling of gay charts for purposes of statistical analysis was cut off at 160, although more have been accumulated since. None of the theories presented here have been proved true with 100 percent accuracy, though all are supported by approximately 90 to 95 percent of the charts.

Some allowance for error must be granted, since all birth dates, times, and places have been given by the individuals without being supported by the author's research into official birth records. In several cases, the birth data originally given proved to be incorrect, and the individuals concerned provided the correct information later. The statistics were changed accordingly in those cases. There may still be some errors.

The full final statistical analysis could not have been completed without the invaluable assistance of Christopher Riccella, and I am extremely grateful to him for his help, concern, and encouragement.

In addition to Warren Bayless at Hay House, without whom *Gay Signs* might never have been written or published, I wish to express my deep thanks to Louise L. Hay for her encouragement and her generous offer to write the Foreword, to Denise Groce, associate editor, for her careful reading and editorial work on the manuscript, to Susan Sennett for her caring, and to Laura Wilson for her considerable effort in seeing the book through.

And finally, I wish to thank the 160 participants in the survey, those known to me and those unknown, some of whom may not even be aware they are a part of the statistics.

—J.E. Kneeland

GAY SIGNS

Introduction

ASTROLOGY AS AFFIRMATION
OF IDENTITY

An astrology book especially for gays?

Yes.

Astrology is much more than the horoscope in the newspaper that tells everyone of a certain sign—male or female, straight or gay, young or old—to expect the same kind of day. At its best, astrology is a highly individualized metaphysical science that helps in the struggle toward understanding Self and toward accepting life's purpose. It can be a means of affirming those special, distinctive characteristics that make one person different from all others—a part of nature, unique and beautiful, and worthy of love.

Like snowflakes, no two astrological charts are precisely the same. Even twins, born moments apart, have slight variations that make each an individual, marvelously different from all other living persons. Again, like snowflakes, there may be patterns that are similar, connecting some while distinguishing from others, and that adds to the beauty of the natural phenomenon.

There are astrological patterns that apply specifically to homosexual men, planetary relationships that are a part of nature's purpose and design. While every gay person is beautifully unique, many share characteristics or qualities that link them in spirit or life purpose. Many face the same—or similar—challenges.

This fact alone warrants an astrology book especially for gays.

Throughout history, society has attempted to repudiate homosexuality as unnatural and perverse, as if homosexuals were somehow less than human or chose to be different from heterosexuals. This book may do nothing to change society's attitude, but it is hoped that it may encourage homosexuals to refuse to accept that view, for they are truly a good and positive part of nature. They are themselves natural.

And all that is natural is beautiful.

Astrology can help to confirm this by giving a degree of objectivity to life's events and challenges, allowing the gay person to view the feelings, the problems, and the sometimes overwhelming negatives of his life in a more affirmative light. Nature, through the planetary aspects, does give the homosexual some unusual burdens and difficult relationships to deal with, but nature does not usually give more than an individual soul can handle.

Many astrologers divide the planets into benefics and malefics, good and evil. However, those astrologers miss a great deal of what the heavens have to offer. The distinction between good and bad is a superficial one. Ultimately, all planets and aspects are beneficial, resulting in spiritual growth, a part of the grand design of the universe. For example, the restrictions, the hardship, and the feelings of guilt attributed to the planet Saturn must exist for the sake of the much more important sense of achievement and personal reward received for effort expended. The lies and deception and insecurity of Neptune, not to mention the problems of drugs and alcohol, are necessary for that planet to give inspiration, creativity, and the fantasy of theater and film. The anger, the quarrelsomeness, and the hurtfulness of Mars must exist for the energy and force to act vigorously and decisively.

The lesson of astrology is that every "negative" has a positive, and the challenge for each individual's chart is to take what might appear to be problems and turn them to benefits. To some extent, our individual identities are defined by the stars, and the important events of our lives may be preordained or destined, but we do have some control over the way we accept our Selves and how we confront and build upon our fate.

Our objective in life is to grow spiritually. Each day, the planets give us choices, some of them more important than others. If we choose to fight what is given, to deny our individual destinies, we will feel continually thwarted and frustrated. If we choose to ignore our planetary configurations, we drift aimlessly, feeling lost. But if we choose to face our true natures, to accept what has been handed us by fate, we can proceed to recognize our life challenges, to cope with them actively, and to flow with the forces of nature toward a joyous spiritual affirmation, filled with limitless blessings.

It must be acknowledged that no astrology book can hope to cover each individual's unique identity or special life's challenge. That can be accomplished only by calculating and reading the individual chart. However, there are a great many characteristics and challenges that groups of people share.

There is one astrological factor that virtually all gay men have in common, and that is the nature of homosexuality itself. (However, as will be shown, the term "homosexual" is an inaccurate definition of the special nature of gays, just as the term "gay" is inadequate to express the specialness that distinguishes the spirits of this group of people.) A great many share other astrological characteristics, some generational, others based on planetary relationships that recur periodically with every generation. Finally, there are some qualities that almost all gays of a particular Sun sign or Rising sign will have in common.

The objective here is to provide guidance in understanding the spiritual challenges associated with being gay, utilizing astrology. Admittedly, there are problems with attempting to do this within the pages of a book. It is important to realize that all natives of a specific Sun sign are not completely alike. Some of what appears under your sign will apply to you, while other parts may not. In some ways, your Rising sign is even more important than your Sun sign. (It is dependent upon your time and place of birth.) To determine your Rising sign, or Ascendant, requires precise mathematical calculation, along with a book known as a "table of houses." * We will give a generalized method for you to approximate this, but we cannot be precise.

Each person participates in the life challenges of a number of signs, not just the Sun sign and Rising sign, because of specific placement of other planets, by sign as well as by "house." For this reason, it is helpful for one to read the descriptions of all of the signs, unless the details of the individual chart are known. The placements of the Moon, Mercury, and Venus are extremely important, and in gay charts, some of the slow-moving planets, such as Uranus, Pluto, and Neptune, are critical.

If the problems or life challenges of any sign seem to be ones you can identify with, it is quite likely that that sign is significant in some way in your chart. By reading with a selective and discerning eye, you may benefit by accepting only the passages that you feel you can relate to in some aspect of your life.

This cannot be an instructional book on how to construct and interpret horoscopes; but, in order to understand much of what follows, some basic terminology and concepts need to be explained.

TWELVE SIGNS/TWELVE HOUSES

Virtually everyone today knows the twelve signs of the Zodiac. For those who can't recall them all in order, they are Aries, Taurus, Gemini, Cancer, Leo, Virgo, Libra, Scorpio, Sagittarius, Capricorn, Aquarius, and Pisces. They do not

---

I use Dalton's Table of Houses, Macoy Publishing and Masonic Supply Company, Inc., copyright 1975.

correspond precisely to the twelve months of the year, which were developed to approximate the Moon's cycles, but the annual placement of the Sun. The four Cardinal signs of the Zodiac begin the seasons, starting with the Spring Equinox (Aries), proceeding to the Summer Solstice (Cancer), followed by the Autumn Equinox (Libra), and concluding with the Winter Solstice (Capricorn).

Much of the significance of the twelve signs is determined by what is happening to the Sun at the particular time. The two Equinoxes, which begin Aries and Libra, are the days that are divided equally between darkness and light. The Summer Solstice (Cancer) is the longest day of the year, and the Winter Solstice (Capricorn) is the shortest.

The twelve signs, each of which is made up of thirty degrees of a circle, also form Twelve Houses. In the basic horoscope, the order of the houses is synonymous with the signs, beginning with Aries. Each house governs a specific aspect of life. In the basic chart (not the individual or personal chart), the Twelve Houses are as follows:

- First House (Aries)—governs Self, appearance, personality; keynote, "I am."
- Second House (Taurus)—governs money, possessions, and values; keynote, "I have."
- Third House (Gemini)—governs mind, communication, short trips, brothers and sisters; keynote, "I think."
- Fourth House (Cancer)—governs home, mother (in a male chart, generally), real estate, and old age; keynote, "I feel."
- Fifth House (Leo)—governs children, romance, speculation, and entertainment; keynote, "I will."
- Sixth House (Virgo)—governs service, occupation, health, and small animals; keynote, "I analyze."
- Seventh House (Libra)—governs marriage, partnership, relations with other people in general, and obvious enemies; keynote, "I balance."

- Eighth House (Scorpio)—governs sex, inheritance, partnership or marriage finances, and death; keynote, "I desire."
- Ninth House (Sagittarius)—governs the abstract mind, higher mind, philosophy or religion, higher education, long distance travel, and publishing; keynote, "I see."
- Tenth House (Capricorn)—governs reputation and honor, profession, the father (in a male chart, generally), and public recognition; keynote, "I use."
- Eleventh House (Aquarius)—governs friendships, social groups and organizations, and hopes and dreams; keynote, "I know."
- Twelfth House (Pisces)—governs confinement, secret enemies, institutions, large animals, and self undoing; keynote, "I believe."

As can be seen by the keynote phrases for each sign/house, the order or progression of houses represents twelve stages of spiritual growth or evolution, beginning with physical awareness of existence and ending with abstract faith. The keynote phrases define the essence of the signs and houses in their simplest forms.

Unless one has Aries Rising, however, the individual or personal chart will not have these signs governing these houses. (Even some Aries Rising will have variations, because of what are called "intercepted" signs.) The house breakdown for your chart is dependent upon what your Ascendant, or Rising sign, is.

ASCENDANT/RISING SIGN

The Rising sign is that sign that appears on the eastern horizon at the time of birth. In the individual chart, that sign governs the First House, and the signs that follow govern the houses that follow (with the exception of charts having intercepted signs; a great many gay charts do have interceptions).

For full benefit from the material that follows, it is important that the reader knows his Rising sign. If you have had your chart done and are aware of your Ascendant, you will not need to follow the suggestions for determining it, which are imprecise and risky, at best. (Following them will not always produce the Ascendant. Precise determination depends upon latitude and longitude, the season of the year, and whether standard time was in effect at birth.)

If you do not know what time you were born, attempt to find out. In recent years, most states require the time of birth on birth certificates. If this does not give you the information, ask family members. (Mothers are generally not very precise, however, because most were too busy to look at the clock.) Once you have the time, make use of one of the two simplified techniques that appear in Chapter 3 (see pages 36 and 39) for approximating your Ascendant.

If, when you read the description of that sign, you do not identify, try reading the sign preceding or following. In the individual chart, the houses (or pie slices) are rarely exactly thirty degrees each. You will recognize your Ascendant when you read it. The Rising sign is usually more accurate a definition of Self than the Sun sign is.

QUALITIES/ELEMENTS

The signs of the Zodiac are further defined by three qualities and four elements. Each sign has its own special combination of quality and elements. The three qualities are Cardinal, Fixed, and Mutable. The four Cardinal signs are those that represent the change of seasons—Aries, Cancer, Libra, and Capricorn. Natives of these signs are characterized by drive, initiative, a need to move and change things. Sometimes, however, they lack staying power. The Fixed signs are those that follow the Cardinals—Taurus, Leo, Scorpio, and Aquarius. They occur at the peak of the four seasons, when they are "fixed." Those born in these signs are stubborn, persistent, resistant to change; they also have considerable personal charm and are very resourceful. The last four are the Mutable signs—Gemini, Virgo, Sagittarius, and Pisces— occurring as the seasons are on the wane, subject to "change." Those born under these signs are flexible, changeable, and adaptable; they are often thought to be "wishy-washy," but this quality tends to permit them always to learn and to grow, remaining young in mind and spirit.

The four elements are Fire, Earth, Air, and Water. The Fire signs—Aries, Leo, and Sagittarius—are generally energetic, enthusiastic, and optimistic. The Earth signs—Taurus, Virgo, and Capricorn—are practical, cautious, and sensual. The Air signs—Gemini, Libra, and Aquarius—are communicative, imaginative, and intellectual. The Water signs— Cancer, Scorpio, and Pisces—are sensitive, emotional, and "fluid."

Combining qualities and elements, the nature of the twelve signs work out as follows:

- Cardinal Fire—Aries
- Fixed Earth—Taurus
- Mutable Air—Gemini
- Cardinal Water—Cancer
- Fixed Fire—Leo
- Mutable Earth—Virgo
- Cardinal Air—Libra
- Fixed Water—Scorpio
- Mutable Fire—Sagittarius
- Cardinal Earth—Capricorn
- Fixed Air—Aquarius
- Mutable Water—Pisces

From this, it can be seen that the nature of the signs has been derived more from tangible qualities on earth than from clusters of stars in the heavens. At least a part of the significance of signs comes from the seasonal changes of the year, and another part from what was considered in ancient times to be the four basic elements of life.

RULERSHIP

Each of the twelve signs of the Zodiac have been assigned a planetary ruler. And this, in turn, means that each of the Twelve Houses have rulers. The planet that rules the Ascendant and the planet that rules the Sun in an individual chart have a great deal of significance. (There is also a chart ruler, the planet nearest the Midheaven to the west, but that must be determined through delineation of an individual horoscope.) The movement of the rulers of Ascendant and Sun sign, and the aspects they make, are influential in both actions and reactions to events.

The rulers of the twelve signs are as follows:

- Aries—Mars
- Taurus—Venus
- Gemini—Mercury
- Cancer—Moon
- Leo—Sun
- Virgo—Mercury
- Libra—Venus
- Scorpio—Pluto
- Sagittarius—Jupiter
- Capricorn—Saturn
- Aquarius—Uranus
- Pisces—Neptune

Most of these planets are named for gods of ancient Greece and Rome. Their "rulership" of signs in the heavens cannot be accepted literally, but their mythology can tell us much about ourselves through the symbolism they offer to their signs. As the god of war, Mars contributes action, rashness, force, and vigor to the native of Aries. Venus, the god-

dess of beauty and the arts, as well as of nature, strongly influences Taurus and Libra toward peace and harmony. Mercury, the fleet-footed messenger, causes Gemini and Virgo to
concentrate on communication and service. Jupiter, god of
wisdom, makes Sagittarius generous and expansive and outgoing. Saturn, the timekeeper, the gatekeeper, makes
Capricorn very concerned with time and with management of
the material world. Pluto, god of the underworld, makes Scorpio rather private and greatly concerned with sex and death.
Uranus, watcher over heaven, causes Aquarius to be high-
minded, inventive, and freedom loving. Neptune, god of the
sea, contributes a quiet, placid nature to Pisces, while making
him creative and inspirational.

●   ●   ●

The various forces at work within a particular astrological
sign have a purpose, both physical and spiritual. At times,
they may seem to create problems or conflicts, but they also
strive toward resolution and spiritual growth. It is not expected that the reader will accept a mystical belief that stars
billions of miles away forming a configuration that may or
may not resemble an earthly form, or planets circling the Sun
like the earth does, could be guiding or controlling the mil-
lions of humans walking the earth. It is what they have been
made to represent as facets of a universal spirit or consciousness that has significance, and that can aid us toward understanding and affirming ourselves.

PART I

WHAT MAKES A
SIGN GAY?

Chapter 1

THE GAY RULER—URANUS

Gay astrological charts are as distinctive and as diverse as heterosexual charts, but there is one factor that distinguishes them from almost all others—a relationship between the planet Uranus and the Moon. For the average reader, accustomed only to a knowledge of Sun signs, this concept may seem rather formidable at first. However, an understanding of Uranus and its influence on the Zodiac is essential to the special spiritual challenges of homosexuals.

Astrology has its origins in a number of divergent ancient civilizations, and it has changed and developed over the centuries. As currently practiced in the western world, it utilizes symbols from Greek and Roman mythology to convey its deeper meanings.

MYTHOLOGY

Although Uranus was not discovered until March 13, 1781, the choice for its name was highly significant. Uranus (or Ouranos) was the progenitor for all of the Greek and Roman gods. He symbolized Heaven, and he mated with Gaea, the Earth, to produce first a number of hundred-handed monsters, then the Cyclops, and finally the Titans. Uranus hated his children, who were tied to the earth, so Mother Earth appealed to her children to destroy their father. Only one—Saturn (or Cronus)—responded. Saturn castrated his father and took his place as the supreme god, later to be displaced by one of his own sons—Jupiter (or Zeus).

Each of these first three omnipotent gods have planets named for them, and each rules an astrological sign. Uranus rules Aquarius; Saturn rules Capricorn; and Jupiter rules Sagittarius. Two of the brothers of Jupiter have application to astrology as well—Neptune (or Poseidon), which rules Pisces, and Pluto, which rules Scorpio. Three of Jupiter's children are involved in astrology, each having a different mother. Mercury (or Hermes) rules both Virgo and Gemini; Venus (or Aphrodite) rules both Libra and Taurus; and Mars (or Ares) rules Aries.

The other two signs of the Zodiac—Leo and Cancer—are ruled not by planets, but by the luminaries—the Sun and the Moon, respectively. (However, the two do appear in mythology as two of the Titans—the Sun being Helios, and the Moon being Selene, or Luna.)

As strange as it may seem, the mythological symbolism of the planets applies quite accurately to the astrological signs they rule. In this age of space exploration, we have been able to see photographs of distant heavenly bodies in great detail, and we have learned about the physical nature of the planets. To apply human qualities to them, however godlike in nature, would appear to be naive.

But the qualities of the ancient Greek and Roman gods, and the relationships among them, continue to apply to individual horoscopes.

For gays, the nature of Uranus and its relationship to each of the other planets and signs is extremely important.

THE NATURE OF URANUS

In astrology, all of the planets and the luminaries have both positive and negative attributes. Uranus is no exception. As the planet of freedom, it is also the representative of insecurity and even trauma. It signifies the higher mental powers that result in scientific advancements such as electricity and electronics, but because genius is erratic it causes disruption and upheaval. Indeed, Uranus, the original god of Heaven, fathered monstrous creatures as well as gods, and he caused earthquakes, extreme weather such as tornados and hurricanes and electrical storms. Yet he, in combination with the Earth, produced the entire pantheon of gods and humanity itself.

His son Saturn castrated him, making him impotent, yet his influence continued to be felt. Without Uranus, we would have no knowledge, genius, invention, truth, humor, creativity, revelation, insight, or science. Astrology itself would not exist. To possess those positive attributes we value so highly, we must also accept and understand what we consider negative attributes—crime, war, violence, chaos, explosions, and the upheaval of nature.

We must also accept homosexuality and bisexuality, for Uranus rules that as well. Though many may consider this to be one of its negative attributes, the genius, brilliance, and creativity of homosexuals throughout history tends to contradict this.

THE INFLUENCE OF URANUS

Because it is one of the outer, slower moving planets, the influence of Uranus is generally considered (by most astrologers) to be primarily on society as a whole rather than on individuals, for an entire generation may have Uranus in the same sign. However, research indicates it also influences the individual strongly through its specific house placement in charts and through aspects made to it by the faster moving planets, such as Mars, Venus, Mercury, and the Moon and Sun.

It is its relationship to the other heavy, slow-moving planets—Pluto, Neptune, Jupiter, and Saturn—that creates the generational social trends.

Most of these relationships would be too technical, even

tedious for detailing here. But one is crucial to the gay astrological chart—that of Uranus and the Moon.

In the survey taken of 160 homosexual and bisexual men, more than ninety percent had aspects of the Moon to Uranus. In virtually all of 160 charts of purely heterosexual men, there was no relationship between the placement of Uranus and the Moon whatsoever. The only exceptions were the charts of heterosexuals closely linked to homosexuals and the charts of heterosexuals who were actors or comedians. (The exceptions in both cases were roughly ten percent of the poll.)

For those not versed in the details of astrology, it may be necessary to explain what an "aspect" is. The astrological chart is formed in a circle surrounding the earth, that circle being the path followed by the Sun, Moon, and planets, as they pass through twelve configurations of stars that comprise the astrological signs—Aries, Taurus, Gemini, Cancer, Leo, Virgo, Libra, Scorpio, Sagittarius, Capricorn, Aquarius, and Pisces.

Mathematically, the circle is divided into 360 degrees, with thirty degrees allocated to each sign. Two planets are considered to aspect when they appear approximately in the same degree in the same or two different signs. These "aspects" are conjunction, semi-sextile, sextile, square, trine, quincunx, and opposition, and a variable of five degrees is allowed in calculating the aspects.

Two planets are in conjunction when they appear within five degrees of each other in the same sign. They are semi-sextile when they are placed similarly in adjacent signs (or thirty degrees apart), and they are sextile when they are approximately sixty degrees apart. All three of these aspects, along with the trine, which is 120 degrees apart, are considered harmonious relationships.

The square, which is a separation of ninety degrees, the quincunx, which is 150 degrees, and the opposition, which is 180 degrees, are considered to be stressful or difficult.

Any of these aspects, whether harmonious or stressful, when they occur between Uranus and the Moon, appear to result in homosexuality or bisexuality. The aspects that appeared most frequently in the charts of the 160 gay men polled were the sextile (representing just over nineteen percent) and the trine (just over eighteen percent), both harmonious aspects. Fewer than four percent had the least favorable relationship—that of the opposition between Uranus and the Moon.

The quincunx, which is not entirely unfavorable, but tends to focus the relationship in an unusual way, was the third most frequent—appearing in over fourteen percent of the charts. The most favorable, the conjunction, occurred in just under nine percent of the charts, while the semi-sextile and the square were represented in just over ten percent each.

WHY URANUS AND THE MOON?

Although there are a number of other planetary relationships that occurred frequently in the 160 charts analyzed, the connection between Uranus and the Moon was the one factor that linked almost all of them together. This applied, no matter what the age of the subject was; the oldest was born in 1915, and the youngest in 1970. Since Uranus and the Moon are in aspect approximately one-third of the time, it was interesting to note that this related very closely to the incidence of male homosexuality in society generally.

Why should a relationship between Uranus and the Moon be a significator of homosexuality? Neither is considered to be a "sexual" planet. In human or personal terms, Uranus is primarily mental or intellectual, while the Moon is concerned with the emotions.

This tends to imply that "homosexuality" is not so much a "sexual aberration" as was once considered as it is a mental and emotional relationship that finds outlet or expression through sex—a spiritual rather than a physical challenge.

Uranus frees the emotional nature from conventional responses, and the Moon nourishes the mind (sometimes clouding it as well) through feelings. Perception and conception function together to produce creativity. This facet of the relationship between mind and soul does not automatically find physical outlet through gay sex, however. It is another of the Moon's functions that makes homosexuality not a choice but a necessity in most cases.

In astrology, as in most mythologies, the Moon represents the Mother, Eve, the female sexual and reproductive system. It is fecundity, or fertility, the instinctive urge to create new life through the planting of seeds. In heterosexual charts, Uranus does not interfere with this instinctive urge; there is no other alternative for creativity and productivity, because the primal god of the heavens functions independently of the emotional nature.

In gay charts, Uranus both links the homosexual male to the emotional nature of the mother and frees him from her. The creative urge becomes mental and spiritual in nature, disassociated from the urge for reproduction. Sexuality, the need for physical expression, is something quite separate. The nature of sexuality, however, varies in homosexual charts—in some becoming an expression of pure, platonic love or spiritual love; in others a means of defining ego; and in some a purely physical release.

THE CHALLENGE OF URANUS-MOON

The connection between Uranus and the Moon should not be looked upon as a negative aspect. Although bisexuals may have a degree of choice in the selection of sexual partnership, those who are strictly gay are given no alternatives. The negatives associated with homosexuality come from a narrow-minded segment of society that fears what it cannot understand.

The Uranus-Moon connection is a special challenge that God, or the Life Force, gives to gays. It is not a physical challenge, but a spiritual one. It is a challenge to understand and to accept love in its purest and deepest form.

There are several levels to the lessons of Uranus and the Moon. The first, and the most basic, is to learn acceptance of Self. Being gay is nothing to be ashamed of. Gay is good because it comes from God, and that Cosmic Force does not create anything that is ugly or sordid. Man does that.

When one accepts himself as beautiful, his challenge then is to love himself—to see the beauty within that transcends the physical and to appreciate it without reservation. This is possibly the most difficult stage of the gay challenge, for gays tend to feel an emptiness within, a lack that stems from society's disapproval (and therefore also the family's disapproval) or from the disassociation with the instinct for physical reproduction.

Inevitably there is an inclination to attempt to fill this feeling of emptiness from external sources. Most often, gays attempt to find partners who will supply what they see as a lack in themselves. Until they are able to perceive that there is truly nothing lacking; however, this search for love is usually frustrated by a series of unsuccessful relationships. Frustration drives many gays to other means of filling the emptiness. But alcohol, drugs, and fantasies are ultimately defeating.

All that is truly lacking at this stage of the gay challenge is love of Self. A full appreciation of one's own inner beauty is the only thing that can fill the sense of emptiness. And only after that emptiness is filled with self-love can the gay fully love another gay, sharing spiritually as well as physically.

The lesson that Uranus must give to the emotional Moon is that freedom and respect are essential to gay love. The natural enemy of Uranus is his son Saturn, who wishes to restrict him and to render him impotent. Love cannot be restrictive; it cannot be taken forcefully or imposed upon another; it must be freely given as something one possesses securely within himself. It is the love that one possesses; never the lover.

It is first and foremost a love of the spirit, the soul; and the physical is merely an expression of what is shared. Ultimately, in the greater design of the heavens, the sex of homosexuality is transitory, producing no physical children. It is the love of the soul and the spirit that produces, by freeing the lovers to create in other ways.

URANUS AND THE MOTHER

Naturally, some will argue that this is a simplistic view of homosexuality, that it cannot be the interaction of planets in the heavens that creates gays. There are physical, scientific explanations that are more rational and reasonable, and therefore more credible. Astrology is not intended to compete or to contradict these explanations, but rather to reinforce them on a metaphysical level, shedding additional light that the strict scholarship of science might exclude.

There is one factor in the relationship of Uranus and the Moon that might be considered negative. Since the Moon represents the Mother, as well as the emotional nature, and since Uranus represents disruption, upheaval, and violence, as well as freedom and creativity, there is some indication that homosexuality is related to emotional disturbances inflicted upon the mother during pregnancy.

In the poll taken of homosexual charts, those subjects who were aware of conditions of their mothers' pregnancies confirmed that there were disruptive influences. In some cases there was physical abuse; in others extreme fear or trauma.

Recent scientific studies have been moving toward this view, indicating that hormonal changes occur as a result of physical difficulties. One such study involved mothers who were pregnant during the blitz in London; the results indicated a higher than average number of homosexual males born to these women who were upset by the wartime shelling and destruction.

Yet even this negative view of the causes of homosexuality has its positive side. It was this generation, borne of war, that initiated the major move toward attempting to end the horrors of war for all time, seeking peace and love.

Indeed, Uranus rules some aspects of war, but it also rules civilization, directing science, creativity, and the higher mind toward a better world.

Chapter 2

LOVE AND SEX—VENUS, MARS, AND PLUTO

The challenge of sexuality for gays is almost as important as the challenge of love. Indeed, sexuality for both homosexuals and heterosexuals has become a special concern today, with the development and spread of AIDS and other new sexually transmitted diseases. But once deep love has been accepted, the challenge of sex becomes easier; it may, in fact, take care of itself, for the two are inextricably intertwined.

For heterosexuals, the astrological significators of sex are Venus, Mars, and Pluto, and the sexual nature of the individual is determined by relationships between these three planets. While all three do play a part in determining the sexual nature of homosexuals, the patterns seem to be different, though not as clear-cut as the Uranus-Moon relationship.

PLUTO

The sexual nature of the individual is ruled by the planet Pluto. In mythology, Pluto ruled the underworld, or death, as well as wealth and precious metals. All things hidden or subconscious fall within his sphere—including the unconscious urge for physical reproduction and sexual gratification. Sex connected with Pluto is pure lust, unrelated to love, however. Passion is his domain, the pure physical need for release.

Because the planet Pluto moves so slowly, it is represented in only three signs—Leo, Cancer, and Virgo—in the charts of those surveyed. In the years since 1970, it has passed through Libra and into the sign it rules, Scorpio. Naturally, the nature of the signs has applied both to heterosexuals and homosexuals.

However, the house placement of Pluto in gay charts has shown a marked preference for the Ninth, the house of Higher Mind, of philosophy, higher education, publishing, and long distance travel. Almost twelve percent of gay charts have Pluto placed here, strongly influencing the Midheaven, and therefore acting as ruler of the entire chart. Just over eleven percent have it in the Twelfth of secrecy, self-undoing, and spiritual regeneration, and a similar number have it in the Seventh House of partnership and marriage.

In astrology, Pluto rules far more than sex. However, when it relates to either Mars or Venus, it connects pure lust to the nature of love.

VENUS AND MARS

In a very high percentage of gay charts, Venus, Mars, and Pluto do not seem to relate to each other. Venus and Mars are relatively fast moving planets, and they aspect each other—as well as the other planets—quite frequently, but in 63 percent of the charts of homosexuals and bisexuals polled, Mars (representing the masculine principle) and Venus (representing the feminine principle) do not aspect each other at all. In fact, most of those who did have the planets in aspect were those who considered themselves bisexual. The only exception was in the category of Venus conjunct Mars (positioned within five degrees of each other), the connection that is often referred to as the "Charlie Chaplin aspect,"* which

---

Throughout his life, Charlie Chaplin was noted for his romantic prowess with younger women. In the 1940s, this included a paternity suit which made the headlines.

represents a large sexual appetite, from earliest years until the end of life.

Even this connection (which occurs approximately once a year) showed up in only eight percent of the gay charts.

In Greek and Roman mythology, Venus represents Love and Beauty. Although the Moon represents the mothering or reproductive side of women in astrology, Venus is the pure feminine principle—the representative of female as lover and beloved. This does not mean that she applies only to female charts; Venus represents divine love—and even illicit delights—for males and females, heterosexuals and homosexuals. She is pleasure and harmony, expression and sensuality in all forms.

Mars is representative of the masculine principle; it is energy, force, and drive, for males and females, for heterosexuals and homosexuals. It is as active as Venus is peaceful and passive, and it can be violent, hurtful, combative, and destructive.

Sexual gratification is achieved through the relationship of the two planets—aided by a link to Pluto—with each opposing force affecting the other and modifying it. Some charts that do not have a link between Venus and Mars are aided by one or the other in aspect to Pluto. Two-thirds of all charts should have Venus and Mars aspecting. Approximately seventy-five to eighty percent of all charts should have a link between at least two of the three planets.

It is for this reason that significance must be attached to the fact that Venus and Mars do not aspect in 63 percent of the cases, Venus and Pluto do not aspect in 60 percent, and Mars and Pluto do not aspect in 65 percent. And a great many of the cases where aspects do occur are cases of bisexuality.

THE VENUS-MARS-PLUTO CHALLENGE

What this suggests for gays is a second major challenge. The feminine Love does not connect to the masculine energy, making the balance between the two difficult and causing considerable insecurity in love relationships. Lust and love seem to be two separate and unrelated urges, no matter how hard the individual attempts to bring them together.

The result may be a continuing frustration as the gay moves from one unsuccessful relationship to another, always seeking the person who can fulfill his desires and needs. The challenge of Venus, Mars, and Pluto not connecting is to realize that no one can fulfill his desires and needs except himself. The search for perfect love must begin with the Self. Perfection exists only in the beauty of one's imperfections.

The disparate strains of Venus (harmony, contentment, and beauty), Mars (energy, sexual dominance, and forcefulness), and Pluto (lustfulness, desire for release) must be understood and accepted as good and positive attributes within the Self. They can be—and often are—united by some other force within the person. The love expression that results is no less beautiful and perfect than heterosexual love.

Astrologically, the forces that facilitate the unity and expression of homosexual love are frequently supplied by other planets. The two that seem to occur most often are Saturn and Neptune.

THE SATURN CONNECTION

In virtually all of the 160 gay charts analyzed, Saturn was in aspect either to Venus or Mars, or to both. The one aspect that occurred most frequently—in over fifteen percent of the cases—was Venus quincunx Saturn (150 degrees apart), a relationship that is generally considered to focus the energies of one planet or the other in a special or unusual direction. Almost the same percentage, however, had Mars semi-sextile Saturn (thirty degrees apart), a relationship that is similar to the quincunx but with a greater combining of energies.

The least common aspect for both Mars and Venus with Saturn in gay charts was the conjunction, alignment in the same degrees of the same sign, the aspect that would combine the energies most strongly.

In the case of Saturn, however, this is not necessarily a bad thing.

It should be remembered that Saturn (or Cronos) was one of the Titans, the one who deposed and castrated his father Uranus, only later to be deposed by his son Jupiter (or Zeus). The original function of Saturn in the earthly domain was to serve as the keeper of Time. He meted out both rewards and punishment with strictness and severity, demanding a careful accounting for time and effort.

Astrologically, Saturn serves those functions and more. He governs both responsibility and guilt; he both restricts and repays; he is concerned with age or aging and with the past. Saturn also categorizes, puts things in pigeon-holes. Saturn is the teacher, as well as the administrator.

Saturn Aspecting Venus

Saturn aspecting Venus tends to look upon love as a reward, as something one deserves or earns. As such, there may be a great concern with responsibility or with guilt. There is an inclination for the person with this aspect to associate love with feelings of guilt; but it is important to accept this as a challenge toward responsibility, the positive side of Saturn's nature.

Responsibility in love is always important, but it is particularly important in gay love. Maintaining a balance between selflessness and selfishness is a part of Saturn's call for responsibility to achieve security in love, a sense of equality and fairness between partners.

Saturn is considered a karmic planet, and the aspects he creates in an individual chart indicate areas in which lessons must be learned. Saturn in aspect to Venus is meant to teach love, and he generally does this in stages. Often, in youth, love is confused with physical beauty, for Venus does not see the difference, so concerned is she with appearance and material goods. But Saturn is age and endurance, and he will exact retribution if an individual fails to accept his lessons.

The bloom of youth passes too swiftly, and the physical beauty associated with it will inevitably change, perhaps even fade away completely. Most gays are aware of this, and they fear it, doing everything possible to maintain the appearance of youth. Eventually Saturn teaches them that this physical appearance is not essential to love, but all too often it is a hard lesson. Saturn's retribution may be loneliness and bitterness, if love remains dependent upon superficial qualities.

Another facet of Saturn's challenge is for the gay to avoid segmenting or compartmentalizing love. Of course, most people do tend to divide love into categories—friendship, love of parents, love of children, platonic love, sexual love. However, the person who has Saturn aspecting Venus tends to carry that categorization further, dividing the love of partners into spiritual and sexual love, increasing the tendency toward promiscuity.

Saturn asks that the person look beneath the physical beauty for the spiritual beauty and see sex as an expression of the deepest love of two souls in union, giving and accepting on an equal basis, each seeking to appreciate the beauty and the flaws of a separate and unique individual.

Saturn Aspecting Mars

Saturn aspecting Mars may be somewhat more difficult than Saturn aspecting Venus, but it does not present an insurmountable challenge. Saturn tends to restrict the masculine principle within the gay man, causing one to withhold his energy and forcefulness—or even to turn it destructively on himself.

But Saturn will give great rewards if his challenge to Mars is met. The masculine energy that exists within the gay man, if turned outward creatively, can produce phenomenally. Saturn builds and structures, and its uniting with Mars' forcefulness and strength can be a positive relationship.

The most frequently occurring connection between Mars and Saturn in gay charts is the semi-sextile, the closest possible after the conjunction, indicating that the results of effort expended can be rather swift and noticeable.

In loving, sexual relationships, Saturn will repay for energy and strength devoted to a partner. The sharing of strength between two men is a part of what homosexuality is all about. It more than doubles what one man alone can accomplish, especially when done with genuine love and acceptance. (Interestingly, partnership in astrology is represented by the sign Libra, the sign in which Saturn is exalted and Mars is in its detriment.)

THE NEPTUNE CONNECTION

Neptune Aspecting Venus

Neptune aspecting Venus challenges the gay native to understand the depth and scope of spiritual love and to direct it positively.

In mythology, Neptune was the god of the seas, son of Saturn and brother of Jupiter. Astrologically, he rules all things that are without boundaries or form. In addition to water and liquids, Neptune is concerned with things spiritual, with imagination, with fantasy and creativity. He rules film, music, photography, and abstract art, as well.

In a very high percentage of the gay charts analyzed, Neptune aspected either Venus or Mars or both (only a few less than Saturn aspected). In almost 57 percent of the charts, Neptune related to Venus, while in 54 percent it aspected Mars.

In aspect to Venus, Neptune becomes especially concerned with art and creativity. However, it may also become preoccupied with fantasies of love and sex, or even pornography, and it may involve alcohol or drugs. In love relationships, Neptune can cause jealousy, possessiveness, and deception.

The challenge of Neptune and Venus should become automatically clear—to direct the energies of Venus' love toward Neptune's spiritual side, thereby defeating the planet's negative or destructive tendencies. Neptune challenges the individual to have faith in love and trust in the lover, allowing the union of spirits to free both to live more creatively. The love of each is meant to inspire the other, both within the relationship and in the outside world.

Neptune Aspecting Mars

Neptune aspecting Mars can be a very troublesome connection, and its challenge is a serious one. It is this relationship that lures gays out to the bars every night. Neptune's alcohol and drugs, seeking evenings of fantasy and pleasure, can weaken the energy of Mars; Neptune's enticement to promiscuity can then make way for infections and sexual ailments, sapping Martian strength.

The challenge of Neptune relating to Mars is to perceive inner strength, so that the fantasy life, the escape from reality into an alcohol or drug induced dream world is unnecessary. Each person, whether heterosexual or homosexual, has the strength and energy of Mars to rely on. Being gay does not mean that one is not a man, even though Neptune may attempt to cloud that perception within.

THE CHALLENGE OF THE NEPTUNE-PLUTO ERA

Since shortly after World War II, the two slowest moving planets in the Zodiac—Neptune and Pluto—have been in sextile aspect with each other, even though they have each moved through three signs. The effect of this relationship has been a sexual revolution, with both positive and negative results for gays.

Neptune led the way as it passed through Libra, the natural sign of partnership and marriage, with Pluto following from Leo, the sign of entertainment, pleasure, and risk taking. Gradually, Neptune began to dissolve the old boundaries of marriage and close relationships. Neptune utilized all of its tangible assets—film, alcohol, drugs, mobility, art, music, fantasy, and imagination—to achieve its ends in the sign of deep love. Its intangible attributes—spirituality and creativity—were held back, as personal ethics and morality became confused.

It was aided by Pluto, keeping pace stealthily from sixty degrees back in Leo. Pluto is not only the planet of sexuality and the subconscious; wherever it passes, it destroys and rebuilds on a newer—and presumably better—basis. It began to contribute its qualities to those of Neptune, the two working in unison toward common goals. Placed in Leo, it started tearing down old concepts of entertainment and pleasure and creativity. Movies, theater, art, and music changed drastically, as sexuality and eroticism became an integral part of leisure time escape.

Late in the 1950s, the two planets changed signs, signaling a new phase of their common undertaking. Neptune moved into Scorpio, the sign ruled by its partner Pluto. The interaction between the two became even more pointed. In Scorpio, the house of sexuality, the subconscious, partnership finances, legacies from the past, and death, Neptune's tendency to dissolve boundaries became extreme, especially in the early 1960s, after becoming fully established in the new sign.

The mass media was proclaiming it the era of the sexual revolution, unaware that other facets of Neptune were quietly at work. The planet's rule of infection and viruses became directed toward sexual diseases, spread by the breakdown of restrictions on sexual promiscuity and aided by increased use of Neptunian drugs and alcohol.

Simultaneously, Pluto was establishing itself in the sign of Virgo, the natural sign of health, medicine, clothing, food, work, and service to humanity, preparing to destory old definitions of these factors and to establish new ones. In the beginning, its work was hidden, secretive. Working closely with Neptune in Pluto's sign, it contributed chemical additives to food and to clothing, pollution to the air in general and especially to the workplace through recirculated air conditioning. And all of this, combined with the increased sexual promiscuity, affected the health of human beings.

During 1971, the third phase of the partnership between Neptune and Pluto began, as Neptune moved into Sagittarius and Pluto into Libra. In the natural sign of philosophy, higher knowledge, growth, expansion, and long-distance travel, Neptune broke down more boundaries, spreading its influence. "Consciousness expanding" drugs were given intellectual sanction; religious boundaries were dissolved as people returned to more primitive beliefs in search of meaning; and old forms of higher education were forsaken for new ones.

Pluto began to assume greater importance in the interplay as it moved to the point in Libra that Neptune occupied when their connection began. Neptune having dissolved old boundaries of marriage, partnerships, and personal relationships, Pluto now destroyed them completely, ready to create new concepts and approaches.

In 1978, a new factor entered the relationship. Uranus, ruler of homosexuality, disruption, upheaval, and social movements, moving faster than either Pluto or Neptune, had passed Pluto in the early 1960s. Now—with Neptune midway through the sign Sagittarius and Pluto halfway through Libra, the critical points of change—Uranus reached the midpoint of Scorpio, aspecting both planets equally and focusing the efforts of each onto itself.

The result of this special connection would not be seen until 1981, and then not truly evidenced to the general population until late 1983, when Pluto and Neptune again changed signs, with Neptune moving into Capricorn and Pluto into its own sign, Scorpio.

Capricorn, ruled by Saturn, began to place restrictions on Neptune's negative side, with efforts to restrain the usage of drugs and alcohol, the uncontrolled pollution, and the rising rate of infectious diseases. Now in the sign it rules, Pluto became concerned with reassessing its basic nature, scrutinizing the true meaning of sexuality and even the life experience called death.

The focus of attention of both planets was Uranian—the homosexual population. And the reason was a new disease, known as AIDS, Acquired Immune Deficiency Syndrome.

THE AIDS CHALLENGE

By 1988, AIDS was no longer primarily a concern for gays; it had become a challenge for the entire population, homosexual or heterosexual. However, it is significant that gays were given the challenge first. Unlinked to the regenerative facet of sexuality, it would be up to them to seek and uncover the spiritual side of love and sexuality and to formulate the new definitions that humanity would need for the twenty-first century.

As frightening as AIDS may be, it will ultimately have its positive side. It is a challenge that will be met, and the result will be an increased capacity for love, both of Self and of others.

Astrologically, a major step forward should have been made by mid-February of 1988, when Saturn and Uranus both entered Capricorn, virtually on the same day. At first, this might not have appeared to be positive for gays, for Uranus is not comfortable in the sign ruled by the son who deposed him, and there may have been restrictions placed on homosexual activities, perhaps even involving the law.

However, Saturn is at his most powerful and most beneficent in Capricorn. He will repay fairly for efforts expended toward the public good. Ultimately, Capricorn is the sign of public recognition and success.

This success may not be perceived until late 1989, when Saturn reaches conjunction with Neptune in Capricorn, restricting the disease itself. And the final resolution of the AIDS challenge may not take place until late 1991 or early 1992, when all four of the heavy planets are aspecting in separate signs and houses, at the critical halfway points. Pluto will still be in his own sign of Scorpio, having destroyed old concepts of sexuality and formulated the new. Uranus and Neptune will be in conjunction sixty degrees away, halfway through Capricorn, while Saturn has moved on thirty degrees ahead midway through Aquarius.

In a rare occurrence, Saturn and Uranus will work together rather than against each other, for they are in each other's signs (what is referred to as mutual reception), and each acts as if it is the other, thereby placing three of the four in their home signs and houses, all working together for the social good. (Incidentally, in May of 1992, Mars and Venus, the planets of love and sex are each in the signs they rule— Taurus and Aries—so that five of ten planets control their own signs, something that happens rarely in the Zodiac.)

What does this mean for the AIDS challenge and for gays?

It would appear that gays will be in the forefront of establishing new definitions and boundaries for love and sex. Love of Self, love of partners, and love of society should be perceived as one, united for the common good. Selfishness and selflessness can join; and homosexuals and heterosexuals may work together in understanding and mutual acceptance.

With Pluto at the critical degree of Scorpio that signifies cancer, the solution to AIDS may also be a cure for that long dreaded disease, and with Neptune at the critical degree of Capricorn, this may also involve restrictions on chemicals, alcohol, and drugs.

Chapter 3

SUN SIGNS AND RISING SIGNS

Some challenges are common to all gays; others are unique to individuals. Within this work, the closest we can approximate the individual challenges is to consider the nature and concerns of the Sun signs and the Rising signs, along with the various combinations of the two.

Most people are aware of their Sun signs, because all that is needed is the date of birth. They read their daily Sun sign horoscope in the newspaper and assume that is all there is to astrology. However, in many—if not most—cases, the Sun sign is of less importance than the Ascendant, or Rising sign, which is dependent upon the time of day or night one was born.

In the formation of individual natures and challenges, the number of astrological variables is virtually limitless. Indeed, it is safe to say that there have never been two individuals with precisely the same combination of personality traits and spiritual challenges. There are some similarities that allow for generalizations, and these pertain to the combinations of Sun signs and Rising signs, which will follow in Part II.

THE ASCENDANT OR RISING SIGN

To determine the Ascendant or Rising sign with the precision necessary to erect an individual chart requires mathematical calculations, utilizing the exact time of birth with longitudes and latitudes, along with a reference book that lists a "table of houses." It is not the object here to teach astrology.

However, it is important for the reader to have at least a rough idea of what his Rising sign is.

There are ways of approximating this, so long as one knows the time of his birth.

The simplest—but crudest and least accurate—is to visualize the placement of the Sun in relationship to the location where one was born.

Imagine the earth surrounded by a circle that is divided equally into twelve segments. (See Figure 1.) An "X" is placed at the top of the earth, directly beneath the area designated "Midheaven." If you were born at about noon, the Sun would be placed at the Midheaven; if at midnight, it would be exactly opposite, at the position labeled "Nadir." If you were born at dawn, the Sun would be at the left, at the position of the Ascendant; if at sundown, at the right, on the Descendant.

Halfway between dawn and noon, the Sun would be halfway between the Ascendant and the Midheaven; and so on around the chart, moving clockwise.

Using this system as a guide, approximate the position of your Sun in one of the twelve segments of the circle, and label it with your Sun sign. Following the order of the signs throughout the Zodiac—Aries, Taurus, Gemini, Cancer, Leo, Virgo, Libra, Scorpio, Sagittarius, Capricorn, Aquarius, Pisces—label all the other segments.

The sign closest to the left side of the chart—at the dawn position—should be your Ascendant or Rising sign. What the Ascendant is, in fact, is the sign that is rising over the eastern horizon at the time of birth.

In figuring this, remember that during the summer months, in many years, Daylight Savings Time was frequently used. If you know it was in effect when and where you were born, subtract one hour from your time of birth.

Also, it is important to understand that, at certain times of the year and on certain parts of the globe, the Sun is not in an arc that places it directly overhead. This may create what is called "interceptions"—making some of the twelve segments larger than thirty degrees and others smaller, so that the sign placement will not be precise. (This is why an accurate chart requires mathematical calculations.)

If the description of your Ascendant is not accurate, read the one before or the one after for determining personality and appearance.

Another technique that may be somewhat more accurate utilizes a chart. (See Table I.) However, it is again necessary to subtract one hour if Daylight Savings Time was in use at your birth, and there is still the possibility of sign interceptions.

To use Table I, locate your Sun sign at the top. Then follow the column down to the approximate time of your birth. The result, in most cases, will be the Rising sign.

The Ascendant determines the placement of all other planets in the individual horoscope, because it sets the pattern for all of the twelve houses—with it being the First, the house of Self, personality, and physical appearance. It indicates the way the person is perceived by the outside world, though it is not a superficial house. It does signify how the individual defines himself to the world as well, by stating, "I am."

As indicated in the Introduction, each house and each sign make a statement about the Self. To determine the specific motto for your Ascendant, you can complete the statement, "I am because...," by using the sign's statement. The twelve possible mottos are as follows:

- Aries—"I am because I am."
- Taurus—"I am because I have."
- Gemini—"I am because I think."
- Cancer—"I am because I feel."
- Leo—"I am because I will."
- Virgo—"I am because I analyze."
- Libra—"I am because I balance."
- Scorpio—"I am because I desire."
- Sagittarius—"I am because I see."
- Capricorn—"I am because I use."
- Aquarius—"I am because I know."
- Pisces—"I am because I believe."

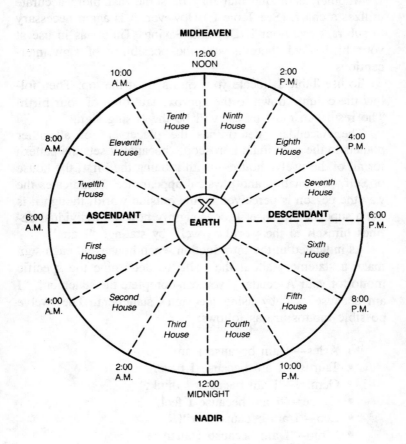

Figure 1

THE RELATIONSHIP OF SUN AND ASCENDANT

The other factor in one's definition of Self is the Sun sign, which represents the ego and the will. Working together with the Rising sign, it completes the definition of one's nature.

It is for this reason that one would read the description of both Sun sign and Ascendant, to combine the two, for a full picture of himself. One or the other may seem to be a stronger influence, perhaps because of placement in the chart, or possibly because of other planets in conjunction. In some signs and houses, the Sun may be weaker or stronger than the Ascendant.

There is also the factor of aspect. When the Sun and the Ascendant are in degrees that relate to each other, they may work closely together for a stronger personality—or, in some cases, work against each other. The two tend to work best together in cases of sextile (sixty degrees, two signs away on either side) and trine (120 degrees, four signs away), and to some extent semi-sextile (thirty degrees, the next sign in either direction).

Normally one would consider a conjunction to be a positive aspect. However, in the case of Ascendant and Sun, it produces the "double" sign, which tends to make the individual rather one-sided.

Sun and Ascendant tend to work against each other—or at least in a stressful relationship—when they are square (ninety degrees) or opposition (180 degrees). The squares are three signs either side of the Ascendant, roughly at the top of the chart or at the bottom. The opposition is the Descendant.

It is, of course, necessary to know the precise degree of the Ascendant to be able to determine if it is in aspect with the Sun. However, there is a way of determining the approximate house placement of the Sun in an individual chart. The locations in Table II can give a rough idea.

The Sun is generally stronger than the Ascendant in cases where it is above the horizon—in houses Seven through

Table I

TABLE OF ASCENDANTS

SUN	ARI	TAU	GEM	CAN	LEO	VIR
AM						
12–2	Cap	Aqu	Pis	Ari	Tau	Gem
2–4	Aqu	Pis	Ari	Tau	Gem	Can
4–6	Pis	Ari	Tau	Gem	Can	Leo
6–8	Ari	Tau	Gem	Can	Leo	Vir
8–10	Tau	Gem	Can	Leo	Vir	Lib
10–12	Gem	Can	Leo	Vir	Lib	Sco
PM						
12–2	Can	Leo	Vir	Lib	Sco	Sag
2–4	Leo	Vir	Lib	Sco	Sag	Cap
4–6	Vir	Lib	Sco	Sag	Cap	Aqu
6–8	Lib	Sco	Sag	Cap	Aqu	Pis
8–10	Sco	Sag	Cap	Aqu	Pis	Ari
10–12	Sag	Cap	Aqu	Pis	Ari	Tau

Twelve. These persons, born during the day, are usually more outgoing than those born during the night, with the Sun in houses One through Six, who tend to be somewhat shy. This is a generalization, however, and therefore may not apply in all cases. There are many other planetary aspects that can counteract—or even contradict—this.

HOUSE PLACEMENT OF SUN

The Sun In The First House

The Sun in the First House is an indication of good health and a strong constitution. It automatically implies a "sunny"

Table I (cont.)

TABLE OF ASCENDANTS

SUN	LIB	SCO	SAG	CAP	AQU	PIS
AM						
12–2	Can	Leo	Vir	Lib	Sco	Sag
2–4	Leo	Vir	Lib	Sco	Sag	Cap
4–6	Vir	Lib	Sco	Sag	Cap	Aqu
6–8	Lib	Sco	Sag	Cap	Aqu	Pis
8–10	Sco	Sag	Cap	Aqu	Pis	Ari
10–12	Sag	Cap	Aqu	Pis	Ari	Tau
PM						
12–2	Cap	Aqu	Pis	Ari	Tau	Gem
2–4	Aqu	Pis	Ari	Tau	Gem	Can
4–6	Pis	Ari	Tau	Gem	Can	Leo
6–8	Ari	Tau	Gem	Can	Leo	Vir
8–10	Tau	Gem	Can	Leo	Vir	Lib
10–12	Gem	Can	Leo	Vir	Lib	Sco

disposition and attractiveness, as well as a unified personality and will. Persons with this aspect usually have considerable ambition and a great will-power; they frequently succeed at whatever they undertake, rising to great heights.

However, on the negative side, they are challenged to deal with a strong ego and a considerable amount of vanity. They may be so single-minded in their desire to succeed that they will be insensitive to the feelings or interests of others, and they must work to overcome this tendency or they may find themselves "alone at the top."

With the emphasis of First House on physical appearance, and its challenge of "vanity," one would expect a great many gays to have the Sun placed here. Indeed, a higher than chance number did have the Sun in the First in the survey

Table II

SUN TO ASCENDANT

TIME OF BIRTH	SUN PLACEMENT
4:00–6:00 AM	First House
6:00–8:00 AM	Twelfth House
8:00–10:00 AM	Eleventh House
10:00–Noon	Tenth House
Noon–2:00 PM	Ninth House
2:00–4:00 PM	Eighth House
4:00–6:00 PM	Seventh House
6:00–8:00 PM	Sixth House
8:00–10:00 PM	Fifth House
10:00–Midnight	Fourth House
Midnight–2:00 AM	Third House
2:00–4:00 AM	Second House

taken—over eleven percent. However, it was not the placement that was highest, nor even the second highest. Truly, the challenge for a great many gays is the Self and the appearance, but there appear to be other challenges that are more significant.

The Sun In The Second House

The Sun in the Second House is greatly concerned with money and with material possessions, but it may also indicate a very loving and a very giving person. This position may give security, through what one possesses, both materially and emotionally. He likes pleasure and will share his pleasures.

There are negatives, however. The person with Sun in the Second House is challenged to avoid being overly materialistic, to be wary of giving "things" rather than giving of Self. He must guard against devoting himself totally to the acquisition of money and try not to display his wealth or possessions merely to gratify his own ego.

In the survey of gay charts, just over eight percent had Sun in the Second House, slightly above what would be expected from chance (7.5 percent). This suggests that gays are no more concerned with materialism than is the general population. It also implies that the challenge of giving and sharing of love is no more difficult for them than for others.

The Sun In The Third House

The Sun in the Third House indicates one whose greatest interest is in intellectual pursuits, in education or in some form of communication, especially in writing. There is a strong ambition, but it is not always fulfilled, especially if the Sun is square the Ascendant. The ego and the personality may, at times, be at odds with each other, causing them to feel torn, or pulled in different directions.

In some cases, persons with Sun in the Third House are challenged to avoid an overemphasis on intellectualism. They may tend toward snobbery or pedanticism, and may concentrate on platonic, mental relationships at the expense of genuine love.

Over eleven percent of gays in the survey had the Sun in the Third House, indicating that matters of basic communication and mental pursuits are of greater concern to them than to the general heterosexual population. Since many have Sun here square the Ascendant, it may indicate that the challenge to justify or unify the inward and the outward Self is a significant one.

The Sun In The Fourth House

The Sun in the Fourth House signifies one whose great emphasis is on home and family. Gays with this aspect generally have a strong tie to the mother, and they may prefer the homemaker role to going out into the world with a career. They are loyal lovers, and may profit from real estate, landscaping, or interior design.

The negative factor here is a challenge to avoid being overly jealous or possessive of the partner or lover. There may also be a problem in achieving the security they so desperately need at home, especially during youth, because their lives may seem to be always an uphill struggle, so far is their Sun from the Midheaven. (There is also the fact that the Sun is not comfortable in the house ruled by the Moon.)

From the usual preconceptions about homosexuality, one would expect an unusually high number to have Sun in the Fourth House, which would indicate a strong link to the mother. However, in the survey, only nine percent had this placement, just a little higher than chance.

The Sun In The Fifth House

The Sun in the Fifth House indicates a great interest in entertainment and a focus on creativity, which may be directed toward the arts. It is especially powerful in this house, for it is the ruler of Leo, the natural sign of the Fifth. Romance and adventure are of great importance to persons with Sun placed here. Life must be one long love affair for them—or one affair after another.

There are many challenges for gays born with Sun in the Fifth House. They may love risk-taking for its own sake, and they are inveterate gamblers (usually lucky, however). They need to be wary of too great an emphasis on pleasure-seeking, and to try to avoid losing true love by seeking the thrill of constant one-night stands. They may perceive themselves as perennial children, never wanting to grow up.

The percentage of gays with Sun in the Fifth House was one of the surprises of the survey. Only 5.6 percent of the poll had this placement, considerably lower than chance. One would have expected far more than chance, considering the extensive social life of gays. This, combined with the low number with Sun in the Eighth House, suggests that the outward appearance of "homosexuality" has little to do with its real nature, and that the challenge of gays is not so much a physical as a spiritual one.

The Sun In The Sixth House

The Sun in the Sixth House suggests a great concern with health, work, and service. On the positive side, the person with this position might seek work of a medical nature, seeking truly to serve and care for others. He may love clothing, dressing well, and he may shower his affection on a pet or pets. He is a good and devoted worker, and he may pay great attention to his health and to his diet. Also, he is likely to be an excellent cook.

However, the negative side presents the gay with this placement with a great challenge. His constitution may be weak, and he may be susceptible to frequent illnesses. In his work, as in his relationships, he needs affirmation from others; he must learn to appreciate himself, gaining strength from that, rather than from seeking approval from outside.

In the survey of gay charts, the fewest number had Sun in the Sixth House—just over 3.7 percent, only half the number one would expect from chance. This would indicate that matters of health and service do not represent a significant challenge for a great many gays.

The Sun In The Seventh House

The Sun in the Seventh House gives a great deal of emphasis to marriage and partnership. This placement may create a devoted lover who will put much effort into any partnership, whether personal or business. He will tend to see himself as reflected in the eyes of others. He is very likeable, and invariably is popular. He may achieve success and is good with anything dealing with partnership and other people in general.

On the negative side, the person with Sun in the Seventh House may place too great an emphasis on others, especially partners, allowing himself to be completely dominated by them. His challenge is to stand up for himself without becoming argumentative or willful.

Sun in the Seventh House also appeared in a relatively low number of gay charts—only five percent in the survey.

The Sun In The Eighth House

The Sun in the Eighth House indicates a concern with partnership finances or the money of others, as well as a great preoccupation with sex. Those who have this aspect generally profit from inheritances and from the money of the life partner. They may also be greatly concerned with spiritual matters, seeking to understand Death and the nature of God.

The challenge of the negative side of this aspect is to avoid too great a preoccupation with sex and death. The native needs to be wary of seeking his identity through sexual activity, or be overly concerned about the satisfaction of his partners. Thwarted ambition may also be a concern, and there must be an effort to avoid bitterness, for recognition may not come until after death, and there may be continuing frustration at not having acquired money on one's own.

In the survey of gay charts, Eighth House placement of Sun was extremely low, representing just over four percent of the total. This tends to confirm the thesis that sex is of less concern to "homosexuals" than love. Very few gays seem to find their identities through sexual activity.

The Sun In The Ninth House

The Sun in the Ninth House places the person in the public eye, usually with an emphasis on higher education, law, religion, travel, or publishing. It indicates much ambition, and a deep spiritual or intellectual nature. Ambitions generally meet with success, and the person usually has a great effect on the growth or expansion of others. The person may also have talents or interests in several areas.

The challenge of this Sun placement is somewhat similar to that of the Sun in the Third. There can be a tendency toward condescension, intellectual snobbery, or religious hypocrisy or dogma, with efforts at forcing views on others. The person with this Sun placement must also endeavor to avoid undertaking too many projects at the same time.

Interestingly, in the study of gay charts, the only house placement for the Sun that was precisely the percentage of chance—7.5 percent—was the Ninth House. This would indicate that questions of higher mind and philosophy do not vary greatly whether one is straight or gay.

The Sun In The Tenth House

The Sun in the Tenth House is usually a significator of much public success in life. It indicates great ambition and probably a large ego. In most cases, the person with Sun in the Tenth had a good father or father figure, and he handles responsibility well. There is a quality of dignity or nobility in his bearing, and there is considerable outward strength.

However, there may be a lack of inner, or spiritual, depth; and, if the Sun is square the Ascendant, an inability to unify the inner and outer Self. The challenge of Sun in the Tenth House is to avoid ruthlessness or unscrupulousness in achieving ambitions, to acquire a degree of consideration for human failings, both in himself and in others. Without this, there is a risk of the person losing all he has sought so vigorously.

A great many gays appear to have Sun in the Tenth House. In the sampling, more than twelve percent had this placement, ranking second behind Sun in the Twelfth House. This was an unexpected placement for the gay Sun, as it is generally considered by psychologists that gays do not have a strong father figure. It may be that the challenge here to unify the inner Self with the outer is significant.

The Sun In The Eleventh House

The Sun in the Eleventh House indicates one who seeks his identity through friendships and group associations. He is extremely popular and attracts friends easily. He has high ambitions, and may achieve them, though often it is through powerful or influential associates. He may have a good mind, possibly of a scientific bent, and he could have concerns of a humanitarian nature.

The challenge for this person is to learn the value of individual love, avoiding seeing others as a part of an impersonal social group. He needs to be wary of a tendency to dominate or use his friends and associates for his own ambitions.

The placement of Sun in the Eleventh House was unexpectedly low, in the survey of gay charts—just over 5.6 percent, considerably lower than chance. The reason it was unexpected was that, if any house can be considered the natural house of homosexuality, it would be the Eleventh.

The Sun In The Twelfth House

The Sun in the Twelfth House indicates a person with a strong spiritual nature, one with a great need for creative expression. However, he may have a degree of shyness or a desire for seclusion. To achieve his ambitions, he may feel that self-sacrifice is necessary, or he may be forced to remain behind the scenes. To him, his own soul is of greatest concern.

His work may be associated with institutions such as hospitals, prisons, or retirement homes, or he may choose an occupation that he follows alone or in seclusion. Whatever he does, he needs to feel that he is serving others.

The challenge of Sun in the Twelfth is to avoid his tendencies for self-sacrifice becoming self-destructive. He must fight having his shyness become extreme neurosis. In relationships, he must endeavor to keep from secretly manipulating others to satisfy his vague or insecure egotism.

In the sampling of gay charts, the highest percentage had Sun in the Twelfth, significantly higher than chance—a full fifteen percent. This would indicate that a great many gays are challenged to deal with spiritual matters. The challenge for them to deal directly with the outside world and to avoid seclusion (or the "closet") is an important one.

●　　●　　●

The relationship of Sun and Ascendant—or ego and personality—appears to be an important part of the gay challenge, judging from the placement of the Sun in the houses, according to the survey. An unusually high number of gays had the Sun in either the Tenth or the Third, in square aspect to the Ascendant, focusing the challenge toward a need for unifying aspects of Self. A great many also had the Sun in either the Twelfth or the First, with a significant percentage having Sun conjunct the Ascendant, emphasizing the personal or spiritual nature of the challenge.

Indeed, it is incredible to consider that exactly half of the survey—80 of the 160—had the Sun placed in one of these four houses, which might be considered the least "sexual" of all the houses of the Zodiac. Only twenty percent had the Sun placed in the houses one would have expected—the Fifth, Seventh, Eighth, and Eleventh—the ones that would tend toward the "sexual" facets of "homosexuality." And these are the ones that would have confirmed the most common preconcep-

tions about gay life, the houses that are concerned with pleasure, love affairs, partnership, blatant sexuality, friendship, and group activities.

This tends to indicate that the gay challenge is one of
the spirit and the Self, one of love and understanding, rather
than a challenge of the physical, the material, and the purely
sexual.

PART II

THE CARDINAL SIGNS

SEASONAL BEGINNINGS

Life is a process of growth, transformation, and change, marked by the passage of time. On a yearly basis, the changes on earth parallel the changes taking place in what appears to be the path of the Sun through the heavens. Four times a year, the Sun, the light-giving, life-giving force, seems to set itself on a new course, the earthly season is altered, and living things pass into a different period, some dramatically, others imperceptibly.

Astrologically, the seasonal beginnings are marked by the Cardinal signs—Aries, Cancer, Libra, and Capricorn. The nature, or quality, of these signs is determined by what is happening on earth as a result of the apparent change of course of the Sun. When the Sun enters the configuration of stars known as Aries, spring begins, and life seems to burst forth anew on earth. It is the Spring Equinox, when the periods of light and darkness are approximately equal in length. The Sun enters Cancer at the Summer Solstice, when the period of light is longest and the night is shortest. It enters Libra at the Autumn Equinox, a second time of equal light and dark; and Capricorn at the Winter Solstice, when the night is longer than the day.

Individuals born during the time the Sun is in one of these four "turning points" are heavily influenced by the quality of "beginnings." They are characterized by an energy and a forcefulness not evident in the other signs. They show a great deal of initiative and wish to act immediately and decisively. They are the born leaders of the Zodiac, not necessarily because they have the ability to organize or persuade, but because they set out a course of action and expect others to fall in line.

Generally they succeed, primarily because they do not acknowledge failure or defeat. When they do fail, it is because of overconfidence or insensitivity to the needs or objectives of others.

To the Fixed and Mutable signs, they seem naive, brash, impatient, and foolhardy, unable—in their desire to deal with the present—to comprehend the lessons of the past or to perceive the needs of the future. The Cardinal signs relate best to other Cardinal signs, though Aries and Libra do have some problems with Cancer and Capricorn because of the incompatibilities of Fire and Air with the Water and Earth signs. Cardinal signs have their greatest difficulties with the Fixed signs, because they have little patience for stubbornness or implacability. They do get along somewhat better with the Mutable signs, who are always willing to adapt even though they may feel somewhat abused by the Cardinals.

Fortunately, very few people are purely Cardinal, purely Mutable, or purely Fixed, but are combinations of the qualities and elements represented by the Twelve Houses. If an individual with Fixed or Mutable Sun sign and Ascendant has qualities of Aries, Libra, Cancer, or Capricorn in some facet of his life, it is likely that important planets appear in those signs in his horoscope.

In the random survey taken of gay signs, 22.5 percent had Cardinal signs on the Ascendant, and 28 percent had the Sun in Cardinal signs. (Chance would be 33 percent.) Aries represented the largest number of Cardinal Sun signs, with 9.3 percent of the total, but the fewest Rising signs, with 2.5 percent. Libra represented the largest number of Ascendants at 7.5 percent, while there were only 5.6 percent with Sun in Libra. There were 6.8 percent with Sun in Cancer, and 6.2 percent had Sun in Capricorn. There were 7.5 percent with Capricorn as the Rising sign, and 5 percent had Cancer Rising. (Chance would be 7.5 percent.)

Chapter 4

CARDINAL FIRE—ARIES

(March 21–April 19/20)

Applies to Aries Sun sign, Aries Ascendant, and those with Mars on the Ascendant.

RULER—Mars
MOTTO—"I am."
SYMBOL—Ram
POLARITY—Positive/Masculine
COLOR—Red
KEY WORDS—Action, Initiative, Self-Assurance
MALE IDOLS—Elton John, Marlon Brando, Chuck Connors
FEMALE IDOLS—Bette Davis, Joan Crawford, Gloria Swanson

THE ARIES LOOK

The first thing noticeable about the man with strong Aries influence is the aura of confidence. He knows what he wants and is out to get it. This may be a blatant masculinity or simply the appearance of constant activity or aggressiveness. Different degrees of Aries look different, but generally he gives the appearance of the athlete—tall, with broad shoulders and strong limbs, but with a lean, spare body. The Aries will usually have a rather long, strong neck, a long or narrow face, and a prominent forehead, with piercing dark eyes and dark brows. The hair will generally be black or reddish, and the complexion will be swarthy or somehow reddish or pink in hue.

In dress, the Aries will generally choose clothes that suggest masculine activity, being most comfortable in jogging shorts or jogging suit or sweats. Those who are older or more conservative will wear clothing that suggests some sort of male uniform—bush jackets, shirts with epaulets, surgical greens, or old army fatigues.

If going to a costume party, Aries will likely choose to appear as a soldier, a policeman, a knight, a football player, or a hunter.

THE ARIES NATURE

Aries epitomizes the masculine principle, but this does not mean that an Aries cannot be gay, or even effeminate. Aries women, such as Bette Davis and Joan Crawford, are strong and self-assertive, yet appealingly feminine. While most gay Aries will look like athletes or sportsmen, some may become so obsessed with activity and the present that they come off like fussy old-maid schoolteachers, though they are rarely aware of the effect they create.

Whatever the case, you cannot keep a gay Aries down, and you cannot ignore him. Aries are invariably strong personalities. They are who they are, and it doesn't matter what others think of them.

Aries is the sign of the natural First House of the Zodiac, and as such it is greatly concerned with identity, Self, personality, and appearance. This, in combination with the Cardinal quality and the Fire element, makes Aries the most action oriented sign. Ruled by aggressive, driving, ambitious, active Mars, the pure Aries is an originator, an achiever, a sportsman, a talker, and a leader.

Aries rushes headlong at his goals and is highly competitive. Not only does he want to be the best at whatever he undertakes, he feels he has to be the best. He has to prove himself, to himself as well as to others. His ego is so strong he may feel that he is invincible, heedlessly placing himself in positions of risk or danger, as he attempts to achieve success, power, fame, or even material goods.

In social situations, Aries is known to monopolize conversation, and all too often he talks only about himself, his possessions, his goals, his achievements. He doesn't mean to be rude or boring, however; his is an unconscious egotism, and he assumes everyone else is interested in his concerns. And he is not always wrong. His mind is as active as his body, and he can be extremely witty.

Aries is a strong individualist, with a belief in freedom and independence, and a great instinct for survival. He does not like to be bossed or directed by others, unless that person is at least as strong as he is. He respects aggressiveness from others, for he understands it; sometimes, it is the only way he can be made to listen to the ideas or opinions that do not agree with his own.

He is generally quick-tempered, and may be inclined to physical fights, but his anger doesn't last long, and he doesn't hold grudges. Even though he may have been violent, or may have said cruel, vicious things in anger, he can't understand why others don't forgive and forget as easily as he does.

Gay Aries can be a passionate lover. Certainly he has a strong sexual desire, and he is almost always sexually attractive. However, he has difficulty maintaining sexual relationships over a long period of time. As with most of his actions, Aries lacks "staying power" in a relationship, and indeed is such an individualist he does not truly understand the meaning of "partnership" so essential to love. (The reason for this is that Libra, the natural partnership sign, is the one in opposition to Aries, and Mars, ruler of Aries, is in detriment there.)

THE ARIES CHALLENGE

No astrological sign exists without imperfections. One of Aries' little flaws is his tendency not to believe this fact. Aries is inclined to believe he is perfect, that there is nothing to achieve by looking inward. Once Aries realizes that there are challenges or obstacles to overcome within his own makeup, there is no stopping him, however. He will attack them with the same vigor he would to conquer a mountain peak.

Because Aries rushes headlong at his goals, he has to beware of being too rash or hasty. He needs to learn to think, or even to plan, before acting, to make sure the goal is truly what he wants or even something worth achieving. Because of his headstrong nature, he is somewhat accident prone, and should learn some degree of caution.

His life's challenge is to learn to be aware of the needs of others, to learn patience, to learn to listen with as much energy as he talks to others, and to learn to complete one project before beginning another.

This is more difficult for an Aries to achieve than it might seem to be to one of the more receptive signs. Aries doesn't know that he seems arrogant or pompous or self-obsessed. There is no intentional malevolence or calculated malice in the Aries. He has no idea that his words or actions may hurt someone; when his rash words or acts inflict pain, he isn't aware of the fact. He is as naive and as innocent as a child when it comes to his effect on others.

Love is the ultimate challenge for Aries. If he can learn to be as sensitive to the needs of another person as he is to his own, if he can understand why others do not operate with the assurance and determination that he does, then he will truly have accomplished the goals of his astrological sign.

ARIES RISING

Aries Rising with Aries Sun

> *"I am because I am; my will/ego finds expression through the fact that I am."*

The Sun in this combination will most likely fall into the First House or the Twelfth. If the Sun is in the First, the ego expression finds outlet through matters related to the personality and appearance; if in the Twelfth, through matters of spiritual regeneration, solitude, institutions, or inhibitions or restrictions he places on himself.

In either case, Mars rules both Ascendant and Sun, providing considerable energy and force to the identity, as well as ambition. This is truly a fiery individual.

This is perhaps the most egocentric of all the possible combinations of the Zodiac (with the possible exception of the double Leo, who tends to be more vain than self-assured). The double Aries has no need for any other purpose in life but his mere existence. He is a natural leader, but other factors in his chart must give him the incentive to know what and who he must lead.

He is the most natural, instinctive of men. He could be a fighter, a military man, an adventurer, a soldier of fortune. He could be a surgeon, a fireman, an actor, a stuntman, an explorer. He could be virtually anything he chooses, or anything his other planets permit.

His challenge is to discover that which is outside himself, to see and understand what motivates others, and to learn to love and care for those around him, those who so willingly follow his lead.

Aries Rising with Taurus Sun

> *"I am because I am; my will/ego finds expression through what I have or possess."*

The Sun in this combination will most likely fall into the Second House or the First. If the Sun is in the Second, the ego expression finds outlet through matters related to money, possessions, or the loving, giving nature; if it is in the First, it finds outlet through the personality and the appearance.

Mars rules the Ascendant, and Venus the Sun. If the Ascendant and Sun are in semi-sextile relationship, this can be a strongly sexual combination. There can be some internal stress for the individual, however, as the Ascendant is Fire while the Sun is Earth in nature, causing the practicality and the materialism of the ego to restrain the ambitious Self.

There must be a creative solution to the stress between the active needs of the Ascendant and the peaceful, rural, practical needs of the ego. This native might choose to be a farmer or a rancher, raising cattle, or he might build and run a nursery for plants and flowers. If his Second House Taurus Sun runs in the direction of money or finances, he might be an insurance investigator. If possessions or collectibles are his metier, he might collect or buy and sell antique guns or military memorabilia.

His challenge is typically Aries—to seek to discover what makes others tick, to understand the needs of others, to learn to love without being possessive, while avoiding putting all his Martian drive into making money and acquiring material possessions.

Aries Rising with Gemini Sun

"I am because I am; my will/ego finds expression through the fact that I think (or have opinions)."

The Sun in this combination will most likely fall into the Third House or the Second. If the Sun is in the Third, the ego expression finds outlet through matters related to communication, education, and brethren; if it is in the Second, it finds outlet through money and possessions, and perhaps the loving, giving nature.

Either way, the two work well together, for the Air of the Gemini Sun feeds the Fire of the Aries Ascendant in a creative, productive mixture, so that the ego and will are able to accomplish the ambitions of the Self without stress.

If the Gemini Sun is in the Third House, this native might be a teacher at a military school, or he might be a writer of action and adventure novels. But he might as easily be a race-car driver, or he could be a newspaper reporter or television reporter covering wars or accidents or sports events.

He will certainly be one of the most talkative or communicative of all the combinations. He has plenty of opinions, and will not hesitate to express them aggressively.

His challenge is to learn to be more practical and down to earth, as well as to learn to listen to those he loves and cares about. He must also beware of exhausting his Martian energy by his Gemini activity. He may dance all night, but sometimes he must remember to sleep.

Aries Rising with Cancer Sun

"I am because I am; my will/ego finds expression through my feelings."

The Sun in this combination will most likely fall into the Fourth House or the Third. If the Sun is in the Fourth, the ego expression finds outlet through matters related to the home, mother, or real estate; if in the Third, through matters associated with communication, education, and brethren.

This is a stressful relationship, though not entirely unproductive. The Water of the Cancer Sun, especially when in square aspect, tends to put out the Fire of the Aries Ascendant, making it necessary for the native to work extremely hard to accomplish his goals. He can succeed, but often through indirect means.

It may take some time to discover his goals. He could be a land or real estate developer, or he could be a security guard for a large high-rise apartment building or condominium. But his Cancer Sun could take him to another extreme, causing him to be guided more by his feelings and his concern for family. This could be a difficult combination for a gay, causing him to devote his energy to taking care of his mother, or to serve as a "houseboy" for someone else's family, or he might become a professional genealogist. He might also make a career of buying old homes and restoring them, then selling them at a profit.

His challenge is to find unity between his active Ascendant and his passive, shy Sun, and to become more outgoing, enjoying the company of others.

Aries Rising with Leo Sun

"I am because I am; my will/ego finds expression through my will."

The Sun in this combination will most likely fall into the Fifth House or the Fourth. If it is in the Fifth, the ego expression will find outlet through matters related to entertainment, love affairs, romance, speculation, or children; if in the Fourth, it will find outlet through matters connected with the home, mother, or real estate.

Either way, it is an excellent mix of two Fire signs. The ambitions of the Aries Ascendant and the need to express himself succeed through the strong ego and the powerful will of the Leo Sun, with the determination of its Fixed nature.

A Fifth House Sun is probably the luckiest of all placements. This could produce a highly successful professional gambler, or one who is lucky in love. Indeed, this combination does produce one who seeks romance and love affairs throughout his life. At his worst, however, it could create someone who seeks to be a child all his life, simply playing the time away.

But normally Aries is exceedingly ambitious, and Leo has the will to succeed at ambitions. If other aspects concur, this native might be an actor on stage or on film, or possibly a stuntman. But he might as easily be an adventurer, one who takes risks simply for the thrill of it, a sky-diver or a balloonist, a race-car driver or a participant in rodeos.

The challenge of this combination is to learn responsibility, to avoid his tendencies to want to be the perennial child, and to work against tendencies to play and have a good time while others pay the piper for his romantic adventures.

Aries Rising with Virgo Sun

"I am because I am; my will/ego finds expression through my ability to analyze."

The Sun in this combination will most likely fall into the Sixth House or the Fifth. If it is in the Sixth, the ego expression will find outlet through matters of work, service, health, clothing, and food; if in the Fifth, through matters of entertainment, love affairs, romance, speculation, and children.

It is not an easy combination, because the Mutable Earth Sun does not mix well with the Cardinal Fire Ascendant, making it difficult—though not impossible—for the native to achieve his ambitions. He must find original, Mutable ways to reach success.

The strong Aries nature is not really comfortable submerging his ego in the service of others, yet he is virtually compelled to do so. To feed the vanity of his Self while not really seeming to do so, he might become an inventive chef specializing in exotic dishes. Another possibility is work in medicine or the health services field. If Mars is well aspected in the individual chart, there is a chance the native could be drawn to a career in surgery, since Mars, the ruler of the Ascendant, rules that facet of medicine.

But the Sixth also rules pets and small animals, so the native could as easily be a veterinarian or a breeder of hunting dogs. There is even the possibility of military service or police work, or the manufacture or creation of men's fashions.

The true challenge of this combination is in discovering how to serve Self and others through the same action.

Aries Rising with Libra Sun

"I am because I am; my will/ego finds expression through my ability to balance."

The Sun in this combination will most likely fall into the

Seventh House or the Sixth. If it is in the Seventh, the ego expression will find outlet through matters of partnership and associations with others; if in the Sixth, it will be through matters of work, service, health, clothing, and food.

It is a positive combination, with the Cardinal Air of the Sun feeding the Cardinal Fire of the Ascendant, though there is the challenge for the native of defining his ego through his relationships rather than through his inner Self. However, this stressful tug of war can be productive and ultimately successful.

The native with this combination could succeed in virtually any sort of partnership. However, his Sun's need to balance might draw him to some sort of career in arbitration, such as a mediator in labor disputes. Because of his ruling Mars and Venus, he could be a marriage counselor. If he wants to be an entertainer, he could be a juggler or a circus performer doing a high wire act in partnership with others.

Aries Rising with Scorpio Sun

"I am because I am; my will/ego finds expression through my desires."

The Sun in this combination will most likely fall into the Eighth House or the Seventh. If it is in the Eighth, the ego expression will find outlet through matters related to partnership finances, sex, heritage and inheritance, or death; if in the Seventh, it will find outlet through matters of partnership and associations with others.

It is not an easy combination, for the Fixed Water of the Scorpio Sun tends to put out the Fire of the Aries Ascendant, or the fire is directed toward sex, creating steam that is in turn frustrating to the ambitions. Whatever the combination, the Eighth House Sun is almost always frustrating for the native, and he must find original, creative solutions to what he wants to achieve in life.

He might be drawn to psychiatry or psychotherapy as a career, or to some form of investigative work, such as a private detective, or even to military intelligence. Depending upon the placement of other planets, he might even become a banker, or a business manager for theatrical or entertainment figures.

Should his ambition be of a purely personal nature, in some creative or artistic field, he may have to come to terms with the fact that his major success will occur after his death, accepting the creative urge and accomplishment as satisfying for its own sake.

Aries Rising with Sagittarius Sun

"I am because I am; my will/ego finds expression through my ability to see or perceive."

The Sun in this combination will most likely fall into the Ninth House or the Eighth. If it is in the Ninth, the ego expression will find outlet in matters related to higher education, philosophy, travel, or publishing; if it is in the Eighth, it will find outlet through partnership finances, sex, heritage or inheritance, or death.

The combination is highly directed toward success, combining Cardinal Fire on the Ascendant and Mutable Fire ruling the Sun, so that the ego is capable of enduring for ultimate achievement. The only difficulty may be a burn-out resulting from efforts to accomplish too much too fast in too many directions.

The mix of Aries and Sagittarius could make this native one of the finest of public speakers, both knowledgeable and persuasive, whether he directs his talents toward education, religion, or world travel. His ego finds fulfillment through the generous sharing of his knowledge and his beliefs, which is one of the factors that would make him an excellent teacher or minister, or even a writer or an editor (though the Aries

Ascendant might make it difficult for him to sit still long enough to convey his words through writing).

The challenge for this individual is to endeavor to listen to others as he expects to be listened to, truly hearing what others have to say, imparting his wisdom according to the needs of those he wishes to share with.

Aries Rising with Capricorn Sun

> *"I am because I am; my will/ego finds expression*
> *through my ability to use."*

The Sun in this combination will most likely fall into the Tenth House or the Ninth. If it is in the Tenth, the ego expression will find outlet through public recognition, honors, success, and the father; if it is in the Ninth, it will find outlet through matters related to higher education, philosophy, travel, or publishing.

Because the Sun is Fixed Earth, in square aspect to the Cardinal Fire Ascendant, this is a stressful combination, but the stress is productive, with positive outcomes, because the Sun is in the Midheaven, the ideal placement for success. The native is almost sure to achieve recognition in the public eye; however, he has the challenge to perceive his inner Self, not relying totally on seeing himself through his success—or through the eyes of others.

To some extent, this combination is a workaholic, for the Aries-Capricorn native is very success oriented; however the Aries Ascendant does allow him to play occasionally, for he must always satisfy himself.

He seeks to be appreciated for his accomplishments, defining himself by the approval of others, and he strives overly hard to deserve that approval. If he is in business, he is an excellent administrator, knowing how to use the talents of his workers, though at times he may reveal an explosive temper. If he is in politics, the interests of his constituency will always be kept in mind, as important to him as his own self-interest.

Aries Rising with Aquarius Sun

"I am because I am; my will/ego finds expression through who or what I know."

The Sun in this combination will most likely fall into the Eleventh House or the Tenth. If it is in the Eleventh, the ego expression will find outlet through friends, group activities, aspirations, or social movements; if it is in the Tenth, it will find outlet through matters related to public recognition, honors, success, and the father.

Either way, the Fixed Air of the Aquarius ego works well with the Cardinal Fire of the Ascendant, with the air feeding the fire for success of personal ambitions as well as group ideals. The native is a born political leader or social activist, though he may have a tendency to prefer socializing with friends, occasionally neglecting responsibilities.

All too often, the Aquarius Sun can be coldly objective, but Aries is one of the most subjective of signs, and so it contributes personal concerns to the humanitarian ones.

The Aries-Aquarian can be a political leader, a crusader for human rights, an organizer for any group activity from unions to social functions to safaris. What he sets out to do he invariably accomplishes with relative ease, using who he knows as well as what he knows.

He has lots of friends, and there is almost a mesmerizing quality about him that attracts others. However, he has a tendency to break with friends after a time, either letting them drift away or losing them because of a loss of Martian temper. His attitude, unfortunately, is rather cavalier—there are always more where those came from.

The challenge of this combination is to learn intimacy—to learn to relate to individuals one on one, endeavoring to keep from thinking of his friends as people he uses to fulfill his own ambition.

Aries Rising with Pisces Sun

"*I am because I am; my will/ego finds expression through what I believe.*"

The Sun in this combination will most likely fall into the Twelfth House or the Eleventh. If it is in the Twelfth, the ego expression will find outlet through matters of spiritual regeneration, solitude, institutions, or inhibitions or restrictions he places on himself; if it is in the Eleventh, it will find outlet through friends, group activities, aspirations, or social movements.

It is usually a very difficult combination, causing considerable frustration for the native. Not only is the Sun in the Mutable Water sign, whose water will tend to put out the Cardinal Fire of the Ascendant, but it is in the sign and/or house that has the most self-destructive tendencies. There is a significant challenge for this native to seek spiritual solutions to his ambitions, rather than to turn his fire against himself.

Like those with the Sixth House Sun, the native with this combination may seek service in some institution, such as medicine, psychiatry, or penology. If Mars and Neptune, the rulers of his Ascendant and Sun, are well placed, he might find the success he desires in military service, either the Navy or the Marines. In some cases, there might be a combination of these, for example a Naval surgeon.

The challenge of this native is to find a productive or creative solution to the great conflict he feels, rather than a self-destructive one, for both facets of his identity must be fulfilled. He must have his aggressive Martian ambitions, yet find his ultimate accomplishment in matters that are Neptunian, spiritual, and service-oriented.

Chapter 5

CARDINAL WATER—CANCER

(June 22–July 22)

Applies to Cancer Sun sign, Cancer Ascendant, and those with Moon on the Ascendant.

RULER—Moon
MOTTO—"I feel."
SYMBOL—Crab
POLARITY—Negative/Feminine
COLOR—Yellow orange
KEY WORDS—Home, Family, Sensitivity, Protection
MALE IDOLS—Yul Brynner, Tab Hunter, Jan Michael Vincent
FEMALE IDOLS—Susan Hayward, Ginger Rogers, Barbara Stanwyck

THE CANCER LOOK

One doesn't always notice the distinguishing characteristics of the gay Cancer immediately. Cancers aren't really shy, but they sometimes seem to be, because they are the quietest, most conservative of the Cardinal signs.

Usually, the first thing noticed about someone with heavy Cancer influence is the dimple in the chin. The next thing is the eyes, which are rather round and impassive. The eyes may be of any color, but in purest form are gray to gray-green. The Cancer face is generally round and firm, and sometimes there are dimples in the cheeks as well as in the chin, though not always. Except for the eyes, the features are generally rather small or delicate. The hair may be brown or blond and is usually rather straight. When it is brown, there is a tendency to premature graying; when it is blond, it tends toward the platinum shade.

The Cancer's body is relatively short in stature, though strong and sturdy. The chest, or the upper body, is generally proportionately larger than the lower, with slim hips and legs and large or barrel chest, with slender arms.

Cancer does not stick to a single style of dress, but changes clothes with his changes of mood, which are frequent. However, he rarely wears anything outlandish or outrageous. The most extreme choice for him would be to dress entirely in white, reflecting the Moon, which is his ruling planet.

There are some cases of transvestism among Cancers, and a great many others would choose drag if attending a costume party.

THE CANCER NATURE

Like the other Cardinal signs, Cancer is assertive, but he does not appear to be, because he never approaches anything directly and because he frequently changes his mind. Because of the element of water in its nature, Cancer is the most sensitive of the Cardinal signs, yet it is the most dynamic of the Water signs.

The emotional nature of gay Cancer rarely shows on the surface, and especially not in public. Like the crab that is their symbol, Cancers build a protective shell around them to protect their extreme vulnerability. Because the Moon is their ruler, they tend to feel everything more strongly than other signs. Once they have been hurt, they try desperately to avoid being hurt again, generally unsuccessfully.

Under any circumstances, Cancer is a complex sign. Gay Cancer is even more complex, requiring much understanding from others yet very reticent about sharing the feelings that would help others to understand.

Cancer is devoted to home and family. His motivations, and his accomplishments in life, are all directed toward building a home and toward protecting it. He can succeed in anything so long as he has a home and family to reflect his success. This presents a very special problem for gay Cancer, whose first inclination is to marry heterosexually even when he knows he is gay. Some find an outlet by remaining devoted to their mothers, others by attempting to establish gay relationships in which they serve as the domestic partners, keeping house and playing the role of wife. In keeping house, no one is cleaner or more efficient than the Cancer.

Sometimes these solutions work, but not always. Often, it is necessary for Cancers to create a family atmosphere among their friends or to form close platonic relationships with women, in order to achieve the security and stability so essential for them to operate.

Once they have that security, there is no stopping them. Cancer is a very creative sign, the most sensitive and artistic of the Cardinal signs. Born at the time of the Summer Solstice, when the days are longest and the night is shortest, they are outwardly very bright and cheerful and positive. They endeavor to hide or conceal whatever is dark or negative. They are "self-starters," with plenty of initiative, and can work very well alone, or when delegated authority.

Like the other Cardinal signs, however, they lack staying power, primarily because of the changeability of their emotions. They are at their best when they have someone or something they can nurture. They do well in public relations, promoting others; in building or decorating houses; landscaping; selling real estate; with nurseries or flower shops; as architects or builders; managing nursing homes; or in almost any of the creative arts.

In love, Cancer is a devoted partner, some might feel too devoted. They are the most loyal of the signs, yet they expect—even demand—loyalty from their partners. They are generous with their love, even to the point of smothering the lover. And they are as possessive as they are passionate. When they have been hurt, they will never forget, but will nurse the hurt, bringing it up repeatedly in disputes. If anyone should attack or threaten them or their mates, they will fight tenaciously.

THE CANCER CHALLENGE

The life challenge for the gay Cancer is to learn to understand and to cope with his emotional nature, to become more trusting of others and less possessive of those he loves. Cancers must discover that pain is not quite so painful when it is not nursed, and that they should let go of old resentments to make way for new joys.

It is important for them to realize that they do not have to sidestep to avoid confrontations, that expressing their thoughts and feelings directly and openly will mean less pain and suffering, for them as well as for those they love.

CANCER RISING

Cancer Rising with Cancer Sun

"I am because I feel; my will/ego finds expression through my feelings."

The Sun in this combination will most likely fall into the First House or the Twelfth. If the Sun is in the First, the ego expression finds outlet through matters related to the personality and appearance; if in the Twelfth, through matters of spiritual regeneration, solitude, institutions, or inhibitions or restrictions he places on himself.

With the Moon ruling both the Ascendant and the Sun, this is truly an emotional person, though he may have difficulty expressing the emotions, especially when the Sun is in the Twelfth House. If it is in the First House, his ego is very strong, and he may be somewhat vain as well. The emotions he feels have a tendency to be directed entirely toward the Self, and probably held deep beneath the surface. He feels a great affinity for women, and has a strong link to his home.

As he has a tendency to approach everything indirectly, it is a part of his challenge to learn to be more direct with people, especially when it concerns his feelings.

To him these feelings are what make him special; he identifies himself by them, and generally his ambitions are directly related to them. It is love and security that are of primary importance, but he also has a great need to feel productive in some way.

A love partnership is critical to his feelings of success, but he must be wary of becoming overly possessive or protective of the person he loves.

Cancer Rising with Leo Sun

"I am because I feel; my will/ego finds expression through my will."

The Sun in this combination will most likely fall into the Second House or the First. If the Sun is in the Second, the ego expression finds outlet through matters related to money, possessions, or the loving, giving nature; if it is in the First, it finds outlet through the personality and the appearance.

To some extent, this combination is a stressful one, because the Cardinal Water Ascendant has a tendency to dampen the Fixed Fire of the Leo Sun. However, if the Ascendant and Sun are in semi-sextile aspect, they can work together (in a steamy mixture) to acquire the material goods that the home-loving Cancer deems important to security.

The Fixed Leo Sun is determined to work his strong will in the acquisition of money and possessions, if it is in the Second House, willing himself to have as much as possible for the sake of his ego.

Yet, because of his Ascendant, he feels very strongly, and he is torn sometimes between his emotional needs and his strong will to be out in the world making more money. Often, this person will strike a compromise, entertaining in his home for business reasons, displaying what he has acquired of a material nature—perhaps some collectibles—to let others become aware of his success.

Cancer Rising with Virgo Sun

"I am because I feel; my will/ego finds expression through my ability to analyze."

The Sun in this combination will most likely fall into the Third House or the Second. If the Sun is in the Third, the ego expression finds outlet through matters related to communication, education, and brethren; if it is in the Second, it finds outlet through money and possessions, and the loving, giving nature.

Either way, the two work well together, for the Cardinal Water Ascendant feeds and nourishes the Mutable Earth Sun, the emotional Cancer Self being part of what the analytical Virgo ego seeks to understand and communicate.

This is an ideal combination for a writer, particularly a writer involved with poetry or romance novels or books about women and/or the home. It is also good for a teacher or a psychotherapist or marriage counselor, anyone who is called upon to analyze emotional matters and communicate understanding. Since Cancer resists straightforward expression, however, he is more comfortable with the written word.

The challenge for this combination is to learn to deal with matters related to the public and to the inner spirit. Virgo, as an Earth sign, is both sexual and practical, but his rather schoolmarmish attitude, when combined with the almost shy home-loving nature of Cancer, tends to hold this native back somewhat. He needs to learn to get out into the world and experience and to integrate his experiences into his spiritual nature.

Cancer Rising with Libra Sun

"I am because I feel; my will/ego finds expression through my ability to balance."

The Sun in this combination will most likely fall into the

Fourth House or the Third. If the Sun is in the Fourth, the ego expression finds outlet through matters related to the home, mother, or real estate; if in the Third, through matters associated with communication, education, and brethren.

This is a stressful relationship, especially if the Sun should be square the Ascendant, but it can be a productive one. The emotional nature of the watery Cancer has difficulty mixing with the airy mentality of Libra, which has difficulty balancing the extreme personal feelings this Ascendant experiences.

However, if the Libra Sun is in the Fourth House, it is in the natural house of Cancer, so the ego is capable of dealing with the home-loving, feminine feelings. It could turn to real estate to find its need for balance, or perhaps interior decorating, or some form of art or crafts that fulfills Libra's need for beauty.

Both the Ascendant and the Sun are ruled here by feminine planets, the Moon being the mothering, productive instinct and Venus being the loving, artistic, harmonious aspect of woman.

The challenge for this native is likely to be that of full communication and development of the active intellect. He needs to develop the will and determination to go out into the public and seek recognition for himself, separate from partners.

Cancer Rising with Scorpio Sun

"I am because I feel; my will/ego finds expression through my desires."

The Sun in this combination will most likely fall into the Fifth House or the Fourth. If it is in the Fifth, the ego expression will find outlet through matters related to entertainment, love affairs, romance, speculation, or children; if in the Fourth, it will find outlet through matters connected with the home, mother, or real estate.

This is an excellent mix of two Water signs. The emotional Cardinal Water of the Ascendant can be quite ambitious at times, and when it mixes with the sexy, creative Fixed Water of the Scorpio Sun is one of those times—especially when the two are trine from the First to the Fifth House. The one defines itself through feelings, and the other through desires.

The real danger for this individual is that he can be so much in love with Love that he will forget about other facets of love, living for the romance of the moment, going from one love affair to the next, without dealing with such mundane matters as career, education, work, or home. His challenge is to come to terms with his ambitions and to find a practical way to accomplish them.

This native is probably a very talented individual, and he is certainly one of the luckiest of the Zodiac. If other aspects confirm, he could be an actor or an entertainer, perhaps a film or television personality. If the Cancer Ascendant can keep his emotions from showing, this combination could also be a professional gambler.

Cancer Rising with Sagittarius Sun

"I am because I feel; my will/ego finds expression through my ability to see or perceive."

The Sun in this combination will most likely fall into the Sixth House or the Fifth. If it is in the Sixth, the ego expression will find outlet through matters of work, service, health, clothing, and food; if in the Fifth, through matters of enter--tainment, love affairs, romance, speculation, and children.

There is some strain in this combination between Cardinal Water and Mutable Fire. The excessive Cancer emotions tend to put out the fiery ambitions of Sagittarius, which tend to go off in all directions anyway. The Cancer side wants to sit at home with a loving partner; the Sagittarius side wants to go out and explore the world, meeting new people and developing his mind.

However, to achieve unity between the two sides of the identity—the personality and the ego—this native must find ways that feelings and mental perceptions can work together. This is a part of his challenge. If the Sun is in the Sixth House of work and service, the Jupiter ruler of his Sun might combine with the Moon ruler of his Ascendant to breed champion dogs or cats, or to running a pet shop. (The Sixth also rules pets and small animals.) If other factors in the chart confirm this, he might as easily be a fashion illustrator or be an airline attendant. He might also be in the catering business.

Cancer Rising with Capricorn Sun

"I am because I feel; my will/ego finds expression through my ability to use."

The Sun in this combination will most likely fall into the Seventh House or the Sixth. If it is in the Seventh, the ego expression will find outlet through matters of partnership and associations with others; if in the Sixth, it will be through matters of work, service, health, clothing, and food.

This is a positive combination, with the Cardinal Water of the Ascendant nourishing the Cardinal Earth of the Sun, though as with all Seventh House placements of the Sun, there is the challenge for the native to endeavor not to define his ego through his relationships, but to discover his inner Self.

The Capricorn ego must learn to use his Cancer feelings as easily as he uses the partnerships that come to him so naturally, both personal and business partnerships. With Saturn ruling his Sun, he has the ability to organize and to structure matters of business, and he works according to a strict ethic.

A part of his challenge is, in fact, to endeavor not to be too strict in his partnerships, and not to be too hard on himself. In his personal partnership, this individual is most likely to settle down with one lover for a lifetime, or at least have the desire to.

Between his two rulers, Saturn and the Moon, he is much concerned with times and tides, and he may seek a career dealing with either or both. If other factors confirm, he might be involved in the legal or judiciary system in some way.

Cancer Rising with Aquarius Sun

>*"I am because I am; my will/ego finds expression through who or what I know."*

The Sun in this combination will most likely fall into the Eighth House or the Seventh. If it is in the Eighth, the ego expression will find outlet through matters related to partnership finances, sex, heritage and inheritance, or death; if in the Seventh, it will find outlet through matters of partnership and associations with others.

This is not an easy combination, for the Cardinal Water of the Ascendant and the Fixed Air of the Sun merely coexist, unable to mix productively. Whatever the combination, the Eighth House Sun is almost always frustrating, and the native must find original, creative solutions to what he wants in life.

It is possible for this native to achieve this, for the Moon is productive and Uranus, ruler of his Sun, is creative, ingenious, and original. However, it is also freedom loving, while the Moon is home loving. If the Sun is in the Eighth, in quincunx aspect to the Ascendant, this might produce a comedian with a very strange humor directed toward sex and death and parentage.

The combination of the Ascendant's feelings and the Sun's knowledge might also produce a psychiatrist or a sex-therapist, or even someone who runs a computer dating service. It might also produce a counselor on death and dying.

Cancer Rising with Pisces Sun

>*"I am because I feel; my will/ego finds expression through my beliefs."*

The Sun in this combination will most likely fall into the

Ninth House or the Eighth. If it is in the Ninth, the ego expression will find outlet in matters related to higher education, philosophy, travel, or publishing; if it is in the Eighth, it will find outlet through partnership finances, sex, heritage or inheritance, or death.

This is one of the best combinations for Cancer Rising, having Cardinal Water on the Ascendant and Mutable Water ruling the Sun. It is especially beneficial if the Sun is in the Ninth, trining the Ascendant. The extremely emotional nature of the Self works with the emphasis on faith and beliefs of the ego, in the house of the higher mind and the higher spirit. It is an ideal combination for a minister or priest, theologian or professor of philosophy. It is also excellent for metaphysics, or one involved in the occult. It could as easily be representative of one who works on cruise ships.

With such an emphasis on the emotions, the mind, and the spirit, the challenge of this combination is to seek to develop the physical side, to avoid becoming too much of an ascetic, too deeply involved in an internal world.

Cancer Rising with Aries Sun

"I am because I feel; my will/ego finds expression through the fact that I am."

The Sun in this combination will most likely fall into the Tenth House or the Ninth. If it is in the Tenth, the ego expression will find outlet through public recognition, honors, success, and the father; if it is in the Ninth, it will find outlet through matters related to higher education, philosophy, travel, or publishing.

Because the Sun in this combination is Cardinal Fire in square aspect to the Cardinal Water of the Ascendant, this can be a stressful relationship, but it could be one oriented toward public success. The watery emotions of the Self and personality tend to put out the fiery ambitions of the Sun, but as the

Sun is in the Midheaven, it can overpower the retiring nature of the Ascendant.

This individual might seek a career in the military or law enforcement, or he might go into politics or even fire-fighting. (The combination of water and fire in the latter would be ideal.)

However, whatever he does, he tends to be very concerned with himself and with his own feelings. His challenge is to try to understand the feelings and concerns of others, and to share his own with them.

Cancer Rising with Taurus Sun

"I am because I feel; my will/ego finds expression through what I have."

The Sun in this combination will most likely fall into the Eleventh House or the Tenth. If it is in the Eleventh, the ego expression will find outlet through friends, group activities, aspirations, or social movements; if it is in the Tenth, it will find outlet through matters related to public recognition, honors, success, and the father.

The water of the Cardinal Ascendant nourishes the earth of the Fixed Sun, producing a creative and successful combination, especially if the Sun is in the Eleventh. The feelings natural to Cancer can easily be directed toward social causes,and loving, Venus ruled Taurus, which is also quite practical, utilizes all he has to serve others in this position.

This person can be a good politician or a social worker; he can also be a professional party-giver or host, with an extensive social life. However, his tendencies toward materialism and personal comfort can, at times, work against his professional concerns for others. He is challenged to acquire some of the nature of the Twelfth and Sixth Houses—spiritual development and true work and service to others.

Cancer Rising with Gemini Sun

"I am because I feel; my will/ego finds expression through my ability to think (or have opinions)."

The Sun in this combination will most likely fall into the Twelfth House or the Eleventh. If it is in the Twelfth, the ego expression will find outlet through matters of spiritual regeneration, solitude, institutions, or inhibitions or restrictions he places on himself; if it is in the Eleventh, it will find outlet through friends, group activities, aspirations, or social movements.

Ordinarily, the Twelfth House Sun is one of the most difficult of placements. However, because of Gemini's ability to think, this can be fairly positive. Gemini's mind is capable of understanding the Cancer Ascendant's deep feelings, despite the fact that his Mutable Air merely coexists with Cancer's Cardinal Water.

The danger, of course, is that Gemini's capacity for thought can be a crude form of opinionation, working to the native's detriment. A part of the challenge of this combination is to seek the positive side of Gemini's dual nature.

The feelings and the thoughtfulness of Cancer-Gemini could produce a priest, one with a deeply spiritual nature, or a minister. Or he could be a prison counselor or a probation officer, or he could be a medical administrator with a special concern for patient welfare.

Chapter 6

CARDINAL AIR—LIBRA

(September 23–October 22)

Applies to Libra Sun sign, Libra Ascendant, and those with Venus on the Ascendant.

RULER—Venus
MOTTO—"I balance." or "I justify."
SYMBOL—Scales
POLARITY—Positive/Masculine
COLOR—Green
KEY WORDS—Balance, Harmony, Partnership
MALE IDOLS—Montgomery Clift, Johnny Mathis, Gore Vidal
FEMALE IDOLS—Julie Andrews, Rita Hayworth, Angela Lansbury

THE LIBRA LOOK

At any gathering of gays, more than likely the "prettiest" faces in the room will have a strong Libra influence. Ruled by Venus, Libra generally sets the standard for beauty. Usually Libra is tall and well-formed proportionately, though tending to slenderness or lankiness. The face may be somewhat round or oval, with dimpled cheeks, classical features, and an impeccably clear complexion. The hair is generally straight, and may range in color from auburn to blond to flaxen. When genetics permits, Libra will be likely to have blue eyes. In some cases, the eyebrows may be noticeably heavy or darker than the hair.

Libra's tendency towards prettiness can reach the extreme of effeminacy or an androgynous appearance. This may be combined with a softness or a sweetness to the voice.

In dress, Libra almost invariably keeps up with the

fashions or trends of the time, or will be careful to follow the dress code for the occasion. But one thing is consistent about Libra's attire: he will always have everything perfectly coordinated, so that all colors harmonize and the overall effect is pleasing to the eye.

It may take Libra forever to get dressed to go out, not because he is slow but because he has difficulty choosing what to wear.

If attending a costume party, Libra will be likely to pick his apparel on the basis of whether or not it is pleasing to the eye. If he has a date for the party, he may attempt to match whatever his partner is wearing.

THE LIBRA NATURE

Libras generally give the impression of having it all—looks, brains, and talent. And to some extent, they do. They carry with them all the blessings of the Autumn Equinox, when light and darkness are of equal duration, in the season of bounteous harvest. But that isn't enough to satisfy Libra, who knows that winter is coming, but is able to cope only with the present.

Libra is one of the most sociable of the signs, not to mention the most charming and gracious. When Libras smile, which they do often, hearts beat a little faster.

Libra is quite aware of the effect he has on others, both because of his looks and because of his charm. Some consider Libra to be vain, but this is not quite true. It is more that he has a fine appreciation of beauty, harmony, and comfort; and—assuming that others are just as appreciative—he seeks to please. To some extent, the obsession with his looks and with what others think of him is calculated; abhorring ugliness and unpleasantness, he wants others to be as beautiful and as charming as he is.

Being both artistic and refined, gay Libra can accomplish much, especially in fields where aesthetics and personality are important. An Air sign, he has very creative ideas, and is exceptional at setting projects into motion. But he very quickly needs the help or the approval of others in order to continue. It is not because he is lazy, but because he—like the other Cardinal signs—lacks staying power. Without help or approval, he begins to doubt himself and his creative efforts.

Some consider Libra to be indecisive, but that is not quite true. It may take him some time before he will make important decisions, but he does make them, after carefully perceiving and analyzing all options. It is in making the little choices in life where Libra has great difficulty—choosing what clothes to wear, selecting food from a menu.

His ability to see all sides of an issue makes Libra a great mediator in disputes. He is just and fair toward others, and he expects others to treat him the same way.

In love, Libras are rather difficult to understand. The driving force behind this Cardinal Air sign is the need to achieve partnership, a loving union with one other person. Yet he has great difficulty achieving it. Surprisingly, as beautiful as Libras are, they are not very passionate, and indeed not very sexual. They prefer the mental, emotional, and psychological sustenance of a relationship, and sex just seems to get in the way. They want approval, support, and reinforcement from others.

Often, the only ones who truly understand their needs are other Libras.

THE LIBRA CHALLENGE

The life challenge for the gay Libra is to learn to love himself, to realize that the kind of support and approval he seeks from others will always be inadequate so long as he does not truly believe in himself first.

The greatest barrier to Libra's perceiving this fact is his great preoccupation with surface matters. Aware of his own beauty and charm, he tends to doubt the depth of his spirit and mind. He fears he may truly be "just another pretty face." These fears are unfounded, of course, and often it takes another Libra for him to see his own problem. It is, for him, like looking in a mirror. By perceiving the foolishness of another's fears, he sees his own.

Ultimately, gay Libra will realize that it is loving rather than being loved that comes first; then all blessings follow.

LIBRA RISING

Libra Rising with Libra Sun

"I am because I balance; my will/ego finds expression through my ability to balance."

The Sun in this combination will fall into the First House or the Twelfth. If the Sun is in the First, the ego expression finds outlet through matters related to the personality and appearance; if in the Twelfth, through matters related to spiritual regeneration, solitude, institutions, or inhibitions or restrictions he places on himself.

The double Libra is extremely concerned with fairness, but such an emphasis on the characteristics of balance can create an individual who is actually rather one-sided. His concept of fairness may be a highly original one, created by himself, and one that only he believes in. By nature, the airy Cardinal sign Libra directs its energy toward partnership or union with others, balancing the needs of Self with the needs of lover or business partner. In this case, all that energy is directed toward the Self and the ego, the house that is opposed to its natural home.

The efforts of this individual will be to find balance within himself, a balance between loving and being loved. His challenge will be to seek partnership, and to learn to balance his own needs and desires with those of others, which is the very nature of his sign.

Libra Rising with Scorpio Sun

"I am because I balance; my will/ego finds expression through my desires."

The Sun in this combination will fall into the Second House or the First. If the Sun is in the Second, the ego expression finds outlet through matters related to money, possessions, or the loving, giving nature; if it is in the First, it finds outlet through the personality and the appearance.

Venus rules the Ascendant, and Pluto the Sun. If the Ascendant and Sun are in semi-sextile relationship, there can be a focus on matters of sex and love. However, the desires that define the ego may concentrate on money or material goods, and there can be some internal stress because the Ascendant is Cardinal Air and the Sun is Fixed Water, two elements that coexist but do not mix.

The challenge for this native is similar to that of the double Libra, a need to learn to balance partnership, though the emphasis here is directed more toward sex or partnership finances.

Libra Rising with Sagittarius Sun

"I am because I balance; my will/ego finds expression through my ability to see or perceive."

The Sun in this combination will most likely fall into the Third House or the Second. If the Sun is in the Third, the ego expression finds outlet through matters related to communication, education, and brethren; if it is in the Second, it finds outlet through money and possessions, and perhaps the loving, giving nature.

The Cardinal Libra Air works well with the Mutable Sagittarius Fire, especially when the Sun is in sextile aspect to the Ascendant. Not only does the air feed the fire to achieve the native's ambitions, but the weighing and balancing characteristics of Libra's nature is in tune with the Sagittarius ego's eagerness to explore and perceive and acquire knowledge.

In the Third House, the Sun seeks to communicate, to learn, to write, to shine and reflect itself through those it considers brethren. It is an excellent combination for a teacher, and quite good for a writer as well, though this individual wishes always to be fair and aesthetically pleasing. If he is a writer, he might choose to write non-fiction, particularly works concerned with travel, philosophy, religion, or law.

His challenge is to learn pragmatism or practicality, to seek to deal with matters of finances and personal as well as partnership security. He must find something that will pull him down to earth, help him to come down from his ivory tower and deal with reality.

Libra Rising with Capricorn Sun

"I am because I balance; my will/ego finds expression through my ability to use."

The Sun in this combination will most likely fall into the Fourth House or the Third. If the Sun is in the Fourth, the ego expression finds outlet through matters related to the home, mother, or real estate; if in the Third, through matters associated with communication, education, and brethren.

Although this combination of Cardinal Air and Cardinal Earth can be somewhat stressful, it can also be rather productive in square aspect. Air and earth coexist and do not mix. Libra is idealistic, aesthetic, and desirous of loving partnership, appreciating things that appeal to the mind and the senses. Capricorn is practical, serious, responsible, and businesslike. Furthermore, each sign is in the house opposed to its natural placement. This is particularly difficult for the Capricorn Sun, which would prefer to be out in the public eye, not quietly tucked away in the home.

Either by choice or by restriction, this native might find

it necessary to work from his home, perhaps as an artisan or craftsman. However, he might as easily build homes, as an architect, a contractor, or a carpenter, for Saturn, ruler of Capricorn, is concerned with building and structuring. He is also concerned with time and the past, so he might find fortune through renovating old homes.

His challenge is to learn to deal with his concept of self as separate from partners and to establish himself in his rightful place as a leader. He must also find some way to connect his mental and aesthetic interests with his practical, orderly, responsible tendencies.

Libra Rising with Aquarius Sun

> *"I am because I balance; my will/ego finds expression through who or what I know."*

The Sun in this combination will most likely fall into the Fifth House or the Fourth. If it is in the Fifth, the ego expression will find outlet through matters related to entertainment, love affairs, romance, speculation, or children; if in the Fourth, it will find outlet through matters connected with the home, mother, or real estate.

This is an excellent mix of two Air signs, though both are in the opposite houses of their natural placement. Though others might consider this native something of a "space ship," he will surely be highly creative. The aesthetic need for balance within the Libra Ascendant works with the brilliant mind and knowledge of the Aquarian Sun to produce an individual with potential for success in a variety of fields. He could be an abstract painter or sculptor; he could be very inventive in the electronics field; or he could work in some capacity in the entertainment field, perhaps in film, either in front of or behind the camera.

His challenge is to find some means of grounding his airy ideals, to come out of himself and to perceive what the world is really like among ordinary people.

Libra Rising with Pisces Sun

"I am because I balance; my will/ego finds expression through my beliefs."

The Sun in this combination will most likely fall into the Sixth House or the Fifth. If it is in the Sixth, the ego expression will find outlet through matters of work, service, health, clothing, and food; if in the Fifth, through matters of entertainment, love affairs, romance, speculation, and children.

This is not an easy combination. The Cardinal Air Ascendant has difficulty with the Mutable Water Sun. There is an inner tension between the loving, balancing aspirations of the Self and the spiritual, sensitive ego, with the Neptune-ruled Sun in the Sixth House of work, service, and health. This individual tends to be too self-effacing for his own good. He has a strong belief in work, and he will do virtually anything to please, even though it may be detrimental to his own interests.

His challenge is to learn to stand up for himself, to turn the passivity of his Neptune rulership to the higher, more creative facets of his Sun. Medicine would be one of the beneficial choices for his work and service, but work dealing with water or oil or chemicals performed in the outdoors might also satisfy his Libra Self.

Libra Rising with Aries Sun

"I am because I balance; my will/ego finds expression through the fact that I am."

The Sun in this combination will most likely fall into the Seventh House or the Sixth. If it is in the Seventh, the ego expression will find outlet through matters of partnership and associations with others; if in the Sixth, it will be through matters of work, service, health, clothing, and food.

Although there is a tug of war between two opposing

signs, this is a positive combination, with the Cardinal Air of the Ascendant feeding the Cardinal Fire of the Sun. With the fiery Sun in the Seventh House, the natural placement for Libra, this individual successfully identifies himself through his partnerships, both loving and business, to achieve his ambitions in both his personal and professional life.

Love and sexuality are extremely important to him, and he might find a way to have these factors carry over into his professional life, either working with his lover or developing a career that somehow deals with love and partnership—such as a marriage counselor, a divorce lawyer, or a judge.

His challenge is to see others as they truly are, to seek not to be too self-centered.

Libra Rising with Taurus Sun

"I am because I balance; my will/ego finds expression through what I have."

The Sun in this combination will most likely fall into the Eighth House or the Seventh. If it is in the Eighth, the ego expression will find outlet through matters related to partnership finances, sex, heritage and inheritance, or death; if in the Seventh, it will find outlet through matters of partnership and associations with others.

This combination is not an easy one. The Cardinal Air of the Ascendant merely coexists with the Fixed Earth of the Sun, rather than mixing comfortably. The Libra Self wants to achieve, possibly in matters of love or aesthetics; certainly it seeks to balance and be fair. However, the Taurus ego seeks to be comfortable and secure with what he possesses, whether it is inherited money, partnership finances, or his own sexual prowess.

There is one saving factor to this combination, though, and that is that both Ascendant and Sun are ruled by Venus. This unifies this individual into a truly loving person.

His compromise to the pull within himself may be to work in a bank or to handle estates or trust funds for others, or perhaps to work as a stockbroker.

His challenge is to look inward and discover his own spirit, as well as his spiritual needs.

Libra Rising with Gemini Sun

"I am because I balance; my will/ego finds expression through my ability to think (or have opinions)."

The Sun in this combination will most likely fall into the Ninth House or the Eighth. If it is in the Ninth, the ego expression will find outlet in matters related to higher education, philosophy, travel, or publishing; if it is in the Eighth, it will find outlet through partnership finances, sex, heritage or inheritance, or death.

This combination is highly directed toward success, especially success in matters dealing with ideals and the higher mind. The combination of Venus ruled Cardinal Air and Mercury ruled Mutable Air can produce a person who has a brilliant mind. He might be a teacher, perhaps a professor of art, or he could be a writer or a publisher or editor. Whatever he does, his thinking processes are always well-balanced. His speech is usually quite pleasant as well.

His challenge generally is related to the physical sphere. While he might be quite attractive, as most Libra Rising natives are, he needs to become more attuned to his sexual, loving nature, and he may be required to come down to earth and deal with practical mundane matters.

Libra Rising with Cancer Sun

"I am because I balance; my will/ego finds expression through my feelings."

The Sun in this combination will most likely fall into the Tenth House or the Ninth. If it is in the Tenth, the ego expression will find outlet through public recognition, honors, success, and the father; if it is in the Ninth, it will find outlet through matters related to higher education, philosophy, travel, or publishing.

Because the Sun is Cardinal Water and the Ascendant is Cardinal Air, in square aspect, this is a rather stressful combination, but the stress is usually productive, with positive outcomes, because the Sun is in the Midheaven, the ideal placement for success.

Precisely how the deeply feeling nature of the watery Cancer Sun defines itself in the public eye is difficult to say. However, the aesthetic, loving nature of the Libra Ascendant suggests something of an artistic nature. This might signify one who is an actor or an entertainer, someone whose emotions are a part of his public image. If the person is in politics or business, the emotional nature could work to his detriment.

The first challenge for this individual is to find something that will unify the disparate aspects of his identity, then to discover those things that lie beyond his loving and his feeling nature. He needs to learn to unbend and accept life as it comes, to enjoy the moment, without drawing all experience into his sensitive soul.

Libra Rising with Leo Sun

"I am because I balance; my will/ego finds expression through my will."

The Sun in this combination will most likely fall into the Eleventh House or the Tenth. If it is in the Eleventh, the ego expression will find outlet through friends, group activities, aspirations, or social movements; if it is in the Tenth, it will find outlet through matters related to public recognition, honors, success, and the father.

This is an excellent combination of Cardinal Air and Fixed Fire, producing an extremely attractive individual who literally shines among friends and groups. He is an ideal politician or group leader, drawing others by his charisma. The balancing nature of his Ascendant mellows the strong will of his Sun, preventing him from abusing the power that comes naturally to him.

Although the Sun is in the house opposed to its natural placement, Leo becomes quite responsible and considerate of others here. He truly cares about the problems of the world, and endeavors to help resolve them beneficently.

His challenge is to balance his personal, loving relationships as well as he does his social ones, understanding his lover and providing the emotional support that is needed.

Libra Rising with Virgo Sun

"I am because I balance; my will/ego finds expression through my ability to analyze."

The Sun in this combination will most likely fall into the Twelfth House or the Eleventh. If it is in the Twelfth, the ego expression will find outlet through matters of spiritual regeneration, solitude, institutions, or inhibitions or restrictions he places on himself; if it is in the Eleventh, it will find outlet through friends, group activities, aspirations, or social movements.

As with all Twelfth House placements of the Sun, this combination can be a rather difficult one. Cardinal Air and Mutable Earth do not mix, but merely coexist. However, of all the Twelfth House Suns, this can be the most productive one. Not only do the ruling planets of Ascendant and Sun— Venus and Mercury—work well together, but Virgo's ability to analyze enables him to deal well with the spiritual nature of the Twelfth House, while Libra's balancing act gives his other side the ability to deal well with others.

His challenge, of course, is to avoid turning his analytical mind against himself, to keep his thoughts from becoming self-destructive and to prevent his words from working against him with others.

His work might involve writing on spiritual or metaphysical matters, or teaching in institutions such as prisons or hospitals. He could be engaged in medical work, or in the military, though this latter is less likely than some of the other possibilities.

Chapter 7

CARDINAL EARTH—CAPRICORN

(December 22–January 20)

Applies to Capricorn Sun sign, Capricorn Ascendant, and those with Saturn on the Ascendant.

RULER—Saturn
MOTTO—"I use."
SYMBOL—Goat
POLARITY—Negative/Feminine
COLOR—Indigo
KEY WORDS—Responsibility, Conservatism, Ambition
MALE IDOLS—David Bowie, Cary Grant, Johnnie Ray
FEMALE IDOLS—Marlene Dietrich, Ethel Merman, Dolly Parton

THE CAPRICORN LOOK

The first thing noticed about the pure Capricorn is usually his rather prominent jaw and long neck, beneath a long, thin, or narrow face. The second thing is the general impression of boniness or severity of physical makeup. Generally, Capricorn is tall and slender, with a narrow chest and bony legs and knees. The eyes of Capricorn are usually dark, with a rather placid, steady gaze.

Through either appearance or manner, the Capricorn may appear older or more mature than he really is. He tends to dress rather conservatively, and if left totally to his own choices, will pick dark or somber colors.

Capricorn will try to hold onto his old clothes as long as possible, and when he purchases something he expects it to last a lifetime. For that reason, he usually purchases quality in a rather simple style. At the same time, he may pick up a bargain by buying old clothes at a thrift shop. Rarely will he choose something that is trendy or currently fashionable. He feels most comfortable in a business suit or a pair of slacks and an old sweater.

If attending a costume party, gay Capricorn would choose to go as a monk or priest, or even a nun; or he might dress as some prominent figure out of history or possibly as Father Time.

THE CAPRICORN NATURE

Gay Capricorn is extremely ambitious and very career-oriented. He likes dealing with the public and loves positions of authority. He sets goals for himself, and achieves them. Once one goal has been accomplished, however, he must set another, climbing ever higher. To him, success means economic security and material goods, and he achieves it by planning methodically and working hard.

Extremely responsible, Capricorn is the natural "father" of the Zodiac, the efficient executive, who makes rules and lives by them, expecting others to do the same. A workaholic himself, he may be a slave driver to his employees. Discipline, in work and in personal life, is important to him.

He tends to structure everything, making schedules, preparing organizational charts, and even planning his relaxation times well in advance. To him, everything must be in order if it is to function properly.

The problem is, not everything fits into structures and schedules. And it is often the frustration from this fact that causes the lack of staying power for Capricorn. Normally in the position of leadership, it is when his discipline falls apart that he must depend on his followers to take over. He may attempt to take on too much and find out too late that he can accomplish none of them well. Of all the Cardinal signs, Capricorn is the one most conscious of the past and future, because it is ruled by Saturn, the timekeeper. It is the limitations and restrictions of time that drive Capricorn, making him save his money and put it away for his old age. It is his nature as an Earth sign that makes him practical and pragmatic.

Although rather sober and serious, and not very spontaneous, gay Capricorn can be a good lover. Often he chooses partners who are considerably older or younger than he is. As an Earth sign, he is quite sensual, and he has a strong sexual drive. He can be a rock to lean upon, sturdy and reliable, faithful in love, but he expects the same from a partner.

Because his sign is ruled by Saturn, gay Capricorn can have guilt problems to resolve, and some may be related to sex and to his own homosexual nature. The means by which he resolves these problems is determined by the specific sign and house placement of Saturn in his chart. Generally he comes to grips with the problem by age twenty-eight, during the time of his first Saturn "return," the period when his ruler reaches the place when it was at his time of birth.

THE CAPRICORN CHALLENGE

Life challenges for the gay Capricorn are to try to be less critical of others and of Self, to endeavor to allow others to be themselves, and to try to overcome feelings of guilt and melancholy. Because they expect so much of themselves, they sometimes feel that others expect too much as well. They feel overburdened, and must ultimately realize that they do not have to carry the weight of the world on their shoulders.

A sense of loneliness may also be a problem for Capricorn, even in a room full of people. They must come to understand that they create their own isolation, and must break down their reserve and caution to accept the warmth of love and companionship.

Gay Capricorn sometimes has to remind himself that he is a good and deserving person, and it helps to consciously reward himself from time to time. He is able to achieve his greatest success when he understands that true responsibility is free of all motivations of guilt.

CAPRICORN RISING

Capricorn Rising with Capricorn Sun

> *"I am because I use; my will/ego finds expression through my ability to use."*

The Sun in this combination will most likely fall into the First House or the Twelfth. If the Sun is in the First, the ego expression finds outlet through matters related to the personality and appearance; if in the Twelfth, through matters related to the spirit or to service through institutions.

In this combination, Saturn rules both the Ascendant and the Sun, making an extremely serious, responsible, and practical individual. He is very success oriented, and has the capacity to use whatever comes within his sphere toward achieving success—whether it is knowledge, talents, people, or special insights. He not only identifies himself as one who organizes, but he also gets great personal satisfaction from that talent.

However, the great Saturn influence of Capricorn can have its negative side, making him feel guilty or causing him to judge himself and others too harshly. It is a part of his challenge to avoid the negatives of Saturn and strive toward the positives.

He can find success in business or politics, and is superior at any form of administrative work. His practicality, his pragmatism, which stems from his double Earth nature, can be extremely useful to others as well as to himself.

Capricorn Rising with Aquarius Sun

"I am because I use; my will/ego finds expression through who or what I know."

The Sun in this combination will most likely fall into the Second House or the First. If the Sun is in the Second, the ego expression finds outlet through matters related to money, possessions, or the loving, giving nature; if it is in the First, it finds outlet through the personality and the appearance.

This can be a somewhat stressful combination, with the Cardinal Earth of the Self and personality attempting to mix with the Fixed Air of the ego. The individual will eventually have to come to terms with the two distinctly different aspects of his identity. It is possible for him to justify the pragmatic tendency to "use" with his ego's expression through people and things he knows.

With the Sun in the Second House, it is generally his knowledge of money and material possessions that serves his ego, and this can be joined successfully with Capricorn's practicality and ability to organize. The ingenuity of Aquarius in this position can add a degree of social concern or an ability to deal with other people. This individual might succeed easily in merchandising or in sales or in positions of financial authority.

His challenge is to be sensitive to the needs of a partner or lover, to keep from running roughshod over the feelings of other individuals, for Aquarius can be brash and Capricorn can be hard, without intending to be.

Capricorn Rising with Pisces Sun

"I am because I use; my will/ego finds expression through my beliefs."

The Sun in this combination will most likely fall into the Third House or the Second. If the Sun is in the Third, the ego expression finds outlet through matters related to communication, education, and brethren; if it is in the Second, it finds outlet through money and possessions, and perhaps the loving, giving nature.

The Cardinal Earth Ascendant and the Mutable Water Sun work well together. One can jokingly say that it has a tendency to produce mud, but the positive way of looking at it is that the water nourishes the earth, and the earth gives the water form or boundaries, which it does not otherwise have. In this case, the most structured, staunchest of the Earth signs is combining with the most watery and passive of the Water signs.

The Pisces Sun placed in the Third House indicates that the spiritual beliefs of the native find outlet through communication, education, and brethren. This would be an excellent placement for a teacher in a parochial school, or a writer on spiritual matters.

However, the Cardinal Capricorn Ascendant, with its emphasis on using or utilizing its capabilities may be more practical minded, wanting to give greater structure or form to the communication.

The challenge for this native is to come to terms with matters concerning public service and public recognition, to avoid being too shy and retiring.

Capricorn Rising with Aries Sun

"I am because I use; my will/ego finds expression through the fact that I am."

The Sun in this combination will most likely fall into the Fourth House or the Third. If the Sun is in the Fourth, the ego expression finds outlet through matters related to the home, mother, or real estate; if in the Third, through matters associated with communication, education, and brethren.

This is a stressful relationship, though not entirely unproductive. The fire of the Aries Sun tends to scorch the earth of the Capricorn Ascendant, and the earth tends to put out the fire. But Aries is not very comfortable ruling the Fourth House of home, mother, and real estate, anyway, so creative solutions must be found to unite the Self and the ego.

Both being Cardinal in nature, Capricorn and Aries are almost equally ambitious, yet the Saturn ruled goat is more practical than the Mars ruled ram.

Part of the challenge for this individual is to find ways to use the innate strength of the Aries Sun, placed in its weakest position at the Nadir of the chart, to accomplish the goals of both. Real estate is perhaps the ideal occupation for this person, though he may not be satisfied merely with buying and selling, but would want to build and develop as well.

The other part of the challenge is to learn to compromise with those he loves, to settle down and listen as well as to push forward and to talk.

Capricorn Rising with Taurus Sun

"I am because I use; my will/ego finds expression through what I have."

The Sun in this combination will most likely fall into the Fifth House or the Fourth. If it is in the Fifth, the ego expression will find outlet through matters related to entertainment, love affairs, romance, speculation, or children, if in the Fourth, it will find outlet through matters connected with the home, mother, or real estate.

This is an excellent mix of two Earth signs, the one Cardinal and the other Fixed. It should work well for success in the material sphere. Yet, with the Sun placement in the Fifth House, there should be considerable creativity as well.

If the individual is in the entertainment field, he will be more likely to be a producer or director, engaged in some behind the scenes organizational work, than to be a performer. However, the Fifth House is also the house of chance, so he may as easily be involved in the stock market or even in gambling, in both of which he could have success.

The Taurus Sun might also give the native something of a childlike attitude in the Fifth House.

The challenge for this individual is to learn to be more adventurous in his dealings with others, not always to be cautious and concerned with the practical and the material.

Capricorn Rising with Gemini Sun

"I am because I use; my will/ego finds expression through my ability to think (or have opinions)."

The Sun in this combination will most likely fall into the Sixth House or the Fifth. If it is in the Sixth, the ego expression will find outlet through matters of work, service, health, clothing, and food; if in the Fifth, through matters of entertainment, love affairs, romance, speculation, and children.

This is not an easy combination, with the mixing of Cardinal Earth and Mutable Air in quincunx aspect. The air and earth merely coexist, unable to mix. The native must find creative solutions to unify the two disparate aspects of his identity.

Gemini is greatly concerned with his thoughts and his opinions. Gemini Sun is not particularly happy in the Sixth House of work and service and health, though this individual can put his communicative talents to work both in writing and speech in fields involving health, diet, food preparation, pets, and fashion.

In fact, his Capricorn Ascendant virtually forces him to use his talents to their fullest. But he is not entirely happy using them in the service of others, merely working when he wants to create.

The challenge for this individual is to learn to accept the two quite different aspects of his identity, to realize that others are capable of appreciating him for what he is—and not just appreciating, truly loving him.

Capricorn Rising with Cancer Sun

"I am because I use; my will/ego finds expression through my feelings."

The Sun in this combination will most likely fall into the Seventh House or the Sixth. If it is in the Seventh, the ego expression will find outlet through matters of partnership and associations with others; if in the Sixth, it will be through matters of work, service, health, clothing, and food.

As with all Seventh House Sun placements, there is the challenge for this native to go beyond defining his ego through his relationships rather than through his inner Self. The Sun is not entirely comfortable in the watery Cardinal sign of Cancer, which is Moon ruled, but when it is opposed by Saturn ruled Capricorn Rising, there is definitely an internal tug of war. (In some cases, depending upon the placement of Saturn and the Moon in the individual chart, this may have been caused by problems between mother and father.)

But the ultimate result can be quite positive, both creative and productive, and it stems from this stress.

This native must utilize his feelings and his emotions in partnership. In a love relationship, this is ideal. There is the combination of the responsible, mature Self (Capricorn) with the emotional ego reflected through his loved one. But in business partnership, there is a challenge to find some form in which the feelings and the emotions can be used productively.

Capricorn Rising with Leo Sun

"I am because I use; my will/ego finds expression through my will."

The Sun in this combination will most likely fall into the Eighth House or the Seventh. If it is in the Eighth, the ego expression will find outlet through matters related to partnership finances, sex, heritage and inheritance, or death; if in the

Seventh, it will find outlet through matters of partnership and associations with others.

The combination between Ascendant and Eighth House Sun is not an easy one. In this case, it is a combination between Cardinal Earth and Fixed Fire, which do not mix. The fiery Sun scorches the earthy Ascendant, and the earth attempts to quell the fire.

In more realistic terms, this can be seen by the pragmatism and seriousness of Capricorn attempting to restrain the instinctive urge of Leo to be out having a good time, refusing to grow up.

The Leo Sun placed in the Eighth House emphasizes matters of sex and partnership finances, as well as inheritance. While Capricorn wants to save money and invest it wisely, Leo wants to spend it on himself, on entertainment, even on gambling and romantic involvements.

Yet Capricorn can eventually resolve the internal stress, fulfilling at least some of Leo's ambitions through structuring play as well as work.

The challenge for this individual is to give in occasionally, to allow others to lead him at least some of the time, to trust, and, yes, to love. For, ultimately, the deepest conflict of all for this native is between the strong need of Capricorn to control and the strong urge of Leo to will.

Capricorn Rising with Virgo Sun

> *"I am because I use; my will/ego finds expression through my ability to analyze."*

The Sun in this combination will most likely fall into the Ninth House or the Eighth. If it is in the Ninth, the ego expression will find outlet in matters related to higher education, philosophy, travel, or publishing; if it is in the Eighth, it will find outlet through partnership finances, sex, heritage, inheritance, or death.

The trining combination of Capricorn Ascendant and

Virgo Sun is highly directed toward success, combining Cardinal Earth with Mutable Earth. The Virgo Sun, with its inclination to be analytical, is quite comfortable in the Ninth House of the higher mind, philosophy, travel, and publishing. The Capricorn Ascendant encourages the ego to use its resources to the utmost, giving ambition and energy to the usually flexible, Mutable Virgo.

This native could be an excellent teacher or writer, philosopher or travel guide. He could be a good editor as well, with the combination of structure and communication. Because Virgo is the sign of health, medicine, diet, and fashion, his writing, editing, or teaching could be in those fields.

The challenge for this native is to learn to play a bit more, to get out and have a good time occasionally, to unbend and not to be quite so serious.

Capricorn Rising with Libra Sun

"I am because I use; my will/ego finds expression through my ability to balance."

The Sun in this combination will most likely fall into the Tenth House or the Ninth. If it is in the Tenth, the ego expression will find outlet through public recognition, honors, success, and the father; if it is in the Ninth, it will find outlet through matters related to higher education, philosophy, travel, or publishing.

Because the Sun is Cardinal Air, in square aspect to the Cardinal Earth Ascendant, this is a stressful combination, but the stress is productive, with positive outcomes, because the Sun is in the Midheaven, the ideal placement for success. The native should achieve recognition in the public eye, but considerable effort must be expended to accomplish this.

Libra's urge for balance and aesthetics and partnership fulfills the ego through public activities, whether in business, government, or the arts. Capricorn's Cardinal nature, its strength and endurance and pragmatism helps the airy nature of the Libra ego to use its talents for ultimate success.

The challenge for this individual is to become more spiritual in nature, to look within and discover the nature of the inner Self.

Capricorn Rising with Scorpio Sun

"I am because I use; my will/ego finds expression through my desires."

The Sun in this combination will most likely fall into the Eleventh House or the Tenth. If it is in the Eleventh, the ego expression will find outlet through friends, group activities, aspirations, or social movements; if it is in the Tenth, it will find outlet through matters related to public recognition, honors, success, and the father.

In this combination, the Fixed Water of the Scorpio Sun nourishes the Cardinal Earth of the Capricorn Ascendant, while the earth gives form to the water, making this an excellent mixture for success. The Pluto ruled Scorpio ego must fulfill his desires through matters of the Eleventh House— through group associations, friends, aspirations, and social actions and activities.

Pluto's desires may be sexual, but they may also be regenerative, desirous of tearing down old, outmoded structures and building anew. They may also be related to the subconscious, to all matters that are hidden. The Capricorn Ascendant may make use of all these Plutonian qualities to achieve success for the native.

This could make this individual a revolutionary leader, or it could lead him to deal with group therapy or even to organizing parties.

The challenge for this person is to endeavor to uncover his spiritual Self and to direct more of his energy toward loving individual partnership, to become more human, not just humane.

Capricorn Rising with Sagittarius Sun

"I am because I use; my will/ego finds expression through my ability to see or perceive."

The Sun in this combination will most likely fall into the Twelfth House or the Eleventh. If it is in the Twelfth, the ego expression will find outlet through matters of spiritual regeneration, solitude, institutions, or inhibitions or restrictions he places on himself; if it is in the Eleventh, it will find outlet through friends, group activities, aspirations, or social movements.

The Twelfth House Sun is usually a very difficult combination, causing considerable frustration for the native. In this case, the Sun is in Sagittarius, the sign not only of seeing and perceiving, but of growth and outward expansion. It resists the turning inward to spiritual matters that is native to the Twelfth House, not wanting to isolate itself. It is more than just a little uncomfortable, though its Mutable nature does allow it to adapt.

In this case, it is aided by the Capricorn Ascendant, ruled by Saturn, which also restricts and encourages the promiscuous Jupiter ruled Sun to accept the confinement of ego.

When this native accomplishes this difficult spiritual feat, he is able to function well as a unified identity. He may achieve success through metaphysics or through service in medical institutions.

In addition to his spiritual challenge, this native is also challenged to direct some of his energy outward toward other people, learning to share his spiritual discoveries through love.

PART III

THE FIXED SIGNS

SEASONAL PEAKS

Living things are least conscious of their susceptibility to change when seasons are at their peaks—when spring is at full blossom, when summer seems to drift idly and blissfully, when autumn's harvest is done but the cold has not yet set in, and when winter's bleakness seems never-ending. The course of the Sun through the heavens appears not to change, and the pattern of light and darkness is virtually the same from day to day.

Astrologically, individuals born during these periods are considered to be in Fixed signs. When the Sun is at the peak of spring, it is in the sign Taurus; in summer, it is in the sign Leo; in autumn, in Scorpio; and in winter, in Aquarius. Those born under these signs have the nature of the season indelibly imprinted on their characters, rigidly fixed and stubbornly unwilling to change.

They are capable of accomplishing much that the other signs cannot, because they are persistent and persevering. When they are committed to something, their efforts are sustained and unwavering over a long period of time. They allow nothing to sway them from their purpose, no matter whether they are right or wrong. It is this factor that has given them a reputation for stubbornness.

In achieving their ends, they are capable of using—even abusing—the Mutable signs, whom they consider to be "wishy-washy." They may try to do the same with the Cardinal signs, but generally do not have a great deal of success, for the Cardinals are protected by their strong egos.

Fixed signs have no patience for contemplation of the past. They may dream about a rosy future, but seem to get too bogged down in the present to make plans. They depend upon luck and perseverence to achieve their goals. Generally, they are not very good with details, preferring to leave them to others to take care of.

They will almost never admit that they are wrong. For that reason spiritual growth and development is difficult for them. They are capable of learning new things, but only when it suits their already determined goals and objectives.

This makes their life challenges extremely difficult for them. They can accomplish almost anything in the material world, but have to struggle painfully within themselves to achieve their spiritual needs and objectives.

Luckily few people's astrological charts are purely Fixed, but are combined with qualities of Cardinal and Mutable signs. However, a very high percentage of gays have both Sun and Ascendant as Fixed signs. In the survey taken, slightly over twenty percent of all the gays were in this difficult category. Over 38 percent had Fixed Sun signs, while 45 percent had Fixed signs for Ascendants. (Chance is 33 percent.)

The reason for the high incidence of gays born under the influence of Fixed signs is the role played by the planet Uranus. This planet, which is the ruler of Aquarius, is in its detriment in Leo, is exalted in Scorpio, and in its fall in Taurus. Uranus is the planet that rules homosexuality; its natural house is Aquarius, but in that sign its other qualities generally overpower the gay aspect, making the homosexuality largely a mental or intellectual quality.

In the survey, seven percent of those polled had Sun in Aquarius, while 6.3 percent had Taurus Rising. The sign represented by the fewest gays is Taurus, the sign where Uranus has the least power, where it is in its fall. Just over 1.5 percent of those polled had Sun in Taurus, while 5.5 percent had Taurus Rising.

The other two Fixed signs—Leo and Scorpio—were among the "gayest" signs. Scorpio is the sign where Uranus is exalted, where its power is strongest; since Scorpio is also ruled by Pluto, the planet of sexuality, it makes sense that 16.5 percent of those polled would have Sun in Scorpio, while 12.6 percent would have Scorpio Rising. Leo, the sign where Uranus is in its detriment, was represented by 12.6 percent having Leo Sun signs, with 19.6 percent having Leo Ascendant.

Chapter 8

FIXED EARTH—TAURUS

(April 21–May 20)

Applies to Taurus Sun sign, Taurus Ascendant, and those with Venus on the Ascendant.

RULER—Venus
MOTTO—"I have."
SYMBOL—Bull
POLARITY—Negative/Feminine
COLOR—Red orange
KEY WORDS—Possessions, Pragmatism, Obstinacy
MALE IDOLS—Tyrone Power, Rudolf Valentino, Rod McKuen
FEMALE IDOLS—Audrey Hepburn, Elizabeth II, Alice B. Toklas

THE TAURUS LOOK

Contrary to popular belief, Taurus does not always look like a bull. There are two types of Taurus. One fits into the expected mold, being short and stout, with a short neck, wide nose and mouth, thick lips, and dark wide brows. He does indeed look like a bull, and he tends to act like one as well. However, the second type of Taurus is exactly the opposite. Although he is not generally tall, he is slender and regal in carriage, with a striking beauty. The eyes and brows in both types are most noticeable, being large and dark and somewhat impassive. The mouth of the second type will be full, but sensual, and the neck may be long and slender, beneath a rather square jaw. In most cases, Taurus has dark wavy or curly hair.

Gay Taurus may also choose to dress in one of two extremes. He may be totally careless about his appearance, or he may be impeccably neat and precise. In either case, he generally chooses to buy the very best quality, and he makes sure everybody knows the label. He is very fashion conscious, and when he is not a fashion plate, his sloppiness is studied or calculated.

Taurus is highly sensual, and if attending a costume party, gay Taurus will likely choose a costume that is blatantly sexual in nature, or will tend to choose something that will expose parts of his body. Those more conservative might be likely to wear western attire.

THE TAURUS NATURE

The driving force behind Taurus is a need for financial and emotional security. Ruled by Venus, gay Taurus has a fine appreciation of all things beautiful or aesthetic, but being an Earth sign, he is also very practical and pragmatic. He carefully sets out to acquire those possessions that will provide his needed security; once he has them, he does everything possible to protect them.

Although gay Taurus is highly creative, he is more likely to be involved in the buying, selling, or handling of art objects than he is in creating them, because he is exceedingly aware of the value of things, and he rarely takes the risks necessary for an artist. He might be an agent, a dealer in art or antiques, a decorator, or even a banker or stockbroker. Because of his love of nature and gardening, he might also be a landscape architect. Almost always, he combines his artistic nature with his practicality.

Like all of the Earth signs, Taurus enjoys working, and he is very proud of his achievements. Acquiring wealth is one of his great goals, and generally he achieves it, by persevering and working hard.

He must always satisfy the five senses—touch, smell, taste, hearing, and sight. He loves good food, and is an excellent cook, though he may have a tendency toward too much spice or heavy sauces. He enjoys music of all sorts, but generally prefers the softer more harmonious types. He likes being given flowers, and loves perfumes or colognes. Physical comfort is a must, so he chooses always to sit in softly upholstered chairs or sofas, and he adores having a massage.

Very often Taurus chooses his friends or associates calculatedly, deciding consciously whether or not he can use someone to his advantage. This may even apply to a mate. While his love partner must be physically attractive, he must also be financially secure as well as attentive. Gay Taurus expects gifts, and not just on special occasions. He sees objects as tokens of love, as important an expression as sex or affection.

And Taurus is extremely affectionate, perhaps the most affectionate of all the signs. While he is quite sexual, foreplay is an important part of lovemaking to him. He won't tolerate "wham, bam, thank you ma'am."

Taurus is very loyal and devoted to his partner, once he has committed himself, and he expects the same of his partner. He is extremely possessive, and may tend to convey the impression that he "owns" his lover. At the same time, if his partner is loyal to him, he will protect and defend him to the death.

THE TAURUS CHALLENGE

The life challenge for the gay Taurus is a difficult one. He is involved in a lengthy search to discover that things of the spirit are just as important as material possessions. He must learn that there is more to him than what he owns and how much money he has acquired, and that the same is true for the people around him.

This challenge becomes most acute when it comes to his relationship with his partner or lover. He may go through many relationships before he realizes that the ideal mate of his imagination may not really exist. Few love partners want to be possessed or controlled the way a Taurus tends to do.

For this reason, the gay Taurus must learn not to be quite

so jealous and possessive of those he loves. He must come to understand that his partner is a separate individual, who gives his love of his own choice, not because it is expected or demanded. It is important for him to work on getting rid of his obstinacy and inflexibility, especially with those closest to him.

The greatest lesson he can learn is that gifts are of greatest value when they are freely given, not demanded or expected as a matter of course.

TAURUS RISING

Taurus Rising with Taurus Sun

>   *"I am because I have; my will/ego finds expression through what I have."*

The Sun in this combination will most likely fall into the First House or the Twelfth. If the Sun is in the First, the ego expression finds outlet through matters related to the personality and appearance; if in the Twelfth, through matters of spiritual regeneration, solitude, institutions, or inhibitions or restrictions he places on himself.

In either case, Venus rules both the Ascendant and the Sun, providing a very loving and a very sensual nature to the identity. This individual is quite earthy, and probably extremely materialistic, as well as possessive in love.

He both identifies himself through what he has or possesses and satisfies his ego through his money and possessions. He can be warm and affectionate, but extremely stubborn and resistant to change. His career will likely be something related to money or to material goods, yet he enjoys working outdoors, and he prefers to be in rural areas rather than in the hustle and bustle of cities.

His challenge is to develop spiritually, to learn that material goods and money are not all there is to the joy of life, and that love does not involve possessing the loved one.

Taurus Rising with Gemini Sun

"I am because I have; my will/ego finds expression through my ability to think (or have opinions)."

The Sun in this combination will most likely fall into the Second House or the First. If the Sun is in the Second, the ego expression finds outlet through matters related to money, possessions, or the loving, giving nature; if it is in the First, it finds outlet through the personality and the appearance.

Venus rules the Ascendant, and Mercury the Sun. While the mixture of Fixed Earth and Mutable Air are difficult to justify within the Self, they can combine successfully in the semi-sextile relationship to produce one who has a combination of charm and communicativeness, perhaps the ideal salesman.

This combination is quite similar to the double Taurus, because of its emphasis on Second House matters—money and material goods and the loving, giving nature. Yet there is a degree of stress because of the coexistence of earth and air. The ego finds its expression through thoughts and opinions. The Gemini taste in material goods is more important than the goods themselves.

Part of the challenge of this native is to justify the Self's identification through his possessions with the ego's need to express itself through thoughts and opinions concerning money and possessions. Another aspect of his challenge is to seek a spiritual nature to add to his physical and mental facets.

Taurus Rising with Cancer Sun

"I am because I have; my will/ego finds expression through my feelings."

The Sun in this combination will most likely fall into the Third House or the Second. If the Sun is in the Third, the ego expression finds outlet through matters related to communication, education, and brethren; if it is in the Second, it finds outlet through money and possessions, and perhaps the loving, giving nature.

Either way, the two work well together, for the water of the Cancer Sun mixes well with the earthy Taurus Ascendant, and the native is able to express himself quite well, accomplishing his practical Taurus ambitions.

With the Sun in the Third House, Cancer is more concerned than usual with expressing his feelings; his native secrecy and reticence is less severe. He wants to communicate, though it may still not be directly verbal, but may find outlet through writing, though teaching cannot be entirely ruled out. He also has very strong feelings about those he considers his brethren, and he may express them quite openly.

His challenge is to learn to adapt to the needs and concerns of those around him, to become more sensitive to the outside world, and to venture out into the world beyond his neighborhood more often.

Taurus Rising with Leo Sun

> *"I am because I have; my will/ego finds expression through my will."*

The Sun in this combination will most likely fall into the Fourth House or the Third. If the Sun is in the Fourth, the ego expression finds outlet through matters related to the home, mother, or real estate; if in the Third, through matters associated with communication, education, and brethren.

This is a stressful relationship, though not entirely unproductive. The fiery Leo Sun, especially when in square aspect, has difficulty with the practicality of the earthy Taurus Ascendant, which tends to restrain the ego and the will, keeping it from the public eye where it can shine. However, the native can succeed by using his Leo ingenuity.

Leo, being catlike, can almost always land on his feet, no matter what difficulty he faces. His will here finds expression through Fourth House matters—those of home, mother, and real estate. He could be an excellent real estate salesman or land developer, though his Taurus Ascendant might make him always want to keep what he has rather than selling.

His challenge is similar to the other challenges of Taurus Rising individuals, to seek his spiritual side, to open himself up to understanding and dealing effectively with others, especially with the partner or lover.

Taurus Rising with Virgo Sun

"I am because I have; my will/ego finds expression through my ability to analyze."

The Sun in this combination will most likely fall into the Fifth House or the Fourth. If it is in the Fifth, the ego expression will find outlet through matters related to entertainment, love affairs, romance, speculation, or children; if in the Fourth, it will find outlet through matters connected with the home, mother, or real estate.

Either way, it is an excellent mix of two Earth signs, making an extremely practical individual. The flexible, Mutable Virgo ego is able to manipulate to achieve the material success the Taurus Ascendant seeks.

While the Taurus Ascendant is primarily concerned with the acquisition and possession of material goods, the Virgo ego analyzes and works hard to achieve them, willing to be of service to others in the process. While this individual might find a career in entertainment, it is more likely that he will choose something more practical in the Fifth House—such as investments in stocks and bonds or even in the development of new products.

His challenge is to learn to be more adventurous, to be willing to take greater risks to achieve his goals, for the double Earth can be extremely cautious, even when the Virgo Sun is in the house of risk taking.

Taurus Rising with Libra Sun

"I am because I have; my will/ego finds expression through my ability to balance."

The Sun in this combination will most likely fall into the Sixth House or the Fifth. If it is in the sixth, the ego expression will find outlet through matters of work, service, health, clothing, and food; if in the Fifth, through matters of entertainment, love affairs, romance, speculation, and children.

It is not an easy combination, because the Cardinal Air Sun does not mix well with the Fixed Earth Ascendant. The ego wants to achieve more, to be free to create, but the Taurus practicality holds him back, demanding security.

This combination would be the ideal for a mediator in labor disputes, or he could be a breeder of show animals—dogs, horses, or cats. But whatever he does, he must find the balance between his idealistic mental Sun and his practical, materialistic Self.

This is a part of his challenge, but he is also challenged to deal with matters of the spirit as well, delving inward to find the unity of his nature.

Taurus Rising with Scorpio Sun

"I am because I have; my will/ego finds expression through my desires."

The Sun in this combination will most likely fall into the Seventh House or the Sixth. If it is in the Seventh, the ego expression will find outlet through matters of partnership and associations with others; if in the Sixth, it will be through matters of work, service, health, clothing, and food.

It is a positive combination, with the Fixed Water of the Sun enriching the Fixed Earth of the Ascendant, creating one of the most lusty of individuals. However, there is the challenge for the native of defining his ego through his relationships rather than through his inner Self. However, this stressful tug of war can be productive and ultimately successful.

What his ego desires is partnership. Whether that desire can be satisfied by a single partner or not is dependent upon other aspects of his chart. Because of his Taurus Ascendant, he does tend to want to possess his partners, and he can be extremely jealous.

His challenge is to learn to be more trusting of those he loves and works with, to discover that what they give is far more valuable than what he demands of them.

Taurus Rising with Sagittarius Sun

> *"I am because I have; my will/ego finds expression through my ability to see or perceive."*

The Sun in this combination will most likely fall into the Eighth House or the Seventh. If it is in the Eighth, the ego expression will find outlet through matters related to partnership finances, sex, heritage and inheritance, or death; if in the Seventh, it will find outlet through matters of partnership and associations with others.

It is not an easy combination, for the Mutable Fire of the Sagittarius Sun wants to be out adventuring and exploring, while the Fixed Earth of the Taurus Ascendant insists on staying home and being practical. Whatever the combination, the Eighth House Sun is almost always frustrating for the native, and he must find original, creative solutions to what he wants in life.

In the Eighth House, what the Sagittarius ego sees or perceives generally relates to sex, inheritance, or partnership finances. In cases where this relates to financial matters, it can be justified with the Taurus Ascendant's concern with material goods for beneficial results. When it is connected with sexual matters, the challenge for this individual can be a considerable one. For what Taurus has may be love, and what

Sagittarius sees of a physical nature he may venture out to get, for he is quite promiscuous.

His challenge is to learn to restrain himself, to realize that faithfulness to partners is quite important and that his expressions of love can be spiritual as well as physical.

Taurus Rising with Capricorn Sun

> *"I am because I have; my will/ego finds expression through my ability to use."*

The Sun in this combination will most likely fall into the Ninth House or the Eighth. If it is in the Ninth, the ego expression will find outlet in matters related to higher education, philosophy, travel, or publishing; if it is in the Eighth, it will find outlet through partnership finances, sex, heritage or inheritance, or death.

The combination is an extremely favorable one, combining Fixed Earth on the Ascendant with Cardinal Earth ruling the Sun, making a very practical, well-organized individual who can achieve much.

The Capricorn ego uses what his Taurus Self possesses to achieve through Ninth House matters—higher education, philosophy, travel, and publishing. Because he is double Earth, this is usually concerned with subjects of an earthy, practical nature. He might be a teacher of economics, or of manual arts. But Capricorn is also concerned with business and public administration, so he could be concerned with techniques of management or finances.

His challenge is typically Taurus—to seek matters of the spirit, to look within and perceive values beyond the material.

Taurus Rising with Aquarius Sun

> *"I am because I have; my will/ego finds expression through what and who I know."*

The Sun in this combination will most likely fall into the Tenth House or the Ninth. If it is in the Tenth, the ego expression will find outlet through public recognition, honors, success, and the father; if it is in the Ninth, it will find outlet through matters related to higher education, philosophy, travel, or publishing.

Because the Sun is Fixed Air, in square aspect to the Fixed Earth Ascendant, this is a stressful combination, but the stress is productive, with positive outcomes, because the Sun is in the Midheaven, the ideal placement for success. The native is almost sure to achieve recognition in the public eye; however, he has the challenge to perceive his inner Self, not relying totally on seeing himself through his success—or through the eyes of others.

What Taurus has and what Aquarius knows find outlet through business, politics, or the popular arts, demanding public attention and recognition. This is a very social animal, but calculatedly so. He may be perceived as very cold-hearted and ruthless, and to some extent he is. Yet he is sensitive to the way others perceive him, and wants it to be otherwise. This is where the stress comes for him.

His challenge is to delve into his own spirit and realize that what is lacking is a sensitivity to the needs of others, that he must learn to give as well as to receive if he is to have true success as a human being.

Taurus Rising with Pisces Sun

> *"I am because I have; my will/ego finds expression through my beliefs."*

The Sun in this combination will most likely fall into the

Eleventh House or the Tenth. If it is in the Eleventh, the ego expression will find outlet through friends, group activities, aspirations, or social movements; if it is in the Tenth, it will find outlet through matters related to public recognition, honors, success, and the father.

Either way, the Mutable Water of the Pisces ego works well with the Fixed Earth of the Ascendant, with the water enriching the earth for success of personal desires as well as group ideals. The adaptability of the Sun can use Neptunian creativity to achieve the security so necessary for Taurus Ascendant.

In the Eleventh, the Pisces Sun believes strongly in social causes, and it may find outlet through charitable or philanthropic work, perhaps through religious foundations. For possessive Taurus, it is possibly the exception where he truly wants to share what he has with those less fortunate.

His challenge is to learn to love and share personally as well as with the world at large, to focus in on his life partner's needs and realize they are as important as those of society.

Taurus Rising with Aries Sun

> *"I am because I have; my will/ego finds expression through the fact that I am."*

The Sun in this combination will most likely fall into the Twelfth House or the Eleventh. If it is in the Twelfth, the ego expression will find outlet through matters of spiritual regeneration, solitude, institutions, or inhibitions or restrictions he places on himself; if it is in the Eleventh, it will find outlet through friends, group activities, aspirations, or social movements.

It is usually a very difficult combination, causing considerable frustration for the native. Not only is the Sun in the Cardinal Fire sign, where it will tend to scorch the Fixed Earth of the Ascendant, but it is in the house that has the most destructive tendencies, and the Martian quality of Aries can be quite destructive when turned inward. There is a significant challenge for this native to seek spiritual solutions to his ambitions, rather than to turn his fire against himself.

His fiery Aries ego may find outlet through institutions, such as the military or hospitals or prisons, where he can find both the security of regular income and a way of expressing his physical strength and acuity. When he can achieve unity of body, mind, spirit, and material security, he will know he is successful.

Chapter 9

FIXED FIRE—LEO

(July 23–August 22)

Applies to Leo Sun sign, Leo Ascendant, and those with Sun on the Ascendant.

RULER—Sun
MOTTO—"I will."
SYMBOL—Lion
POLARITY—Positive/Masculine
COLOR—Yellow
KEY WORDS—Integrity, Authority, Dignity
MALE IDOLS—Mick Jagger, Andy Warhol, Robert Taylor
FEMALE IDOLS—Mae West, Clara Bow, Jacqueline Onassis

THE LEO LOOK

In a gathering of gays, the person with the largest group of people around him is usually a Leo. At first glance, there appears to be no obvious reason for this. He is not the most beautiful; he is not the most outgoing; if anything, he seems indifferent to the attention. But it is the magnetism of his personality that draws almost everyone to him.

Leo is generally thought to be tall, but that is not always the case; he simply gives the impression of stature by his commanding manner, by his confidence and assurance.

Leo is aptly named; there is about him the indefinable quality of a lion, partly stemming from his regal carriage, partly from his catlike eyes, which are large, usually dark, and sometimes heavy lidded. His stare seems to take in everything and everyone around him without effort.

Leo generally has an oval face, which may become more round with age. His complexion tends to be ruddy, and his hair may be blond, reddish, or brown, but is almost always wavy or curly and thick. Often, the set of his mouth and jaw suggests that he is smiling wryly with some secret known only to him. Some Leos have an overbite, or a slightly open-mouthed appearance, that calls attention to the upper teeth.

Whether he is tall or of medium height, he usually has broad shoulders, and carries himself proudly erect. In middle age, he has a tendency to gain weight around the waist.

Leo dresses tastefully, but with a flair for the dramatic. He may wear subtle, muted shades, but may often set it off with a single bright or startling piece of apparel. Most Leos have a liking for sweaters or for shirts with a soft, plush feel to them, such as velvet or velour. Whatever they wear, they wear proudly, secure that it is right for the occasion.

If attending a costume party, Leo's first choice would be to dress as a king or a medieval prince or a Roman emperor. If in a whimsical mood, he might choose the costume of a cat or a lion. It is unlikely that he would permit his partner or date to select his costume for him, though he might insist that it be picked up and delivered to him.

THE LEO NATURE

Leo is a very social animal. He needs attention, and doesn't like being alone. It's not that he suffers from loneliness, but merely that he prefers to have others around him, the more the merrier. Of course, his ego demands that he has to be the center of attention, though he rarely has to expend any effort to achieve that position—unless there are other Leos around. Surprisingly, he usually does not resent other Leos, but enjoys the spirit of competition.

Gay Leo takes on responsibility without hesitation. He is a very good executive, because he can delegate authority. He expects those who work for him to carry their own weight. He is not particularly good with details, but concentrates on the overall approach. He needs others around him to take care of the small matters, like keeping him organized. The Leo executive has to have a secretary or an assistant; if he does not, his office will always be in chaos, with piles of paper in complete disorder.

Similarly, one should never ask Leo to give directions. Invariably, he will describe everything one will see along the route, telling where not to turn and where not to go. He knows the destination, and he expects everyone else to know.

He is always aware of his own personal goals, and they are usually high ones, which he eventually achieves. Most Leos are quite creative, especially gay Leos, and there are many in the entertainment industry. Leo represents the natural Fifth House of creativity, film, risk-taking, and children. If a Leo is gay and cannot physically have sons and daughters, he will concentrate on creating things as a substitute. He is most effective when working in conjunction with others, serving as the creative leader, with others assisting him. In the arts, this might be the theater, films, music, or collaborative writing.

If Leo's creative urge is squelched, he may become lazy, even embittered. He will be either extremely gracious and charming or utterly obnoxious. If he does not get attention one way, he will attract it another. Sometimes this is calculated. Leo is quite aware of his effect on others, and he may "put on an act" in order to achieve a desired response, quietly and subtly manipulating others. Sometimes this tendency can alienate even close friends.

Leo has a great sense of integrity and a strong belief in fairness, and he expects the same from others. But ultimately, he doesn't care if others disapprove of him, so long as he approves of himself. He will stubbornly follow his own sense of what is ethical. If others do not see that he is right, that is their problem.

In love, gay Leo can be extremely passionate, but he rarely makes the first move in a relationship, not just because his ego cannot bear the possibility of rejection, but because he is extremely proud. If an approach is ill-timed or clumsy, the results could be disastrous. Once a relationship is begun, Leo is extremely giving. He is generous and romantic, focusing all of his love on a single partner.

This can present problems for a relationship. By giving so much, Leo can become quite possessive, feeling that he owns his partner and has the right to control his life completely. For this reason, it is important that Leo's lover be as generous and as giving as he is.

For many gay Leos, life may be an adventure in which they never want to grow up, but enjoy romance, even if it is one romance after another. When an affair ends, Leo wonders why he cannot attract a more constant love, unaware that it is his own inconstancy that is at fault.

THE LEO CHALLENGE

The life challenge for Leos is to learn to avoid excessive pride and egocentricity. For gay Leos, this challenge often focuses specifically on love relationships. Through trial and error, they must eventually come to realize that they do not have to dominate others or control them. True love involves mutual sharing and giving, and does not involve ego games.

They need to learn to let relationships develop and grow gradually, without pushing or expecting passion to remain at the peak of intensity continually, accepting gentle or quiet moments as an integral part of love and caring.

In a similar manner, the challenge for their creative efforts is to learn to organize and to deal with some of the mundane details themselves, accepting what may seem tedious to them as a part of their overall creation.

LEO RISING

Leo Rising with Leo Sun

> **"I am because I will; my ego/will finds expression through my will."**

The Sun in this combination will most likely fall into the First House or the Twelfth. If the Sun is in the First, the ego expression finds outlet through matters related to the personality and appearance; if in the Twelfth, through matters of spiritual regeneration, solitude, institutions, or inhibitions or restrictions he places on himself.

This is possibly the most egocentric of all Ascendant-Sun sign combinations; certainly it is the one with the strongest will to succeed and the greatest ambition, for the Sun rules both Self and ego. In this combination, it is far better for the Sun to be placed in the First rather than the Twelfth House, for at least part of the Leo will can be turned against the Self in the latter position.

With the double Leo Sun in the First, the native can achieve virtually anything he sets out to do, by sheer will power. However, as a double sign, it will most likely choose matters indicated by its natural house; in this case the Fifth. Double Leo will be likely to seek a career in entertainment, perhaps in film, or he will be a gambler, an investor in stocks and bonds, a daredevil of some sort, perhaps a race-car driver or a stuntman.

In his lowest form, he may be a pure romantic, an unregenerate child, wasting his life in pleasure-seeking.

His challenge is to become sensitive to others, both individually and as a group, to realize there is something outside himself, perhaps even someone. He must realize it is as important to love as to be loved.

Leo Rising with Virgo Sun

*"I am because I will; my will/ego finds expression
through my ability to analyze."*

The Sun in this combination will most likely fall into the
Second House or the First. If the Sun is in the Second, the
ego expression finds outlet through matters related to money,
possessions, or the loving, giving nature; if it is in the First,
it finds outlet through the personality and the appearance.

This can be a rather stressful combination, particularly
when the Ascendant and Sun are in semi-sextile relationship,
with the Sun in the Second House. It is a joining of Fire and
Earth, Fixed and Mutable signs. The fire tends to scorch the
earth, and the earth to put out the fire. Leo is willful and ambitious, centering all on himself, while Virgo is analytical and
adaptable, seeking expression through work and service.

There is difficulty in uniting these two factors into an integrated identity, for they seem to work against each other.
But Leo is stronger than Virgo, and will ultimately win, becoming able to utilize Virgo's concerns for getting along with
others and being of use for his own ambitions and concerns.

This combination will probably be involved with matters
of finances and physical possessions; it could be a stock market analyst or a writer on business matters. Or it could be one
who tests products for safety and reliability.

The challenge for this individual is to go beyond unifying
his needs of Self and of service, to perceiving the genuine interests of others, particularly of others who are close to him.

Leo Rising with Libra Sun

*"I am because I will; my will/ego finds expression
through my ability to balance."*

The Sun in this combination will most likely fall into the
Third House or the Second. If the Sun is in the Third, the ego

expression finds outlet through matters related to communication, education, and brethren; if it is in the Second, it finds outlet through money and possessions, and perhaps the loving, giving nature.

This combination works well together, for the Cardinal Air of the Libra Sun feeds the Fixed Fire of the Leo Ascendant. It is a highly creative mixture. The Libra Sun's need for balance finds outlet here through matters of communication, education, and brethren. This individual could be a writer or an artist, or even a teacher, possibly of art. Certainly his sense of aesthetics is important to him.

But the Leo Sun will drive him to success, whatever field he chooses to follow.

The challenge for this native is to seek to become more practical, to plan carefully for his success, to achieve some of the grounding of Earth signs and some of the adaptability of Mutable signs.

Leo Rising with Scorpio Sun

> *"I am because I will; my will/ego finds expression through my desires."*

The Sun in this combination will most likely fall into the Fourth House or the Third. If the Sun is in the Fourth, the ego expression finds outlet through matters related to the home, mother, or real estate; if in the Third, through matters associated with communication, education, and brethren.

The Fixed Water of the Scorpio Sun tends to put out the Fixed Fire of the Leo Ascendant. Ambition is dampened by Scorpio's desires, which may be of either a sexual or a financial nature.

Leo Rising wills for success, but the watery sensual Scorpio Sun is somewhat shy and retiring in this position. The creative solution for this individual will generally center around matters of home and real estate. It is perhaps an ideal combination for an interior decorator or a landscape designer, but the sale of real estate should not be ruled out. Or he may function behind the scenes in some manner.

The challenge for this individual is to learn to adapt, to acquire some Mutable qualities so that he can understand and relate more sensitively to others. He must learn to match his own desires with those of others.

Leo Rising with Sagittarius Sun

"I am because I will; my will/ego finds expression through my ability to see or perceive."

The Sun in this combination will most likely fall into the Fifth House or the Fourth. If it is in the Fifth, the ego expression will find outlet through matters related to entertainment, love affairs, romance, speculation, or children; if in the Fourth, it will find outlet through matters connected with the home, mother, or real estate.

This is an excellent mixture of two Fire signs, especially since the Mutable Sagittarius Sun is most likely to be in the Fifth House, the natural placement for Leo, which appears here on the Ascendant. The sensitivity and perception of Sagittarius gives the strong Fixed will of Leo just what he needs to find success through matters of entertainment, speculation, risk taking, creativity, and children.

This is an ideal placement for an action-oriented actor, particularly in film or television. It is also excellent for a stuntman. However, the double fire must be wary of burn-out. This combination also tends to emphasize too much passion and promiscuity in love affairs and "playing," and the native must avoid taxing his body too greatly.

The challenge is to give himself some self-control, to utilize the Leo will toward success in career. This individual is also challenged to acquire a degree of practicality and caution, to beware of running roughshod over friends and lovers.

Leo Rising with Capricorn Sun

"I am because I will; my will/ego finds expression through my ability to use."

The Sun in this combination will most likely fall into the Sixth House or the Fifth. If it is in the Sixth, the ego expression will find outlet through matters of work, service, health, clothing, and food; if in the Fifth, through matters of entertainment, love affairs, romance, speculation, and children.

This is not an easy combination, for the Fixed Fire of Leo Rising tends to scorch the Cardinal Earth of the Capricorn ego, while the earth tends to put out the fire. Leo's strong will and ambition is not entirely happy with its ego seeking outlet through Sixth House matters.

However, Capricorn's sense of responsibility may find use for Leo's strong will in order to serve a useful function for others. This individual will be a hard worker, and may be involved with medical insurance or management of hospitals. He could, however, as easily be an animal trainer or a restaurant manager.

His challenge is to remember that there are ideals or spiritual goals to be achieved along with his personal ambitions and his practical service.

Leo Rising with Aquarius Sun

"I am because I will; my will/ego finds expression through who or what I know."

The Sun in this combination will most likely fall into the Seventh House or the Sixth. If it is in the Seventh, the ego expression will find outlet through matters of partnership and associations with others; if in the Sixth, it will be through matters of work, service, health, clothing, and food.

Though there is inevitably some stress involved with an opposition between Ascendant and Sun, this can be a highly creative and successful combination because of the mix of the Fixed Air of Aquarius and the Fixed Fire of Leo. Each feeds the other for achievement.

The Aquarian ego seeks fulfillment through partnership, and may indeed identify itself through a lover or business associate. However, his knowledge and his mental powers and his social concerns must enter into the mixture, along with the creative will of the Leo Ascendant.

This individual has many choices of career, though almost all must be accomplished in partnership with others.

His challenge is to become more sensitive to the needs and feelings of those around him, for Leo is naturally self-centered and Aquarius tends to think only of others in groups rather than as individuals.

Leo Rising with Pisces Sun

"I am because I will; my will/ego finds expression through my beliefs."

The Sun in this combination will most likely fall into the Eighth House or the Seventh. If it is in the Eighth, the ego expression will find outlet through matters related to partnership finances, sex, heritage and inheritance, or death; if in the Seventh, it will find outlet through matters of partnership and association with others.

The Eighth House Sun is never an easy position, but this combination may be one of the most difficult ones. Not only does the Mutable Water of the Pisces Sun tend to put out the Fire of the Fixed Leo Ascendant, but the Neptune rulership of the Sun makes the ego extremely passive, more inclined to dream than to achieve, frustrating the Leo Self beyond measure.

Also, the Pisces ego can have difficulties with Eighth House matters. Although Pisces is not uninterested in matters of sex and money, he prefers fantasies to reality. In this position, he finds it necessary to deal with these elements on a spiritual level, incorporating reality into his belief structure.

His Leo will can overpower his Pisces ego to direct his spiritual nature outward toward accomplishment, but it can be exhausting. It can succeed through metaphysics or through psychology, if directed toward sexual therapy or through a spiritual use of money or inheritance.

The challenge for this native is to endeavor to come down to earth, to perceive the tangible, physical world as it truly is, to come out of himself and relate openly to others.

Leo Rising with Aries Sun

"I am because I will; my will/ego finds expression through the fact that I am."

The Sun in this combination will most likely fall into the Ninth House or the Eighth. If it is in the Ninth, the ego expression will find outlet in matters related to higher education, philosophy, travel, or publishing; if it is in the Eighth, it will find outlet through partnership finances, sex, heritage or inheritance, or death.

This is a positive, success-oriented combination of two Fire signs, the one Fixed and the other Cardinal. However, the Aries Sun is positioned in the Ninth House, the natural placement for the third Fire sign, Sagittarius. So, to some extent, this combination utilizes the nature of all of the Fire signs for perhaps the most ambitious, action-oriented of all.

The Mars ruled Sun does have some difficulty expressing its ego through some of the Ninth House matters. Philosophy and higher education and publishing have a tendency toward being somewhat sedentary, and the travel aspect of this house is much more appealing to this native. However, he can be a teacher or writer or minister, if these professions can be related to his need for physical activity and freedom of movement.

The challenge for this native is to acquire sensitivity, to stop and smell the roses, to relax and discover that there can be joy in peace and simple pleasures. He also needs to look around him at those he associates with, and discover beauty within them as within himself.

Leo Rising with Taurus Sun

> *"I am because I will; my will/ego finds expression through what I have."*

The Sun in this combination will most likely fall into the Tenth House or the Ninth. If it is in the Tenth, the ego expression will find outlet through public recognition, honors, success, and the father; if it is in the Ninth, it will find outlet through matters related to higher education, philosophy, travel, or publishing.

Because the Sun is Fixed Earth and the Ascendant is Fixed Fire, this can be a stressful combination, but the stress is productive, with positive outcomes, because the Sun is in the Midheaven, the ideal placement for success. The native is almost sure to achieve recognition in the public eye, yet it may not be easy.

Although the Tenth House is naturally a pragmatic, earthy house, the materialistic earthy Taurus has some difficulty there. He must use what he has or possesses in the public sphere to achieve the success that his Leo Ascendant wills for him. This may be his loving nature or his interest in the outdoors, or it may be his abilities to deal with money.

The challenge for this native—in addition to justifying the two incongruous facets of his identity—is to learn to be more adaptable, to work with rather than against those around him.

Leo Rising with Gemini Sun

> *"I am because I will; my will/ego finds expression through my ability to think (or have opinions)."*

The Sun in this combination will most likely fall into the

Eleventh House or the Tenth. If it is in the Eleventh, the ego expression will find outlet through friends, group activities, aspirations, or social movements; if it is in the Tenth, it will find outlet through matters related to public recognition, honors, success, and the father.

The Fixed Fire of the Ascendant works well with the Mutable Air of the ego in this combination, with the air feeding the fire for success in ambitions. Gemini's emphasis on thoughts and opinions also work well with the nature of the Eleventh House, finding outlet or expression through matters of aspirations, group associations, friends, and social concerns. However, Gemini likes to party, and so does Leo, so these social concerns may tend to be more of an entertaining sort than social activism at times.

It is possible, though, for this individual to take advantage of these tendencies, to become a professional party giver, an organizer of social functions, or even to run a computer dating service.

The challenge for this person is to try to acquire a practical side to his nature, to approach life and loves through a more realistic view.

Leo Rising with Cancer Sun

"I am because I will; my will/ego finds expression through my feelings."

The Sun in this combination will most likely fall into the Twelfth House or the Eleventh. If it is in the Twelfth, the ego expression will find outlet through matters of spiritual regeneration, solitude, institutions, or inhibitions or restrictions he places on himself; if it is in the Eleventh, it will find outlet through friends, group activities, aspirations, or social movements.

This is a very difficult combination, with a strong need for spiritual solutions to inner conflicts. Not only does the Cardinal Water of the Cancer Sun tend to put out the Fixed Fire of the Leo Ascendant, but the Sun is not comfortable in Moon-ruled Cancer, anyway.

The deep feelings of Cancer in this combination tend to turn inward, working against the native, eating away at his soul, aching for expression but totally incapable of coming out fully and openly, no matter how the fiery Self attempts to remedy the situation through exertion of the will.

The native is challenged to seek ego expression through insights into his feelings and his spiritual nature, perhaps to serve in some spiritual advisory capacity for others, through institutions such as hospitals, churches, or prisons. He is also challenged to find partnership that will help him to understand himself, partnership that will allow him to express his feelings through intimacy.

Chapter 10

FIXED WATER—SCORPIO

(October 23–November 21)

Applies to Scorpio Sun sign, Scorpio Ascendant, and those with Pluto on the Ascendant.

RULER—Pluto
MOTTO—"I desire."
SYMBOL—Scorpion
POLARITY—Negative/Feminine
COLOR—Blue green
KEY WORDS—Passion, Regeneration, Secrecy
MALE IDOLS—Rock Hudson, Joel McCrea, Clifton Webb
FEMALE IDOLS—Katherine Hepburn, Jane Alexander, Grace Slick

THE SCORPIO LOOK

There is something blatantly sexual about the appearance of the gay Scorpio. He is not always classically handsome (although he may be), but he is invariably sexy looking. It may have something to do with his dark, watery bedroom eyes. Or it may be related to the sensual set of his full mouth. Or it could be a part of his aggressive, determined manner. Or a combination of all of those factors.

Usually Scorpio is of medium height, with a slight tendency toward overweight, or at least a softness of muscular tissue. However, he is also generally rather strong and healthy. His neck tends to be rather thick or muscular, and he is often somewhat hairy, with coarse brown or black hair on his body as well as his head. Frequently Scorpio chooses to wear a beard or mustache.

His face can be rather wide, and of dark or dusky complexion. Some Scorpios can have very dark, thick, or prominent eyebrows.

Gay Scorpio may choose to dress in a somewhat unorthodox manner, sometimes wearing dark colors, or colors that contrast strongly, such as a black shirt with a white tie. Scorpios like leather, and some may be definitely into leather gear. They are proud of their buns and their baskets, and they may dress to heighten the effect of their sensuality.

More conservative Scorpios (and there are some who are distinctly conservative) will wear more subdued apparel during the workday, but change dramatically for going out at night.

If attending a costume party, gay Scorpio might go as the Devil or as a gangster or as the Grim Reaper. Some might choose Dracula or Frankenstein, or another character from a horror film.

THE SCORPIO NATURE

As the Fixed Water sign, Scorpio has a deeply emotional nature that rarely shows on the surface. Some have compared them to an iceberg, which is "fixed water": like an iceberg, only the tip is visible. What lies beneath the surface can be hazardous.

Among other signs, Scorpios have a rather bad reputation. Some of it may be deserved, but most of it is not. Scorpio does have some destructive tendencies, but they are generally directed more against himself than against others, and the Pluto rulership of Scorpio signifies that the objective of destruction is to create something better. Unfortunately, Scorpio's motivation is never seen clearly by others.

The symbol of his sign is the scorpion, a creature that travels in darkness, and most Scorpios are indeed night people. They like the bar scene and the bathhouse scene.

Secrecy is an inherent part of Scorpio's personality, largely because he is extremely sensitive about what others think of him. Very often, the opposite is true as well. Scorpio is curious—even nosy—about the secrets of others. He has an uncanny knack for finding anything that is hidden or lost. This carries through on virtually all levels. For example, Scorpio loves to discover restaurants or bars that are hidden in out of the way places; and it delights him to find a bargain on sale at a small shop or boutique. But if someone else has the audacity to discover a place or an item before him, he is offended. Uncovering secrets himself is a matter of pride to him.

It is this very quality that contributes to Scorpio's intelligence and creativity. He has a strong need to make a lasting mark on the world around him, because he—of all the signs—is most aware of physical death. For gay Scorpio, this is extremely important, since physical children are generally denied him. He seeks outlet through art or business.

And when he sets his sites on some goal, Scorpio will be extremely tenacious. He has the staying power to see anything through to the very end, even if he faces ultimate defeat. (This, however, is usually not the Scorpio outcome; he will usually win by persistence.) He generally has to do everything himself, for he has great difficulty delegating authority, yet he is also a perfectionist and has a strong desire for power.

Surprisingly, it is the emotional nature of Scorpio that is most significant. He experiences all emotions strongly—from love to hate, from passion to jealousy—yet does not express them fully. Fixed Water cannot allow feelings to flow freely. He has a tendency to live a "soap opera" existence, going from one emotional crisis to another. For all their sensuality—and sexuality—however, Scorpio has a deep spiritual nature, which few people ever see.

Many Sun sign Scorpios also have Mercury in Scorpio. (Some Librans and Sagittarians have this as well.) It is this Mercury placement that gives the gay Scorpio the reputation as a "bitch brilliant." This tendency toward a biting, sarcastic wit is not intended to devastate others, but it unfortunately often has this effect. The Scorpio mind uses it as a defense against its own extreme sensitivity and vulnerability.

There is an intense emotional force behind Scorpio's love life. He has both a great sexual appeal and an enormous sexual appetite, which makes it difficult for him to remain faithful to a lover. This does not mean that he is incapable of loving only one person, but he cannot always master his own passion to know the secrets of others. His infidelities stem as much from curiosity as from lust, and love may have almost nothing to do with them.

The greatest problem for a lover of Scorpio is the tendency to attempt to manipulate relationships. Because of Scorpio's secrecy, those who don't know him well don't often see him pulling the strings, but the Scorpio lover usually sees it and has difficulty dealing with it. However, the good side of this characteristic is that the Scorpio lover rarely gets bored, for there is rarely a dull moment in the relationship.

THE SCORPIO CHALLENGE

Scorpios represent a relatively large percentage of the gay population, so their life challenges are very closely linked to the current challenges of gays in general. Scorpios are capable of being loyal to those they love; but they must learn to be sexually faithful as well. Although they are fascinated with "plumbing," they need to realize that it is not necessary to know all the intimate details of others' secret places.

It is more important to know the emotions of others and to share their own emotions; they very much need to learn to express their feelings, especially with their lovers or partners. Gay Scorpio is challenged to appreciate others as they expect to be appreciated, to avoid hurting others unintentionally, to grant them the freedom and respect they expect for themselves, to avoid jealousy and possessiveness.

They must realize that they are capable of this sort of spiritual growth, for their ruler Pluto is the ruler of transformation and change on all levels, from the physical to the spiritual. They need to avoid cynicism, moodiness, and vindictiveness, striving for the many positive qualities of their sign.

SCORPIO RISING

Scorpio Rising with Scorpio Sun

"I am because I desire; my will/ego finds expression through my desires."

The Sun in this combination will most likely fall into the First House or the Twelfth. If the Sun is in the First, the ego expression finds outlet through matters related to the personality and appearance; if in the Twelfth, through matters of spiritual regeneration, solitude, institutions, or inhibitions or restrictions he places on himself.

Double Scorpio is infamous, and deservedly so, for his entire identity—both personality and ego—is defined by his desires. Both his Ascendant and his Sun are Fixed Water. However, so long as his Sun is in the First rather than the Twelfth House, he can be quite a productive and creative individual.

Although his sexual desires are considerable, that is not all there is to double Scorpio. There is, in fact, a spiritual side to his nature, as there is to all Water signs. In his case, however, it is deeply hidden, even subconscious, difficult even for him to bring to the surface.

As with all double signs, there is a potential self-centeredness to his nature. This is a part of his defense mechanism. He is quite sensitive, and to some extent he is self-destructive; this is especially true when the Sun is in the Twelfth House. It is a part of his challenge to guard against this tendency.

Regeneration is the truly creative side of Pluto ruled Scorpio, and his talent for destruction is to destroy with the objective of creating something better in its place. He may be an artist or he may have talents in financial matters. One extreme possibility for his career is as a mortician, for death is one of his major concerns.

His challenge is to find the security that is a part of the Earth signs, and the discipline that will enable his creative Water to channel itself.

Scorpio Rising with Sagittarius Sun

> *"I am because I desire; my will/ego finds expression through my ability to see or perceive."*

The Sun in this combination will most likely fall into the Second House or the First. If the Sun is in the Second, the ego expression finds outlet through matters related to money, possessions, or the loving, giving nature; if it is in the First, it finds outlet through the personality and the appearance.

This is a stressful combination, because the Fixed Water of the Ascendant tends to put out the Fire of the Mutable Sagittarius Sun, but it can be productive, once the divergent facets of the identity are unified creatively.

The expansive, perceptive nature of Sagittarius seeks outlet for his ego in matters of money, possessions, and love, in the Second House placement. He makes a good stock market analyst or consumer watchdog. With the combination of Scorpio Rising, he could be an excellent marketing analyst in advertising as well, for his desires, translated into the material sphere, can be understood as indicative of society at large.

His challenge, in addition to integrating the two facets of his nature, is to learn practicality and discipline, in this case to keep both his Water and his Fire under control.

Scorpio Rising with Capricorn Sun

> *"I am because I desire; my will/ego finds expression through my ability to use."*

The Sun in this combination will most likely fall into the Third House or the Second. If the Sun is in the Third, the ego expression finds outlet through matters related to communication, education, and brethren; if it is in the Second, it finds outlet through money and possessions, and perhaps the loving, giving nature.

The Fixed Water Ascendant works well in combination with the Cardinal Earth Sun, for the earth gives the water boundaries in which it can work creatively, and the water nourishes the earth. The ego uses Third House matters— communication, education, writing, brethren—to find outlet for its expression, and perhaps also for fulfillment of the physical and spiritual desires of the Scorpio personality.

If this individual is a writer or teacher, it is likely he will be concerned with practical, organizational, or structural matters. He could be a teacher of manual arts, or of civil engineering, or he could be a writer of "how to" books. (Though, for his own pleasure, he could write secretly about his own desires.)

His challenge is to become more actively involved in understanding love as opposed to physical desires, and to learn to communicate that love to those around him without restriction or guilt.

Scorpio Rising with Aquarius Sun

"I am because I desire; my will/ego finds expression through who or what I know."

The Sun in this combination will most likely fall into the Fourth House or the Third. If the Sun is in the Fourth, the ego expression finds outlet through matters related to the home, mother, or real estate; if in the Third, through matters associated with communication, education, and brethren.

This is a stressful combination, though not entirely unproductive. The Fixed Air of the Aquarius Sun and the Fixed

Water of the Scorpio Ascendant merely coexist, unable to mix
and serve each other creatively. The air needs fire and the
water needs earth to function well. And there is also the fact
that the Aquarius Sun, which wants to shine through who and
what it knows, feels hampered in the Fourth House at the
Nadir of the chart.

His ego is compelled to define and express itself through
who or what he knows in relation to home, mother, and real
estate, though the Aquarius nature may bring friends, aspirations, and social concerns into the picture. He may work
from his home, perhaps selling real estate or organizing social functions.

His challenge is to acquire practicality and the drive to
succeed. He must also seek to be more outgoing, not staying
home so much that he loses ambition.

Scorpio Rising with Pisces Sun

*"I am because I desire; my will/ego finds expres-
sion through my beliefs."*

The Sun in this combination will most likely fall into the
Fifth House or the Fourth. If it is in the Fifth, the ego expression will find outlet through matters related to entertainment,
love affairs, romance, speculation, or children; if in the
Fourth, it will find outlet through matters connected with the
home, mother, or real estate.

This is a good mixture of two Water signs, with the Ascendant being Fixed and the Sun, placed in the Fifth House,
being Mutable. While there is some need for earth to give the
water form and direction, the double Water in this case directs
itself toward creativity in entertainment. Because the Pisces
ego is ruled by Neptune, this combination is ideal for one who
works in films or in photography. This individual might be
an actor or a model, with considerable success, if all other
factors indicate.

What Pisces believes and what Scorpio desires make for a highly spiritual person, though there is also much emphasis on pleasure seeking and romance, as well as sex.

The native is challenged to find direction for his spiritual and creative urges. He needs to learn to be practical, to stick to his ambitions with determination, and learn to deal with finances and the material world.

Scorpio Rising with Aries Sun

"I am because I desire; my will/ego finds expression through the fact that I am."

The Sun in this combination will most likely fall into the Sixth House or the Fifth. If it is in the Sixth, the ego expression will find outlet through matters of work, service, health, clothing, and food; if in the Fifth, through matters of entertainment, love affairs, romance, speculation, and children.

This is not an easy combination, for the Fixed Water of the Ascendant endeavors to put out the Fire of the Aries Sun. There is also the fact that the Aries ego feels frustrated in the Sixth House of work and service to others. He wants to go out and achieve for himself, and for his Scorpio desires as well, but is held down by the practical concerns of the Sixth House—work, service, diet, health, clothing, and pets.

This individual must find a creative solution for the two divergent facets of his identity. His fiery Martian ego can make him an excellent craftsman, one who is good with his hands, such as a carpenter or a housepainter or possibly a construction worker. He could be a surgeon, or a proctologist or gynecologist. Yet he is not entirely happy at these tasks.

The challenge for this individual is to find unity in the opposing forces within him; he must seek to perceive the value in practical matters, the qualities of the Earth signs, as well as of matters of the mind, the qualities of the Air signs.

Scorpio Rising with Taurus Sun

> *"I am because I desire; my will/ego finds expression through what I have."*

The Sun in this combination will most likely fall into the Seventh House or the Sixth. If it is in the Seventh, the ego expression will find outlet through matters of partnership and associations with others; if in the Sixth, it will be through matters of work, service, health, clothing, and food.

Surprisingly, this can be an excellent combination, though there is a tug of war between the Fixed Water of the Ascendant and the Fixed Earth of the Sun. Scorpio appears to be the exact opposite of Taurus, and he is, yet the earthy, Venus ruled Taurus is precisely what Scorpio needs to channel his watery desires.

Scorpio's desires, with this placement, can be fulfilled through partnership, while the ego may find expression through what he has in partnership and in relationships with others. He remains rather materialistic, concerned with money and possessions, but he is also very affectionate and loving, rounding out the sexuality of Scorpio.

His challenge is to discover the idealism and the mentality of the Air signs, as well as the ambition of the Fire. He needs to understand intellectually his spiritual nature, and he needs to find the drive to succeed with his Scorpio creativity.

Scorpio Rising with Gemini Sun

> *"I am because I desire; my will/ego finds expression through my ability to think (or have opinions)."*

The Sun in this combination will most likely fall into the Eighth House or the Seventh. If it is in the Eighth, the ego expression will find outlet through matters related to partnership finances, sex, heritage and inheritance, or death; if in the

Seventh, it will find outlet through matters of partnership and associations with others.

This can be a very difficult combination, for the Fixed Water Ascendant merely coexists with the Mutable Air Sun, unable to mix productively. However, the Gemini Sun in the Eighth House is in the natural home of Scorpio, so there becomes an emphasis on matters concerned with sex, partnership finances, inheritance, and death.

This individual is truly preoccupied with sex, and he can overtax himself by too much sexual activity. His Gemini Sun, with its emphasis on thoughts and opinions, knows his ego should be expressed through partnership, yet his extreme promiscuity makes it difficult for him to settle down to the one person he desires.

He is capable of hard work, and he can get satisfaction from a job well done, but he invariably finds himself dependent upon support from family or partners.

His challenge is to learn to become more practical, to learn to stand on his own feet and direct his desires toward accomplishing what he wants. Yet, he must also find the fire and ambition to know what he wants, so that he can achieve this.

Scorpio Rising with Cancer Sun

"I am because I desire; my will/ego finds expression through my feelings."

The Sun in this combination will most likely fall into the Ninth House or the Eighth. If it is in the Ninth, the ego expression will find outlet in matters related to higher education, philosophy, travel, or publishing; if it is in the Eighth, it will find outlet through partnership finances, sex, heritage or inheritance, or death.

This combination is highly directed toward success, with Fixed Water on the Ascendant and Cardinal Water for the Sun, placed in the Ninth House, in trine aspect. There is a great emphasis in this pairing on matters of the spirit, on desires and feelings, however, and there is a need for Earth qualities to give form and direction to the individual.

The ego expression must find outlet through feelings related to Ninth House matters—to higher education, philosophy, travel, and publishing. There are various ways this expression might take form. For example, this would be a good combination for an editor, writer, or publisher of poetry or romance fiction. It might also be ideal for a social director on a "love boat."

The challenge for this individual, in addition to finding the earthy practicality that will channel his spiritual nature, is to seek to develop a higher mentality, an idealism and an education that will help him to understand his spirit.

Scorpio Rising with Leo Sun

"I am because I desire; my will/ego finds expression through my will."

The Sun in this combination will most likely fall into the Tenth House or the Ninth. If it is in the Tenth, the ego expression will find outlet through public recognition, honors, success, and the father; if it is in the Ninth, it will find outlet through matters related to higher education, philosophy, travel, or publishing.

This is a stressful combination, but it can also be a productive, successful one. The Fixed Fire of the Leo Sun is in square aspect to the Fixed Water of the Scorpio Ascendant, and water tries to put out fire. However, the Sun is in the Tenth House, in the Midheaven, a placement that ultimately indicates public recognition and success in one's endeavors.

The Sun is in its own sign of Leo, giving added strength to the will of the ego, so that it can fend off the watery efforts of the personality to deny success. This individual could find his ego outlet in the public eye, possibly in politics or government, in the entertainment field, or in business.

His challenge is to develop a practical plan for success, as well as a way of combining his desires and his will into a unified identity.

Scorpio Rising with Virgo Sun

> *"I am because I desire; my will/ego finds expression through my ability to analyze."*

The Sun in this combination will most likely fall into the Eleventh House or the Tenth. If it is in the Eleventh, the ego expression will find outlet through friends, group activities, aspirations, or social movements; if it is in the Tenth, it will find outlet through matters related to public recognition, honors, success, and the father.

Surprisingly, these two signs work well together. Not only are they in sextile aspect, but the Mutable Earth of the Virgo Sun gives form and direction to the Fixed Water of the Scorpio Sun, although the Virgo Earth does have a tendency to shift and adapt from time to time, sometimes without warning.

Virgo is quite comfortable in the Eleventh House. The ego expression through analysis fits well in the house of friends, group concerns, aspirations, and social concerns, for it is ruled by the other mental planet, Uranus. And Virgo is not as prudish as one usually thinks; all Earth signs are extremely sexual. For that reason, the Virgo ego's analytical ability can understand Scorpio's desires. Once understood, these desires can be dealt with.

The challenge of this combination is to direct the sensual and mental energies outward from the individual, into partnership and friendship and relationships with others generally. This native also needs to acquire more drive and ambition to achieve for Self.

Scorpio Rising with Libra Sun

"I am because I desire; my will/ego finds expression through my ability to balance."

The Sun in this combination will most likely fall into the Twelfth House or the Eleventh. If it is in the Twelfth, the ego expression will find outlet through matters of spiritual regeneration, solitude, institutions, or inhibitions or restrictions he places on himself; if it is in the Eleventh, it will find outlet through friends, group activities, aspirations, or social movements.

The Twelfth House Sun is usually a very difficult placement, and the combination between the Fixed Water of the Scorpio personality and the Cardinal Air of the Libra Sun is no exception, though it may not be as difficult as most other combinations. The reason is that the Libra ego defines itself through balance, and the Scorpio Ascendant is, to some extent, spiritual in nature.

As the Twelfth House is the house of spiritual regeneration, this combination may not be so self-destructive as it can be with other Sun signs. Libra will seek to achieve balance between the inner nature and the outer needs, understanding and aiding in fulfilling the Scorpio desires.

The challenge for this combination is to seek to communicate lovingly and openly toward partners, especially toward the lover, to avoid the tendency of both Scorpio and the Twelfth House Sun for secrecy.

Chapter 11

FIXED AIR—AQUARIUS

(January 21–February 19)

Applies to Aquarius Sun sign, Aquarius Ascendant, and those with Uranus on the Ascendant.

RULER—Uranus
MOTTO—"I know."
SYMBOL—Waterbearer
POLARITY—Positive/Masculine
COLOR—Violet
KEY WORDS—Humanitarianism, Independence, Originality
MALE IDOLS—James Dean, Billy De Wolfe, Ramon Novarro
FEMALE IDOLS—Tallulah Bankhead, Mia Farrow, Ava Gardner

THE AQUARIUS LOOK

Gay Aquarians are almost invariably attractive, though it may be as much their personalities or spiritual natures as it is their physical appearances that draw others to them. Usually, there is a strong aura of masculinity about them. They are tall and well-built; many choose to engage in sports or exercise that will develop their muscularity.

However, they may not be aware of the reasons for this. Their sign is that of the waterbearer, and water is an extremely heavy element to carry. They must be strong, robust, and healthy to bear such a weight. (Symbolically, what they carry is an intense spirituality and intellectualism, confined and concealed within an urn. The motto "a healthy mind in a healthy body" is a very Aquarian one.)

The Aquarian's facial structure is generally rather long or narrow, with some feature or facet slightly unusual or strikingly noticeable. In most cases it will be the nose or the mouth that is prominent, but not always, for Aquarius is a highly individualistic sign.

Contrasting with other aspects of his appearance, the Aquarian's complexion may be delicate or fair, with clear hazel eyes that have a rather sanguine or melancholy set to them. Their hair may vary from sandy to dark; to the Aquarian's frustration, it seems, however, to have a will of its own, with cowlicks or waves that are difficult to control.

THE AQUARIUS NATURE

Aquarius is the sign where Uranus, the planetary ruler of homosexuality and bisexuality, is most comfortable. It is the sign of its home. For this reason, one would expect Aquarians to represent the largest percentage of the gay population. But this is not, in fact, the case. Because Uranus is comfortable in Aquarius, it emphasizes the spiritual rather than the physical side of homosexuality. Most Aquarians, straight as well as gay, feel a strong spiritual bond with those of their own sex as well as with the opposite sex.

Because Aquarius is the waterbearer, many people also think of it as a Water sign, though it is an Air sign. Being the Air sign that occurs at the peak of winter, it carries water. And being Fixed, it generally carries it in the form of snow or ice. The significance of this is that Aquarius can be coldly intellectual, perhaps the most objective of all signs.

In some ways, the Aquarius may seem like a cold, unfeeling machine; indeed, he would like others to think that he is. However, he is generally quite sensitive, and he has an abundance of sympathy for those around him, though it may appear to be rather impersonal because his responses are invariably of an intellectual nature.

Aquarius is the most intellectual of signs, and the one with the greatest degree of social consciousness. The motto of the French Revolution—"Liberty, Equality, Fraternity"—is deeply meaningful to Aquarians, who devote themselves toward achieving an ideal society through social reforms. Their belief in democracy and the "rights of man" is a devout one, and their opinions are extremely liberal ones, so extreme at times that they may become dogmatic and be looked upon as cranks.

We are supposedly approaching the Aquarian Age, yet Aquarius is always uncomfortable with the existing age and the prevailing norms. They can be so unconventional and so uncomfortable with the status quo that they indeed become "rebels without a cause." (It is more than mere coincidence that the star of the film, *Rebel Without a Cause*, was James Dean, an Aquarian.)

Most often, however, they do have a cause, and it is generally a humanitarian one. They affiliate themselves with groups that have social objectives, and they draw others to themselves, inevitably becoming leaders, despite their eccentric temperaments.

Aquarius delights in meeting new people, and it is amazing how they consistently attract others, for they do not really go out of their way to make people like them. They are highly opinionated, very determined, and extremely stubborn. Yet those very qualities can be fascinating to others.

Most Aquarians despise hypocrisy and lies; and they abhor snobbery and affectation. When they perceive those qualities in others, they become like a small child faced with a balloon—they cannot resist puncturing it. They don't mind if they lose or discard a friend, for they will always find new ones. They are so stubbornly sure that their own opinions and ideas are right that they will become argumentative at the drop of a hat. And they cannot understand when others are unreceptive to their ideas.

Generally their arguments and insults are not intended as personal, and they cannot always see why they are taken personally. This is the one blind spot in their usually keen perception and intuition of others. But they don't suffer long from the loss of friends. They move on quickly to new ones. Though, somehow, they do manage to keep many loyal and devoted friends for long periods of time, friends who understand and love them.

When Aquarius has problems, he usually exaggerates them, revealing the restless anxieties that lurk beneath his surface calm.

So strong is the desire for knowledge in the Aquarian that he will constantly ask questions, yet he is so impatient that he will usually go on to the next question before the first is answered.

Sexually, Aquarius may not be an extremely passionate lover, but he can be unconventional, inventive, and imaginative. He is capable of loving one person deeply, though that love may appear to be impersonal, and he may have a desire or need for group sex. It is extremely important for Aquarius' lover to be his best friend as well. It is also necessary that his lover or partner realize Aquarius is faithful in his own way and that he looks upon sex as something quite separate from love.

Aquarius sets his sites on distant goals, and he will almost always achieve them, though it may not seem possible to others, who perceive his actions as too erratic for consistency, for Aquarius does everything in stops and starts. They also have a tendency to take on too many projects at one time, and it seems that they cannot possibly finish them all. However, they are aware of their responsibilities, and they will eventually accomplish everything, if given the opportunity.

For that reason, it is important that Aquarius' partner or lover understand this aspect of his nature and not attempt to interfere, but grant him the freedom he needs to act alone.

THE AQUARIUS CHALLENGE

The life challenge for gay Aquarius is to "stop and smell the roses," to realize that feelings and emotions are as important as ideas and social goals. They must discover that persons are as important as humanity, and that they themselves do not have to be cold efficient machines serving society. Aquarius' own needs are important, as are the needs of those he loves.

Aquarius is also challenged to learn patience, for himself as well as for others, and to admit when he makes mistakes. He can accept himself as imperfect, and as human as those he seeks to serve. The service he performs will be more meaningful when it is done with genuine personal feeling.

He needs to discover the gentle pleasures of intimacy, the simple joys of sights and smells and tastes and sounds, but most important of touch. From time to time he needs to get down off his soapbox and listen—truly listen—to those around him.

AQUARIUS RISING

Aquarius Rising with Aquarius Sun

"I am because I know; my will/ego finds expression through who or what I know."

The Sun in this combination will most likely fall into the First House or the Twelfth. If the Sun is in the First, the ego expression finds outlet through matters related to the personality and appearance; if in the Twelfth, through matters of spiritual regeneration, solitude, institutions, or inhibitions or restrictions he places on himself.

The combination of Aquarius ruling both the Ascendant and the Sun can be a very success-oriented one, but double Aquarius does have his difficulties. He is often described by others as "a know it all." All double signs are rather egocentric, but this one can—without intending to—come off with a superior attitude that annoys those around him. He does indeed know it all, but he must learn not to broadcast the fact constantly.

However, his ego must find its expression through who and what he knows, and it is directed toward the Aquarian concerns—friends, aspirations, social activities, and social action. However, Uranus, ruler of Aquarius, is very creative and freedom loving; it is scientific as well as inventive. In fact, this native has a large choice of careers.

His challenge is to come down from his ivory tower and face reality where ordinary mortals live. He needs to become sensitive to the concerns and feelings of others; indeed, he needs to discover his own feelings as well, and try not to be so caught up in his ideals and his intellectualism.

Aquarius Rising with Pisces Sun

"I am because I know; my will/ego finds expression through my beliefs."

The Sun in this combination will most likely fall into the Second House or the First. If the Sun is in the Second, the ego expression finds outlet through matters related to money, possessions, or the loving, giving nature; if it is in the First, it finds outlet through the personality and the appearance.

This can be a rather stressful combination, for the Fixed Air of the Ascendant merely coexists with the Mutable Water of the Sun, unable to mix creatively. There is also the fact that Neptune ruled Pisces has difficulty with its Sun in the Second House, for it is the least practical and materialistic sign placed in the most practical and materialistic house.

However, it can be quite productive, once a means of unifying the conflicting facets of the identity is discovered.

The Pisces ego finds its expression through beliefs, things of the spirit, imagination, and creativity. This expression in the Second House must find outlet through matters of money and possessions. At the same time, the Aquarian Ascendant is preoccupied with who and what it knows. If the Pisces ego can discover the spiritual in money and possessions and convey its discoveries to the Aquarian personality, unity can be achieved.

The challenge for this combination, in addition to unifying

the identity, is in directing the feelings—particularly feelings of love—toward others. This individual needs to come out of himself and come down to earth occasionally, so that he can accomplish his ambitions.

Aquarius Rising with Aries Sun

> *"I am because I know; my will/ego finds expression through the fact that I am."*

The Sun in this combination will most likely fall into the Third House or the Second. If the Sun is in the Third, the ego expression finds outlet through matters related to communication, education, and brethren; if it is in the Second, it finds outlet through money and possessions, and perhaps the loving, giving nature.

This is an excellent combination of fire and air. The Fixed Air of the Ascendant feeds the Cardinal Fire of the Aries Sun, with great potential for success. When the Sun is in the Third House, the ego expression finds outlet through matters of communication, writing, education, and brethren, ideal for the knowledge of the Aquarius Ascendant.

This individual makes a good teacher or a writer of action and adventure tales.

His challenge is to seek to be more practical, to deal with matters of finances and of love, to think of the needs of others and to learn to adapt to the world around him more readily.

Aquarius Rising with Taurus Sun

> *"I am because I know; my will/ego finds expression through what I have."*

The Sun in this combination will most likely fall into the Fourth House or the Third. If the Sun is in the Fourth, the ego expression finds outlet through matters related to the home, mother, or real estate; if in the Third, through matters associated with communication, education, and brethren.

This is a stressful combination between Fixed Air and Fixed Earth, which cannot mix but merely coexist, but it can be a productive one. With the Sun in the Fourth House, in square aspect to the Ascendant, the expression of ego must find outlet through what this individual has in relationship to home, mother, or real estate.

Since Taurus is ruled by Venus, what he has may be artistic talents, and he may work from home as a painter or sculptor. He may as easily be an interior decorator or a landscape designer, which could unite easily with the Aquarian Ascendant's emphasis on knowledge.

The challenge for this individual is to seek to discover the spiritual within himself and to find the fire of ambition that will take him out of his home into the world among others.

Aquarius Rising with Gemini Sun

"I am because I know; my will/ego finds expression through my ability to think (or have opinions)."

The Sun in this combination will most likely fall into the Fifth House or the Fourth. If it is in the Fifth, the ego expression will find outlet through matters related to entertainment, love affairs, romance, speculation, or children; if in the Fourth, it will find outlet through matters connected with the home, mother, or real estate.

This is an excellent combination of two Air signs. The Fixed Air of the Ascendant mixes extremely well with the Mutable Air of the Gemini Sun, which is in trine in the Fifth House, producing a very creative individual who will be concerned with matters of entertainment, speculation, gambling, and risk taking.

Of course, the double Air nature makes the native rather one sided. The Aquarian is concerned with what he knows, and the Gemini is concerned with his thoughts and his opinions, so this combination is almost totally intellectual or mental. He could be an excellent writer of comedy material, perhaps a writer of screenplays as well. He could be a performer, but other factors in the chart would have to give him the Water necessary for expressing feelings.

The challenge for this individual is to discover the fire of ambition, as well as to develop some of the practical, realistic knowledge of the Earth signs.

Aquarius Rising with Cancer Sun

> *"I am because I know; my will/ego finds expression through my feelings."*

The Sun in this combination will most likely fall into the Sixth House or the Fifth. If it is in the Sixth, the ego expression will find outlet through matters of work, service, health, clothing, and food; if in the Fifth, through matters of entertainment, love affairs, romance, speculation, and children.

This is not an easy combination, because the Fixed Air Ascendant does not mix with the Cardinal Water Sun, but merely coexist. While Aquarius "knows," Cancer "feels," and the two have difficulty meeting and uniting into a single identity.

With the Cancer Sun placed in the Sixth House, the ego expression through feelings must find outlet in matters related to work, service, health, pets, and food. The feelings of the Moon ruled Sun must be ingenious to find outlet through these matters. Perhaps the most likely would be through caring for pets and small animals; this might be a good combination for a veterinarian, for example. It might also be a possibility for a chef or a dietician.

The challenge for this individual, in addition to unifying the two facets of the identity, is to become more practical, especially with financial matters.

Aquarius Rising with Leo Sun

> *"I am because I know; my will/ego finds expression through my will."*

The Sun in this combination will most likely fall into the Seventh House or the Sixth. If it is in the Seventh, the ego expression will find outlet through matters of partnership and associations with others; if in the Sixth, it will be through matters of work, service, health, clothing, and food.

Although there is inevitably stress when the Sun is placed in the Seventh House, opposing the Ascendant, this is a highly positive combination between Fixed Air and Fixed Fire, promising considerable success. However, there is the challenge for the native of learning not to define his ego through his relationships rather than through his inner Self.

The Leo ego finds its expression through its strong will, seeking outlet through partnership. Since the ego here is Leo, this may very likely be partnerships involved in entertainment or creativity. This might be one who produces or directs, or who works behind the scenes in theater or films, utilizing both the Aquarian knowledge and the Leo will to create.

The challenge for this individual is to learn pragmatism, and to seek to delve into the inner Self to discover his spiritual nature.

Aquarius Rising with Virgo Sun

> *"I am because I know; my will/ego finds expression through my ability to analyze."*

The Sun in this combination will most likely fall into the Eighth House or the Seventh. If it is in the Eighth, the ego expression will find outlet through matters related to partnership finances, sex, heritage and inheritance, or death; if in the Seventh, it will find outlet through matters of partnership and associations with others.

The Sun placement in the Eighth House is never an easy one. This combination between Fixed Air and Mutable Earth is particularly difficult, even though the rulers of the two are both mental planets. The Virgo ego in this position finds its expression through analyzing matters of sex, partnership finances, inheritance, and death. But Virgo's tendency to be of service, to work hard, comes into play as well, and this individual may find a career as a sex researcher, or he may become a bank clerk or a manager for a partner.

To unify his identity, he must justify what he learns through his analysis with what his Aquarian Self "knows." Aquarius doesn't really want to learn more, and he must allow himself to bend to the Virgo ego, which is difficult, since Virgo is the mutable, flexible one.

The challenge for this individual is one that is always difficult for Aquarius, to learn to develop spiritually as well as mentally.

Aquarius Rising with Libra Sun

"I am because I know; my will/ego finds expression through my ability to balance."

The Sun in this combination will most likely fall into the Ninth House or the Eighth. If it is in the Ninth, the ego expression will find outlet in matters related to higher education, philosophy, travel, or publishing; if it is in the Eighth, it will find outlet through partnership finances, sex, heritage or inheritance, or death.

This is an excellent combination of two Air signs, the Aquarius Ascendant being Fixed and the Libra Sun being Cardinal. There is much that this individual can achieve. The Libra ego finds expression through its ability to balance in matters of higher education, philosophy, publishing, and travel. In combination with the Aquarian Self's ability to know, this native moves easily forward to accomplish his ambitions.

This individual could find a career through teaching, particularly subjects of social concern or law. He could, however, as easily be a minister or professor of philosophy. If he is involved in publishing, it is most likely that he will edit or produce art books.

His challenge stems from his heavy emphasis on airy mentality, which makes him too one-sided. It is important for this individual to develop both physically and spiritually.

Aquarius Rising with Scorpio Sun

> *"I am because I know; my will/ego finds expression through my desires."*

The Sun in this combination will most likely fall into the Tenth House or the Ninth. If it is in the Tenth, the ego expression will find outlet through public recognition, honors, success, and the father; if it is in the Ninth, it will find outlet through matters related to higher education, philosophy, travel, or publishing.

Although the Tenth House Sun creates a stressful square relationship with the Ascendant, it is almost always a productive combination. In this case, the Fixed Air of the Aquarius Ascendant cannot mix with the Fixed Water of the Scorpio Sun, and the two must find some unity in order to work together for success.

In the Tenth House, the Scorpio ego finds expression through its desires associated with public recognition, career, and success. To some extent Scorpio's natural inclinations toward sex and partnership finances come into play in this accomplishment, and the individual's Aquarian emphasis on knowledge can be utilized as well.

This native could achieve success in business, in politics, or in fields of social service that require him to be in the public eye.

His challenge is to develop the pragmatism of the Earth

signs and the action orientation of the Fire, so that he can channel his watery ego and give life to his airy personality.

Aquarius Rising with Sagittarius Sun

"I am because I know; my will/ego finds expression through my ability to see or perceive."

The Sun in this combination will most likely fall into the Eleventh House or the Tenth. If it is in the Eleventh, the ego expression will find outlet through friends, group activities, aspirations, or social movements; if it is in the Tenth, it will find outlet through matters related to public recognition, honors, success, and the father.

This is a very productive combination of Fixed Air on the Ascendant and Mutable Fire for the Sun. The Sagittarius ego finds expression through its ability to see or perceive matters related to friendship, social activities, social concerns, and aspirations. The natural inclination for Sagittarius to be involved with matters of the higher mind and expansive travel also come into play.

This Mutable Sun is also in the natural house ruled by the Aquarius Ascendant, enabling the ego to adapt to succeed in the ambitions of the Self. This combination has numerous choices of career, either of a Sagittarian or Aquarian nature. He could be in politics, in education, in some social ministry; the possibilities are limitless. He will also be an extremely social animal, with lots of friends.

The challenge for this individual is to learn to be more practical, to realize that he has personal responsibilities as well as social ones.

Aquarius Rising with Capricorn Sun

> *"I am because I know; my will/ego finds expression through my ability to use."*

The Sun in this combination will most likely fall into the Twelfth House or the Eleventh. If it is in the Twelfth, the ego expression will find outlet through matters of spiritual regeneration, solitude, institutions, or inhibitions or restriction he places on himself; if it is in the Eleventh, it will find outlet through friends, group activities, aspirations, or social movements.

The Twelfth House placement of the Sun is almost always a stressful one. This combination is especially so, and the individual here is challenged to come up with creative, original means of uniting the two divergent facets of his identity, the Aquarian Self and personality and the Capricorn ego.

The Cardinal Earth of the Sun merely coexists with the Fixed Air of the Ascendant in this combination, unable to mix. The ego here seeks to find expression through using matters of the spirit, of isolation and solitude, and of institutions. Capricorn, ruled by Saturn, is very uncomfortable here, for Saturn not only wants to be responsible, devoting its positive energies toward structuring and organizing, but when frustrated tends to restrict the individual, becoming preoccupied with guilt.

On the other hand, the Aquarian personality, ruled by Uranus, seeks freedom and independence, wanting to express what it knows.

The challenge for this individual is to seek to incorporate matters of the spirit into his nature, for this will bring him out of himself to deal creatively with his two conflicting forces and avoiding turning them destructively against himself. Religion or metaphysics or service through medical or penal institutions can benefit him greatly.

PART IV

THE MUTABLE SIGNS

SEASONAL CHANGES

As the Sun begins to move away from its extreme, fixed patterns in the heavens, the seasons approach their endings, looking forward to new beginnings. Days grow noticeably shorter or longer again. Living things prepare for maturity or harvest, death or rebirth. The weather seems unpredictable, inconsistent from one day to the next, caught between the old season and the new one to come.

Astrologically, those born during these periods of change are called Mutable. The Mutable signs are Gemini, Virgo, Sagittarius, and Pisces. They are the flexible, adaptable—possibly even unpredictable—signs of the Zodiac; some chidingly call them "wishy-washy," because they are so easily led or influenced by the Cardinal and Fixed signs. But flexibility and adaptability are their means of survival, their way of coping with the stubbornness of the Fixed signs and the egocentricity of the Cardinal signs.

Their natures are very strongly influenced by the seasons that are ending and those that are beginning. Gemini falls between spring and summer; in the human life cycle, they represent adolescence, the culmination of childhood and the beginning of maturity. Virgo comes at the end of summer and the beginning of fall, at the time of harvest, representing the change from maturity to middle age. Sagittarius appears at the culmination of autumn, as winter is about to set in; as such there is a connection between its nature and that of the change from middle age to old age. Pisces occurs at the end of winter, just before spring, signifying death and rebirth.

Because of their special positions in the Zodiac, Mutable signs have an innate understanding of the seasonal changes, an intuitive grasp of the human life cycle. That awareness gives them a strength that the other signs rarely perceive. However, for many who have heavily Mutable charts, the knowledge that all things "must pass away" can also create frustration or a sense of futility in attempting to reach their goals. They must constantly fight the temptation to accept defeat too easily.

This is especially true for the gay Mutable signs. When the special isolating nature of homosexuality is combined with an awareness of the brevity of life, there is a sadness or melancholy that tends toward depression, toward accepting loneliness as inevitable.

In the random poll taken of gay signs, the percentage of distribution among Mutable signs generally was roughly what would be expected from chance. There were 33 percent with the Sun in Mutable signs, while 32.5 percent had Mutable signs for the Ascendant. However, when it came to the specific signs involved, the results were quite different. Sagittarius proved to be the "gayest" of the Mutable signs, with 10.6 percent having Sun in the sign and 13.7 percent having it for a Rising sign. Gemini was represented with just over 8 percent having the Sun in the sign and 7.5 percent for the Ascendant. There were 7.5 percent with Sun in Pisces, while only 5 percent of gays had Pisces as the Rising sign. Interestingly, 6.8 percent of gays had Virgo Sun and 6.2 percent Virgo Ascendant. (Chance would be 7.5 percent for any specific sign.)

Chapter 12

MUTABLE AIR—GEMINI

(May 21–June 21)

Applies to Gemini Sun sign, Gemini Ascendant, and those with Mercury on the Ascendant.

RULER—Mercury
MOTTO—"I think."
SYMBOL—Twins
POLARITY—Positive/Masculine
COLOR—Orange
KEY WORDS—Mentality, Versatility, Nonconformity
MALE IDOLS—Prince, Paul Lynde, Tony Curtis
FEMALE IDOLS—Marilyn Monroe, Rosalind Russell, Judy Garland

THE GEMINI LOOK

No matter how old the Gemini is, there is somehow the appearance of the adolescent or teenager about him. The youthful sparkle remains in his eyes, there is a buoyancy to his step, and his manner shifts mercurially from quiet introversion to peeling laughter. Gay Gemini will generally be relatively tall, but even when he is not, he will give the impression of height by his erect bearing. His body is strong and well made, though usually slender. He may have long arms and legs, which are usually quite active.

Gemini's complexion is most often sanguine in nature, but there is invariably a mischievous sparkle in his hazel eyes. His hair normally has a wave to it, though its color may vary from dark to sandy. The pure Gemini will be likely to have very little body hair.

Gay Gemini chooses clothes with a youthful, casual look to them. He is comfortable in jeans or cut-offs, T-shirts or sweatshirts, but he will also follow the latest trends in young men's apparel, being careful that everything matches perfectly. He tends to wear out shoes very quickly, because of his activity, and if he is financially able, he will change his wardrobe often, growing tired of items before they are out of style.

Similarly, he may change outfits several times a day. If going out for the evening, he may try on everything in his closet before he makes his decision.

If going to a costume party, gay Gemini will strive for originality, and there will usually be something humorous about his choice. He will be likely to look for something that is primitive or childlike in nature—a caveman, an infant in a diaper, Little Lord Fauntleroy, a 1950s teenager, an Indian. Or, if deeply aware of his own nature, he might choose something that displays his two sides—a harlequin, Dr. Jekyll and Mr. Hyde (half and half), or some two-sided character of his own creation.

THE GEMINI NATURE

Gemini is the instinctive charmer of the Zodiac. He is usually the life of the party, the center of attention, chattering away, witty and fun-loving. At first glance, he may appear glib, empty-headed, lacking depth, but appearances are deceiving with Gemini.

He has a great capacity for learning, especially in youth. His mind is quick, and he understands ideas and concepts instantly. He also has an instinctive judgment of people, and he expresses his opinions and thoughts without hesitation.

The Gemini mind is so quick and agile that it may lack concentration; at times it seems impossible to keep it from hopping from one subject to another. If he can hold his interests or activities to two things at one time, Gemini can function extremely well, accomplishing both simultaneously. But he is so nervous and high-strung, even this limitation can be difficult for him. He will tend to feel frustrated and then become depressed.

Extreme mood swings are typical of Gemini, for his nature is dual in every way. Like the early spring, he is both sunny days and sudden storms. There are always two seemingly opposing facets to his nature.

Gay Gemini is highly imaginative and creative, especially with words and with anything that can be accomplished manually. Their objective is communication, and they will put great effort into accomplishing it. They make good writers, salesmen, and teachers. When they have the patience, they are excellent craftsmen.

Gemini must always be moving. He hates to stay at home, and, if forced to do so, will probably spend his time rearranging the furniture. He certainly can't be expected to sit still. He needs to get out and about, even if it is only to wander the neighborhood. He loves to travel, and he enjoys going out, especially out dancing.

If anyone attempts to restrain him or to discipline him, he will rebel. He doesn't like authority, and will fight it even when he knows the other person is right. If there is a rule set, Gemini will break it deliberately, if only to establish his independence. When he has the security of knowing he is appreciated, however, he makes an excellent student, for he is eager to learn and experience anything new.

In love, Gemini may be an extremely difficult partner. His tendency toward detachment or objectivity—even toward emotional ambivalence or coldness—may seem frustrating to others. He may appear fickle, for he is always seeking the new and different, even in relationships. It is almost impossible for him to be held down by a single lover. He has a need for at least two at a time, though another Gemini might supply that need.

The best partner for a Gemini is one who can provide both constant mental stimulation and variety of experience and activities. This may extend to sex, but the physical is of lesser importance to Gemini than the intellectual and emotional.

Even when such a paragon exists, the partnership may not last a lifetime, for lasting relationships border on the impossible for Gemini's restless nature.

The only other alternative is a partner with endless patience and understanding. Gemini does need a partner, if only to have someone to talk to.

THE GEMINI CHALLENGE

Gay Gemini has the mental capacity to understand his challenge, but he lacks the patience and the will-power to deal with it effectively. These are qualities he must endeavor to acquire. He is aware of the duality of his nature, and his greatest challenge is to unify the two distinctive and disruptive poles, so that he can find the inner peace necessary to give and accept love. He does not like what he does to those he loves, but he cannot help himself so long as he is torn by his own inner conflict.

He needs to be wary of criticizing or blaming others for problems or situations he has caused himself. He must learn to cooperate with others and accept the fact that his physical and mental restlessness creates disruption for those around him.

He is also challenged to avoid a tendency toward superficiality or pretentiousness, which is one way Gemini has of avoiding his own inner conflict. He must seek to understand that those he loves—and those who love him—are not necessarily attempting to control or restrict him.

GEMINI RISING

Gemini Rising with Gemini Sun

"I am because I think; my will/ego finds expression through my ability to think (or have opinions)."

The Sun in this combination will most likely fall into the First House or the Twelfth. If the Sun is in the First, the ego expression finds outlet through matters related to the personality and appearance; if in the Twelfth, through matters of spiritual regeneration, solitude, institutions, or inhibitions or restrictions he places on himself.

The combination of Gemini Ascendant and Gemini Sun is, for the most part, a positive one, but it is not an easy one. The double Air mix is difficult enough, but when it is also double Mutable, the native is truly a "space ship" without a flight plan. With the Sun in the First House, double Gemini can have a strong ego, but he is challenged to find ways of expressing it productively.

This individual has an excellent mind, and he is capable of expressing himself very well, though in the double combination he must be wary of being too opinionated rather than thoughtful. Of course, he does have two sides to his nature, and he can be a Jekyll and Hyde, especially when Gemini is doubled.

His ego finds expression through his opinions and his ability to think, and this can find outlet through writing, public speaking, acting, or teaching. He would be an excellent critic, either literary or theatrical, for his opinions are almost always right on target.

But he is challenged to come down to earth and find a direction for his airy thoughts, and to look inward to discover matters of the spirit, truly a difficult task for him.

Gemini Rising with Cancer Sun

"I am because I think; my will/ego finds expression through my feelings."

The Sun in this combination will most likely fall into the Second House or the First. If the Sun is in the Second, the ego expression finds outlet through matters related to money, possessions, or the loving, giving nature; if it is in the First, it finds outlet through the personality and the appearance.

This is not a particularly easy combination, though it can be productive. The Mutable Air of the Ascendant merely coexists with the Cardinal Water of the Sun, unable to mix. However, this individual can, eventually, find ways of unifying thoughts and feelings into his identity.

With the Second House placement of the Sun, the ego finds expression through feelings associated with matters of money, possessions, and love. Since the Sun is Cancer, it also utilizes matters of home, mother, and real estate.

This individual is challenged to become more practical, to learn to deal with the earthly concerns of finances and pragmatism, as well as to develop ambition and directions for his future security.

Gemini Rising with Leo Sun

"I am because I think; my will/ego finds expression through my will."

The Sun in this combination will most likely fall into the Third House or the Second. If the Sun is in the Third, the ego expression finds outlet through matters related to communication, education, and brethren; if it is in the Second, it finds outlet through money and possessions, and perhaps the loving, giving nature.

This is an excellent combination of fire and air. The Mutable Gemini Ascendant feeds the strong, willful, fiery ego of the Leo Sun, for a very creative mixture. With the Sun in the Third House, the ego finds expression through the Leo will, which seeks outlet in matters related to communication, writing, education, and brethren. There is a considerable Fifth House influence as well, bringing in matters of entertainment, speculation, romance, and creativity.

This individual could be a writer, a teacher, an actor, an artist, with considerable success.

His challenge is to learn practicality, dealing with financial matters and security, as well as to delve within to discover his inner Self, becoming more spiritual.

Gemini Rising with Virgo Sun

"I am because I think; my will/ego finds expression through my ability to analyze."

The Sun in this combination will most likely fall into the Fourth House or the Third. If the Sun is in the Fourth, the ego expression finds outlet through matters related to the home, mother, or real estate; if in the Third, through matters associated with communication, education, and brethren.

This is a stressful relationship between personality and ego, though not entirely an unproductive one. Mutable Air and Mutable Earth merely coexist, unable to mix creatively. Without either Fire or Water to feed the Self or his ego, this double Mutable individual has difficulty finding direction for his life.

With the Sun in the Fourth, his ego seeks to find expression through his ability to analyze in matters connected with the home, mother, or real estate. It is likely that he will work from his home, perhaps analyzing and consulting in real estate, though he may also be in sales. He does have a very high mentality, because both his Ascendant and his Sun are ruled by Mercury, and this may give him the means of unifying the two disparate facets of his identity.

He certainly has writing and speaking talents, though he

is somewhat shy and retiring, and he may develop a business that is service related, utilizing his opinions and his analytical abilities.

His challenge is to discover his ambitions and then to direct them; he also needs to come into closer contact with his feelings, to develop spiritually as well as mentally.

Gemini Rising with Libra Sun

> *"I am because I think; my will/ego finds expression through my ability to balance."*

The Sun in this combination will most likely fall into the Fifth House or the Fourth. If it is in the Fifth, the ego expression will find outlet through matters related to entertainment, love affairs, romance, speculation, or children; if in the Fourth, it will find outlet through matters connected with the home, mother, or real estate.

This is an excellent mixture of two Air signs, combining the Mutable Gemini Ascendant with the Cardinal Libra Sun with creative results. As with all combinations of Air signs, there is an emphasis on matters of the mind, on intelligence, thoughts, and ideas. Here, with the Libra Sun in the Fifth House, the ego seeks to find expression through its ability to weigh and balance in matters associated with entertainment, speculation, romance, and creativity.

This individual will be highly artistic, and his talents could find outlet through writing, acting, or painting. Certainly his Cardinal ego is ambitious, and it can give direction to his flexible, Mutable personality productively.

His challenge is to develop both a pragmatic and a spiritual side to his nature, for double Air emphasizes matters of the mind exclusively. He needs to discover his inner Self, and to join that to his expressive outer Self.

Gemini Rising with Scorpio Sun

> *"I am because I think; my will/ego finds expression through my desires."*

The Sun in this combination will most likely fall into the Sixth House or the Fifth. If it is in the Sixth, the ego expression will find outlet through matters of work, service, health, clothing, and food; if in the Fifth, through matters of entertainment, love affairs, romance, speculation, and children. This is not an easy combination, for the Mutable Air of the Ascendant does not mix with the Fixed Water of the Sun. With the Scorpio Sun in the Sixth House, this becomes especially difficult, for the lustful desires of the ego must find expression in matters related to work, service, health, pets, diet, and clothing.

But the Fixed Scorpio ego is stronger than the Mutable Gemini personality, and it will find ways of unifying the two facets of the identity. Scorpio can be quite creative, and he perceives that the thoughts and desires can be joined.

This is an excellent combination for a psychiatrist or psychotherapist. It would also be good for a gynecologist. Fashion design would also be a possibility.

The challenge for this individual is to find a practical means of channeling his energy, utilizing both mind and spirit in ways that will serve himself as well as others.

Gemini Rising with Sagittarius Sun

> *"I am because I think; my will/ego finds expression through my ability to see or perceive."*

The Sun in this combination will most likely fall into the Seventh House or the Sixth. If it is in the Seventh, the ego expression will find outlet through matters of partnership and associations with others; if in the Sixth, it will be through matters of work, service, health, clothing, and food.

This is an excellent combination of fire and air, despite the fact that the Seventh House placement of the Sun gives the native a tendency to see himself reflected through the eyes of his partner or partners. The Mutable Air of the Gemini Ascendant feeds the Mutable Fire of the Sagittarius Sun, which must find its ego expression through its ability to see or perceive in matters related to partnership or other people.

There is, however, in this combination, some influence from the Ninth House, the natural placement of Sagittarius. Matters of higher education, philosophy, publishing, and travel may enter into the partnership concerns, and those factors also work well with the thoughts and opinions of the Self.

This individual can achieve success in any of those fields, continually growing and expanding throughout his life.

His challenge is to seek his spiritual nature, to delve into his inner Self, in order to give depth to his mental nature. He also needs to acquire some degree of practicality as well.

Gemini Rising with Capricorn Sun

"I am because I think; my will/ego finds expression through my ability to use."

The Sun in this combination will most likely fall into the Eighth House or the Seventh. If it is in the Eighth, the ego expression will find outlet through matters related to partnership finances, sex, heritage and inheritance, or death; if in the Seventh, it will find outlet through matters of partnership and associations with others.

This is not an easy combination, for the Mutable Air of the Ascendant merely coexists with the Cardinal Earth of the Sun, unable to mix creatively. Placed in the Eighth House, the Saturn ruled Capricorn Sun has difficulty expressing its ego through using matters of sex, partnership finances, inheritance, and death.

This individual could unify the two distinctly different facets of his identity and find creative outlet through a career as an estate lawyer, or he could be a counselor on matters of sex or on death and dying. It is possible he might be a mortician.

The challenge for this individual is to find his ambition and to follow it through. He also needs to learn to develop his inner Self in a more spiritual form.

Gemini Rising with Aquarius Sun

"I am because I think; my will/ego finds expression through who and what I know."

The Sun in this combination will most likely fall into the Ninth House or the Eighth. If it is in the Ninth, the ego expression will find outlet in matters related to higher education, philosophy, travel, or publishing; if it is in the Eighth, it will find outlet through partnership finances, sex, heritage or inheritance, or death.

This is an excellent combination of two Air signs, with Mutable Gemini on the Ascendant and Fixed Aquarius as the Sun. With the Sun in the Ninth House, trining the Ascendant, the ego finds expression through who and what it knows, connected with matters of higher education, philosophy, travel, and publishing. With Uranus ruled Aquarius as the Sun, it also utilizes matters of friends, group associations, aspirations, and social concerns, for a very strong mentality.

This individual will surely be involved in higher education or in writing or publishing in some way. He has a brilliant mind, and it succeeds in communication.

His challenge is to come down from his ivory tower from time to time to see what the real world is like. He must also endeavor to develop a spirit that will match his mind.

Gemini Rising with Pisces Sun

> *"I am because I think; my will/ego finds expression through my beliefs."*

The Sun in this combination will most likely fall into the Tenth House or the Ninth. If it is in the Tenth, the ego expression will find outlet through public recognition, honors, success, and the father; if it is in the Ninth, it will find outlet through matters related to higher education, philosophy, travel or publishing.

This is a somewhat stressful combination of Mutable Air on the Ascendant and Mutable Water for the Sun. In square aspect, in the Tenth House, the Pisces Sun has some difficulties expressing its ego through beliefs related to public recognition, business management, and success. Also, since Pisces is ruled by Neptune, it is much more comfortable in isolation rather than out in the public eye; it prefers matters of the spirit to matters of the external world.

An individual with this combination could succeed most comfortably in some facet of the arts, perhaps as an actor, perhaps a poet or musician. In other spheres, such as business or politics, he would have difficulty unifying the two distinctly different aspects of his identity.

His challenge, beyond unifying his identity, is to learn to deal with the real world beyond his mind and spirit, to seek to come out of his inner protective shell and relate to others openly and easily.

Gemini Rising with Aries Sun

> *"I am because I think; my will/ego finds expression through the fact that I am."*

The Sun in this combination will most likely fall into the Eleventh House or the Tenth. If it is in the Eleventh, the ego expression will find outlet through friends, group activities, aspirations, or social movements; if it is in the Tenth, it will find outlet through matters related to public recognition, honors, success, and the father.

This is an excellent combination of fire and air. The Mutable Gemini Ascendant feeds the Cardinal Aries Sun, to achieve ambitions successfully. With the Sun placed in the Eleventh House, the ego seeks to find expression through the personality, in matters related to friends, group activities, aspirations, and social movements. This is an ideal combination for a politician, having both Cardinal and Mutable qualities. However, this individual could as easily find success by using his charisma as a professional host.

The challenge for this native is to develop spiritually and to learn to be more practical and down-to-earth.

Gemini Rising with Taurus Sun

"I am because I think; my will/ego finds expression through what I have."

The Sun in this combination will most likely fall into the Twelfth House or the Eleventh. If it is in the Twelfth, the ego expression will find outlet through matters of spiritual regeneration, solitude, institutions, or inhibitions or restrictions he places on himself; if it is in the Eleventh, it will find outlet through friends, group activities, aspirations, or social movements.

This is a very difficult combination of Mutable Air Ascendant and Fixed Earth Sun. The two elements of air and earth merely coexist, unable to mix creatively into a unified identity. In this case, there is the added complication of the Taurus ego finding it extremely hard to feel at home in the Twelfth House, for Taurus, being the most materialistic of signs, is weakened when placed in the most spiritual of houses.

This individual must find some way for his ego expression to achieve outlet through what he has in matters of spiritual regeneration, solitude, and associations with institutions, which is no small task.

This is his challenge, with an additional need to find ways of communicating to partners and other people in general, keeping himself from holding in all that the Gemini Ascendant wants to express.

Chapter 13

MUTABLE EARTH—VIRGO

(August 23–September 22)

Applies to Virgo Sun sign, Virgo Ascendant, and those with Mercury on the Ascendant.

RULER—Mercury
MOTTO—"I analyze."
SYMBOL—The Virgin
POLARITY—Negative/Feminine
COLOR—Yellow Green
KEY WORDS—Order, Service, Discrimination
MALE IDOLS—George Maharis, Earl Holliman, Van Johnson
FEMALE IDOLS—Greta Garbo, Ingrid Bergman, Lauren Bacall

THE VIRGO LOOK

Even though gay Virgo may be quite attractive, he has a way of not being noticed. This may be partly due to his shyness or his quiet manner, but there is also something about his appearance that makes him blend into the background. Generally, he is of medium height, relatively slender (though he does tend to gain weight with age), and with a well-formed and well-proportioned body. His hair is most often brown and straight, varying from medium to dark brown.

His complexion is generally somewhat ruddy, although it may be fairly pale in some cases, and he has a round face with small or delicate features.

Once noticed, however, Virgo's real beauty shines forth from his dark, intelligent, sympathetic eyes, which have a slightly melancholy look, slanting somewhat because of the fact that they turn downwards at the outside, almost in a squint.

Virgo dresses well, though somewhat conservatively. He follows fashion, and longs to wear things that are flamboyant or outrageous, but will invariably choose colors and styles that will keep him from standing out from the crowd. He is extreme in his neatness, and may not show a wrinkle or a soiled spot, even after a long day of work.

He will have a distinctive voice, which in some cases may tend toward being somewhat shrill, thin, or nasal, because— despite the outward appearance of Virgo's calm—he is actually somewhat nervous in nature.

If attending a costume party, gay Virgo will usually choose to wear something indicative of his serious, workmanlike nature. At his most extreme, he might dress as an ascetic, as a monk (or nun), but more likely he will be conservative, wearing the apparel of a doctor (or nurse), a scientist, or a chef.

THE VIRGO NATURE

Virgo is a much maligned sign; he does not really deserve all the jokes made at his expense—not all of them, anyway. He's earned one or two. Gay Virgo is almost always pictured as the fussy, tediously tidy, prim and proper taskmaster— rather like Felix Unger on *The Odd Couple*. To some extent, that is his nature, but it is an unfair caricature, for there is much, much more to him.

Virgo is always attempting to bring matter under the control of mind. With Mercury as his ruler, Virgo places a great emphasis on mentality and language; and with the Sixth House of work and service as Virgo's natural placement, he always wants to put the mind to practical work, for himself and for others.

Whatever Virgo does, he has to feel useful, and he hates to see talent and ability wasted, whether it is his own or someone else's. His sense of perfection can be irritating to those around him, for he will not be satisfied with anything until it is done the very best it can be, and he will not hesitate to offer criticism, though it is almost always constructive criticism.

Virgo is an excellent worker, especially in areas involving criticism or editing or service to the public. Virgo is good with language, and with anything requiring manual dexterity. They are the true craftsmen of the Zodiac, meticulous about details. Careers involving service are best for Virgo, and health care is emphasized. Virgos make good doctors, nurses, and psychiatrists. As they are concerned about diet, they make good cooks or chefs.

Virgo analyzes everything, and usually his analysis is correct, for he is almost invariably intelligent, even when he is deprived of the education he wants. (Those who do not have extensive formal education manage somehow to acquire knowledge on their own.) He has the ability to perceive the whole picture, and then to focus in on specifics, though sometimes he can become too concerned about the details.

But the point of all this mental activity for Virgo is his desire to serve others. Although it would not seem so, from his reserve and his caution, even his remoteness, Virgo loves and cares very deeply. In fact, his sense of self worth seems to be greatly dependent upon his value to others. There is a tendency for Virgo to lack self esteem; he sees himself as imperfect, and needs the appreciation of others to make himself seem worthy.

For a lover, this can sometimes be a problem, for this need of Virgo's may appear to be possessiveness, though it is more likely to be Virgo's desire to be a part of another in order to affirm himself. Gay Virgo can be a true and loyal lover. Despite his quiet, even shy exterior, Virgo can be passionate in sex. In fact, there is more than a small amount of anal eroticism about him, and he has a surprising ability to "get down and dirty." His pleasure in performing a "service" for others plays a part in this.

However, Virgo has a tendency to be slow in committing himself to a partnership, and he generally thinks of the practical considerations, weighing them carefully in making the decision. But once he makes a commitment, he is a devoted partner and lover.

THE VIRGO CHALLENGE

The life challenge for gay Virgo is to become more accepting of human frailty, in himself and in others. He must learn self esteem and self respect, so that he can truly value and respect others. He needs to relax, to try not to control situations and events in order to control his tendency toward worrying and fretting about things that are not within his power.

Virgo's characteristic overworking and overworrying can exhaust him, weakening his constitution and leaving him open to physical and psychosomatic ailments. He is prone toward nervous indigestion and stomach problems generally, and they are almost always attributable to his nervous tension.

A part of Virgo's challenge is to learn to trust, to avoid prejudice and pedanticism and self-righteousness. The love he so desperately needs is dependent upon his willingness to let go and accept his imperfection as something perfect in itself, to let others serve him as he seeks to serve them.

One good thing about Virgo is his mutability; he can change and learn and grow, overcoming his challenge by applying his excellent mind toward understanding.

VIRGO RISING

Virgo Rising with Virgo Sun

> **"I am because I analyze; my will/ego finds expression through my ability to analyze."**

The Sun in this combination will most likely fall into the First House or the Twelfth. If the Sun is in the First, the ego expression finds outlet through matters related to the personality and appearance; if in the Twelfth, through matters of spiritual regeneration, solitude, institutions, or inhibitions or restrictions he places on himself.

The combination of Virgo Rising with Virgo Sun can be a beneficial one, but it is not without its difficulties. As with any double sign, double Virgo is very one-sided and is somewhat egocentric, especially when the Sun is in the First House. Not only is this individual double Earth, but he is double Mutable, which makes him too adaptable for his own good.

He is extremely analytical, being the most mental of the Earth signs, and his ego seeks to find expression through analyzing matters of Self and personality and appearance. This is one of the reasons Virgo seems to be so prim and proper and schoolmarmish (when in fact, he is extremely sexual). With this double placement, factors of work, service, health, diet, pets, and clothing enter into his ego expression.

This individual may have a career in any of those fields, or he may choose to write about the subjects, since Mercury is his ruler.

His challenge is to sustain his ambitions and goals, trying not to be quite so adaptable, and to develop spiritually as well as mentally and physically, to let things go a bit more, not trying to remain in control.

Virgo Rising with Libra Sun

"I am because I analyze; my will/ego finds expression through my ability to balance."

The Sun in this combination will most likely fall into the Second House or the First. If the Sun is in the Second, the ego expression finds outlet through matters related to money, possessions, or the loving, giving nature; if it is in the First, it finds outlet through the personality and the appearance.

This is not an easy combination, but it can be a productive one. The airy Cardinal Sun does not mix with the Mutable Earth Ascendant, but the two merely coexist, and some means must be found to unify them into an integrated identity.

The Libra ego seeks to find expression through its ability to balance in matters related to money, possessions, and love, an earthy concern that is foreign to its nature. However, it brings into the expression its own native concerns with partnership and other people. It is the Ascendant that is the earthy, practical facet of the identity, and Libra can borrow from his analytical ability to produce an accountant or a bookkeeper or a writer on financial matters.

However, Libra would prefer to be an artist or a sculptor, and that is possible in this combination, especially if Saturn is in Libra or Saturn and Venus are in aspect. But it will take considerable effort to achieve success.

The challenge for this native is to develop in spiritual matters, as well as to find the drive and ambition to achieve his goals.

Virgo Rising with Scorpio Sun

"I am because I analyze; my will/ego finds expression through my desires."

The Sun in this combination will most likely fall into the Third House or the Second. If the Sun is in the Third, the ego expression finds outlet through matters related to communication, education, and brethren; if it is in the Second, it finds outlet through money and possessions, and perhaps the loving, giving nature.

This is an excellent combination of earth and water. The Fixed Water of the Scorpio Sun nourishes the Mutable Earth of the Ascendant, and the earth gives boundaries to channel the water. With the Sun in the Third House, the Scorpio ego seeks expression through its desires in matters of communication, writing, education, and brethren. It also brings concerns of sex, inheritance, and death from its own native Eighth House.

This individual could easily be a teacher or writer. If a novelist, his subjects might include sex, death, mystery, crime, and metaphysics.

His challenge is to develop his mind in more intellectual directions, and to find the drive and ambition to succeed.

Virgo Rising with Sagittarius Sun

"I am because I analyze; my will/ego finds expression through my ability to see or perceive."

The Sun in this combination will most likely fall into the Fourth House or the Third. If the Sun is in the Fourth, the ego expression finds outlet through matters related to the home, mother, or real estate; if in the Third, through matters associated with communication, education, and brethren.

This is a rather stressful combination, but it can be a productive one. In square aspect, the Mutable Earth Ascendant cannot mix with the Mutable Fire Sun, but must find some compromise to enable them to coexist within a single identity. However, since both are Mutable, compromise comes naturally to them.

With the Sun in the Fourth House, the Sagittarian ego seeks expression through its ability to see or perceive in matters related to the home, real estate, or mother. It also brings matters of higher mind, philosophy, travel, and publishing from its native Ninth House.

It is very likely that this individual will work at home, either involved in real estate or in writing. If he is a writer, his subjects may be connected to the home or to travel or philosophy. But it is through a joining of his analytical Virgo Self with his perceptive Sagittarius ego that he succeeds.

The challenge for this native is to develop spiritually and intellectually, and to learn to express his love to one person, giving and receiving with openness.

Virgo Rising with Capricorn Sun

"I am because I analyze; my will/ego finds expression through my ability to use."

The Sun in this combination will most likely fall into the Fifth House or the Fourth. If it is in the Fifth, the ego expression will find outlet through matters related to entertainment, love affairs, romance, speculation, or children; if in the Fourth, it will find outlet through matters connected with the home, mother, or real estate.

This is an excellent combination of two Earth signs, with Mutable Earth on the Ascendant and Cardinal Earth for the Sun. Being all Earth, it represents a highly practical individual. With the Sun in the Fifth House, the ego seeks expression through his ability to use in matters of entertainment, speculation, risk taking, romance, and children. Capricorn brings matters of public attention and recognition to the nature, and this makes the combination an ideal one for a director of films and theater. This native might also be involved in investments, utilizing his analytical ability to have a good grasp of the stock market.

His challenge is to acquire some diversity to his identity, to delve into his inner spiritual Self, to acquire some intellectual depth, and to develop the drive to succeed in his goals.

Virgo Rising with Aquarius Sun

"I am because I analyze; my will/ego finds expression through who or what I know."

The Sun in this combination will most likely fall into the Sixth House or the Fifth. If it is in the Sixth, the ego expression will find outlet through matters of work, service, health, clothing, and food; if in the Fifth, through matters of entertainment, love affairs, romance, speculation, and children.

This is not an easy combination, but it can be a productive one if the two distinctly different facets of the identity can be unified creatively. The Mutable Earth of the Ascendant merely coexists with the Fixed Air of the Sun, unable to mix. Moreover, the Aquarius ego is not particularly comfortable in the Sixth House, which is the natural house of the Virgo Ascendant.

The Aquarian ego seeks to find expression here through who or what it knows in matters of work, service, health, pets, diet, and clothing. It can contribute its own Eleventh House concerns of friends, social actions, and aspirations into the mixture, however. By also utilizing the analytical Virgo tendencies toward who and what it knows, it may be able to achieve the unity this individual needs.

It is possible for this native to be a writer or teacher on subjects of health, diet, and medicine, particularly relating the subjects to general social concerns. He can also work in insurance or in a management capacity in hospitals.

His challenge is to develop in spiritual matters, looking into his inner Self for deeper understanding, and to find the fiery ambition for the success he desires.

Virgo Rising with Pisces Sun

"I am because I analyze; my will/ego finds expression through my beliefs."

The Sun in this combination will most likely fall into the Seventh House or the Sixth. If it is in the Seventh, the ego expression will find outlet through matters of partnership and associations with others; if in the Sixth, it will be through matters of work, service, health, clothing, and food.

This is an excellent combination of earth and water, with the Mutable Water of the Pisces Sun nourishing the Mutable Earth of the Virgo Ascendant, and with the earth giving form and direction to the water. When the Sun is placed in the Seventh House, there is almost always a tendency for the native to define himself by seeing himself reflected through his lover or partner. This is no exception, for the double Mutable nature of this individual is quite insecure.

In the Seventh House, the Pisces Sun seeks expression through beliefs related to partnership and other people. However, it also brings in matters of its natural Twelfth House, such matters as spiritual regeneration, solitude, and concerns of institutions such as hospitals, prisons, and the military.

The challenge for this individual is to develop matters of the mind, to strengthen his analytical ability and his belief structure. He also needs to acquire the drive to succeed, despite his mutable nature.

Virgo Rising with Aries Sun

"I am because I analyze; my will/ego finds expression through the fact that I am."

The Sun in this combination will most likely fall into the Eighth House or the Seventh. If it is in the Eighth, the ego expression will find outlet through matters related to partnership finances, sex, heritage and inheritance, or death; if in the Seventh, it will find outlet through matters of partnership and associations with others.

This is not an easy combination, for the Mutable Earth Ascendant and the Cardinal Fire Sun merely coexist, unable to mix easily. With the Sun in the Eighth House, the ego seeks expression through its very existence, related to matters of sex, inheritance, partnership finances, and death. This individual tends to use his appearance and personality to achieve success, and could be a rather ruthless person except for the analytical nature of his Ascendant; for Virgo will attempt to guide his fire away from a total preoccupation with sex toward service through banking, insurance, or estate management.

The challenge for this native, besides unifying the two divergent facets of his identity, is to seek matters of the spirit and of the mind.

Virgo Rising with Taurus Sun

> *"I am because I analyze; my will/ego finds expression through what I have."*

The Sun in this combination will most likely fall into the Ninth House or the Eighth. If it is in the Ninth, the ego expression will find outlet in matters related to higher education, philosophy, travel, or publishing; if it is in the Eighth, it will find outlet through partnership finances, sex, heritage or inheritance, or death.

This is an excellent combination of two Earth signs, with the Mutable Earth Virgo on the Ascendant and the Fixed Earth Taurus Sun. With the Sun in the Ninth House, in trine aspect to the Ascendant, this is a very practical individual who deals well in the real world to achieve success. However, he is somewhat one sided, being double Earth.

With the Sun in the Ninth House, this native seeks ego expression through what it has related to matters of higher education, philosophy, travel, and publishing. Taurus also brings matters of money and possessions and love into the picture, making this combination a good one for management of educational institutions, religious organizations, world tours, or publishing companies.

The challenge for this individual is to develop spiritually and mentally, to give his earthy nature more depth, and to acquire the drive necessary to sustain his success.

Virgo Rising with Gemini Sun

> *"I am because I analyze; my will/ego finds expression through my ability to think (or have opinions)."*

The Sun in this combination will most likely fall into the Tenth House or the Ninth. If it is in the Tenth, the ego expression will find outlet through public recognition, honors, suc cess, and the father; if it is in the Ninth, it will find outlet through matters related to higher education, philosophy, travel, or publishing.

This is a stressful combination, but a highly productive one. The Mutable Earth of the Virgo Ascendant does not mix with the Mutable Air of the Gemini Sun; the two facets of the identity merely coexist. However, they can be united by the fact that the ruling planet for both is Mercury. It is a combination that is very much concerned with matters of the mind, Virgo emphasizing analytical ability and Gemini thoughts and opinions.

With the Sun in the Tenth House, the Gemini ego seeks expression through thoughts and opinions on matters involving the public, business, and politics. It also brings in matters of communication, writing, education, and brethren from its native Third House.

This individual would be an excellent marketing analyst or political analyst. His opinions and analysis of all public matters will demand attention.

His challenge is to develop matters of the spirit, as well as the drive and tenacity to achieve success and sustain it.

Virgo Rising with Cancer Sun

"I am because I analyze; my will/ego finds expression through my feelings."

The Sun in this combination will most likely fall into the Eleventh House or the Tenth. If it is in the Eleventh, the ego expression will find outlet through friends, group activities, aspirations, or social movements; if it is in the Tenth, it will find outlet through matters related to public recognition, honors, success, and the father.

This is an excellent combination of earth and water. The Mutable Earth of the Virgo Ascendant gives form and direction to the Cardinal Water of the Cancer Sun, and the water nourishes the earth. With the Sun in the Eleventh

House, the Cancer ego seeks expression through feelings related to matters of friends, aspirations, social concerns, and social events. Cancer also brings with it matters of home, mother, and real estate.

This individual combines his analytical abilities and his feelings to produce one who may write social commentary or perhaps a society or gossip columnist.

His challenge is to develop in the intellectual sphere and to find the persistence and tenacity to sustain success once it is achieved. He also needs to learn to communicate his feelings openly and freely to his lover or partner.

Virgo Rising with Leo Sun

"I am because I analyze; my will/ego finds expression through my will."

The Sun in this combination will most likely fall into the Twelfth House or the Eleventh. If it is in the Twelfth, the ego expression will find outlet through matters of spiritual regeneration, solitude, institutions, or inhibitions or restrictions he places on himself; if it is in the Eleventh, it will find outlet through friends, group activities, aspirations, or social movements.

This is a difficult combination of earth and fire. The Fixed Leo Fire tends to scorch the Mutable Virgo Earth, and the earth attempts to put out the fire. This individual is challenged to find creative ways to unite the two divergent facets of his identity, by combining his will and his analytical ability.

With the Sun in the Twelfth, the ego seeks expression through will in matters concerning spiritual regeneration, solitude, and service to institutions. However, the deepest challenge for this native is to avoid turning the strong Leo will destructively against himself, for the outgoing nature of Leo is extremely frustrated by this placement.

Positive solutions would be to follow a career in medicine or in penology or even the military, utilizing Virgo's need for service with Leo's need for attention and power.

The challenge for this individual is to acquire spiritual depth as well as the higher mentality to understand the needs of his complex identity. He also needs to learn to express his feelings openly to those he loves.

Chapter 14

MUTABLE FIRE—SAGITTARIUS

(November 22–December 21)

Applies to Sagittarius Sun sign, Sagittarius Ascendant, and those with Jupiter on the Ascendant.

RULER—Jupiter
MOTTO—"I see."
SYMBOL—The Archer
POLARITY—Positive/Masculine
COLOR—Blue
KEY WORDS—Expansion, Generosity, Growth, Exploration
MALE IDOLS—John Davidson, Noel Coward, Dan Dailey
FEMALE IDOLS—Mary Martin, Jane Fonda, Patty Duke Astin

THE SAGITTARIUS LOOK

Even though Sagittarius is among the most handsome signs of the Zodiac, there is something "horsey" about his looks. He is generally rather tall, with a strong, well-built, even muscular body. Though he may give the appearance of long legs, this is usually not so. If anything his legs may be short in proportion to his long torso, which is one of the reasons he may appear to strut or prance when he walks.

He may also have a tendency to stoop or walk with slumped shoulders.

Although the top half of Sagittarius is supposed to be man, while the other half is horse (giving some people cause to refer to him as a "horse's ass"), his long, handsome face tends to show his equine nature. Perhaps it is his straight, narrow, almost Grecian nose, or it may be the straight self-satisfied set of his wide, small-lipped mouth. His eyes are generally dark and clear, with a steady, self-confident gaze, much like that of equus.

Gay Sagittarius usually has rather straight hair, often of an auburn or chestnut hue. However, with age, he may have a tendency toward baldness, particularly at the temples. If Sagittarius has body hair, it may also be fine and straight and lustrous.

His complexion will tend toward ruddiness.

In dress, Sagittarius may run to one of two extremes. Some may choose the "uniform" of the business suit and tie or sport jacket, slacks, and sweater, appearing extremely conservative. Others may go the opposite direction toward a sporty casualness, wearing jeans and boots or running shorts and shoes. Whatever his choice, Sagittarius is invariably impeccably neat in appearance.

If attending a costume party, gay Sagittarius will also tend toward these extremes, but carrying them further. The one may choose the cap and gown of the scholar, or the uniform of the priest, while the other may seek something that will display his fine body, for Sagittarius is an exhibitionist, whether overtly or covertly. He might wear the loincloth of Tarzan or the tunic of a Greek or Roman sportsman. Some with a sense of humor might go as one end of a horse (or both).

THE SAGITTARIUS NATURE

Sagittarius is the least passive of the Mutable signs. Indeed, from his outward appearance, one would not think he could be easily led at all, for he is strong, self-confident, and active. He hates to be confined, and must have freedom of movement and freedom of ideas to the point of suffering from claustrophobia.

But it is his expansive, freedom-loving nature itself that allows him to be influenced by Fixed or Cardinal signs. Sagittarius is generous to a fault; he will "give the shirt off his back." He wants to share everything, both physically and spiritually, and is often disappointed when others do not want to reciprocate.

Accordingly, Sagittarius is the true positive thinker. He will not stay down for long; invariably when he reaches bottom, he fights back against his obstacles with renewed energy. He is an incorrigible idealist, and his is the most enthusiastic sign of the Zodiac. Some of the more cynical signs might call him "Pollyanna," for he seeks to see the best in everyone.

However, gay Sagittarius is really a deep thinker. As the sign of the Ninth House, he emphasizes all of the qualities of the higher mind. He needs intellectual stimulation, as well as spiritual or philosophical growth, or he will feel stifled. He also has the need to travel, for learning more about others as much as for his sense of excitement and adventure.

His world view is a humanitarian one; in fact, Sagittarius is the true "liberal" of the Zodiac, inevitably following a political stance that represents "the good of all," with little regard for self-interest. In relating to others, he is honest and straightforward, and he is naturally outgoing and sociable. He is usually the "perfect gentleman" though, and can be extremely reserved and polite if he feels the occasion calls for it.

He is witty and articulate, and sometimes his barbs can be as cutting to others as Scorpio's. When he pulls an arrow from his quiver and shoots it, it generally goes straight to the target, and he does not understand when it hurts. As the Archer, Sagittarius sometimes tends to shoot too many arrows into the air at one time, undertaking more projects than he can follow up on and complete. It seems there is never enough time for him to do all he wants to do in life; he is almost never bored, perceiving even the most mundane undertakings as adventure.

Although Sagittarius emphasizes the mind and the spirit, he also has great interest in the body, and can be the athlete as well as the scholar. Even if he is not into vigorous activities such as running, tennis, or handball, he will enjoy the outdoors, and may choose golf, hiking, or even just walking.

As a lover, gay Sagittarius may be difficult to understand.

He may swing from extreme passion and vigorous lovemaking to gentle sharing of philosophy or intellectual conversation. He may have a tendency to exhaust a partner, both physically and mentally, for he wants to share everything—every moment, every thought, every experience—with the one he loves.

That is, if he can hold his love down to just one person. For gay Sagittarius has a tendency toward promiscuity. Being half horse, he is the stud of the Zodiac. He has an insatiable appetite and doesn't think there is anything wrong with satisfying it on the spur of the moment. It doesn't mean he loves his lover less; it is a part of his sense of adventure, and his need to experience everything and everyone. He requires a very understanding lover, one who will allow him his freedom yet be willing to share in all he experiences. This might require the patience of a saint, but Sagittarius is himself very sensitive and considerate and can be tamed.

THE SAGITTARIUS CHALLENGE

There is a dichotomy with Sagittarius, almost an hypocrisy. As much as he likes freedom and honesty and openness, he can have a tendency to be dogmatic or overbearing in his expression of his beliefs and ideas. He experiences true shame and contriteness when he is made to realize what he has done, but a part of his challenge is to think before he speaks or acts. He is capable of meeting the spiritual challenges of his life, if only he is able to perceive what they are.

Sagittarius has a tendency to be undisciplined and haphazard, even unreliable at times. Although he is invariably neat in his appearance, he has a tendency to be sloppy or messy in his surroundings.

The major challenge for gay Sagittarius is to learn discipline and responsibility. He needs to perceive that his freedom is really meaningless unless it is tempered with responsible caution. It is important for him to realize that true freedom is not dependent upon straying or wandering to other pastures, that sexual promiscuity can cause harm to him and to those he loves, that growing is something two people can do together, not just something he does alone.

He must learn to focus his love, not scatter it to the winds. For time is the enemy of Sagittarius, and as age creeps upon him, he may find he has wasted much of his energy and have deep regrets.

SAGITTARIUS RISING

Sagittarius Rising with Sagittarius Sun

> **"I am because I see; my will/ego finds expression through my ability to see or perceive."**

The Sun in this combination will most likely fall into the First House or the Twelfth. If the Sun is in the First, the ego expression finds outlet through matters related to the personality and appearance; if in the Twelfth, through matters of spiritual regeneration, solitude, institutions, or inhibitions or restrictions he places on himself.

The combination of Sagittarius Ascendant with Sagittarius Sun can be a very productive one, though, as with most double signs, it is a very one-sided, egocentric combination. Being both double Mutable and double Fire can make this native very ambitious but also very flexible and adaptable. With the Sun in the First House, the Sagittarius ego seeks expression through its ability to see and perceive matters related to Self, personality, and appearance. However, the ego also can find expression through the native Ninth House matters of Sagittarius—higher education, philosophy, travel, and publishing.

This individual is greatly concerned with personal growth and expansion, and he feels most at home with careers associated with travel and the outdoors. However, his Mutable nature allows him to adapt to expansion within the confines of offices and industry.

The challenge for this native is to develop spiritually, physically, and mentally. He also needs to learn restraint and control so that his perception can encompass the feelings and concerns of others.

Sagittarius Rising with Capricorn Sun

> *"I am because I see; my will/ego finds expression through my ability to use."*

The Sun in this combination will most likely fall into the Second House or the First. If the Sun is in the Second, the ego expression finds outlet through matters related to money, possessions, or the loving, giving nature; if it is in the First, it finds outlet through the personality and the appearance.

This is not an easy combination of Sun and Ascendant, but it can be productive, once the native is able to discover a means of unifying the two diverse facets of his identity. The Mutable Fire of the Sagittarius Ascendant tends to scorch the Cardinal Earth of the Capricorn Sun, and the earth endeavors to put out the fire. This tension is increased by the fact that the ruler of Sagittarius, Jupiter, is the natural enemy of the ruler of Capricorn, Saturn, for the two work in opposite directions, the one for expansion and the other for restriction.

The ego of the Capricorn Sun seeks expression through its ability to use matters of money, possessions, and love. It also brings factors from its native Tenth House, matters of public recognition, business, and politics. If the ego can find ways of using what the Sagittarius personality sees or perceives, the two can be united productively.

The challenge for this individual is to develop matters of the spirit and the intellect, and to learn to communicate effectively feelings of love and caring.

Sagittarius Rising with Aquarius Sun

"I am because I see; my will/ego finds expression through who or what I know."

The Sun in this combination will most likely fall into the Third House or the Second. If the Sun is in the Third, the ego expression finds outlet through matters related to communication, education, and brethren; if it is in the Second, it finds outlet through money and possessions, and perhaps the loving, giving nature.

This is a good and productive combination of fire and air, with the Fixed Air of the Aquarius Sun feeding the Mutable Fire of the Sagittarius Ascendant, and the fire giving life to the air. With the Sun in the Third House, in sextile aspect to the Ascendant, the Aquarius ego seeks expression through who or what it knows related to matters of communication, writing, education, and brethren.

This combination can produce an excellent teacher or professor, especially on subjects affecting society as a whole, or on scientific or technical subjects. However, this individual could also write on these subjects as well.

The challenge for this native is to develop spiritually and physically, and to pause occasionally and look at the world the way other, ordinary humans do. He needs to perceive others more accurately and to deal on a more personal level with those he cares about.

Sagittarius Rising with Pisces Sun

"I am because I see; my will/ego finds expression through my beliefs."

The Sun in this combination will most likely fall into the Fourth House or the Third. If the Sun is in the Fourth, the ego expression finds outlet through matters related to the home, mother, or real estate; if in the Third, through matters associated with communication, education, and brethren.

This combination is a rather stressful one, but it can be quite productive. The Mutable Water of the Pisces Sun tends to put out the Mutable Fire of the Sagittarius Ascendant, and the fire tends to turn the water to steam. With the Sun in the Fourth House, in square aspect, the Pisces ego seeks expression through its beliefs related to matters of home, real estate, and mother. It also brings to its expression matters connected with its native Twelfth House, matters associated with spiritual regeneration, solitude, and service institutions.

This is a very spiritual individual, but one who is also extremely shy and retiring. If he does not isolate himself at home, he could be involved in real estate, but only if it fits within his spiritual belief structure. It is more likely that he will engage himself in the arts, as a painter or a poet or a composer of music.

His challenge is to develop his mind and his body, so that he can perceive the real world rather than an idealized one. He is also challenged to deal with practical matters of finances and income.

Sagittarius Rising with Aries Sun

"I am because I see; my will/ego finds expression through the fact that I am."

The Sun in this combination will most likely fall into the Fifth House or the Fourth. If it is in the Fifth, the ego expression will find outlet through matters related to entertainment, love affairs, romance, speculation, or children; if in the Fourth, it will find outlet through matters connected with the home, mother, or real estate.

This is an excellent combination of two Fire signs. The Mutable Fire of the Sagittarius Ascendant is in trine aspect to the Cardinal Fire of the Aries Sun. In the Fifth House, the Aries ego seeks expression through its very existence, utilizing talents involved with matters of entertainment, speculation, romance, and children. This combination could produce an actor of stage and film, or it could create a professional gambler. It might even produce a perennial child, an incurable romantic.

This native is challenged to develop a much rounder sphere of interest, including matters of mind, body, and spirit. He also needs to try not to be so promiscuous in romance, seeking to find one person to love deeply and truly.

Sagittarius Rising with Taurus Sun

"I am because I see; my will/ego finds expression through what I have."

The Sun in this combination will most likely fall into the Sixth House or the Fifth. If it is in the Sixth, the ego expression will find outlet through matters of work, service, health, clothing, and food; if in the Fifth, through matters of entertainment, love affairs, romance, speculation, and children.

This is not an easy combination, for the Mutable Fire of the Ascendant does not mix with the Fixed Earth of the Sun. The fire tends to scorch the earth, and the earth seeks to put out the fire. With the Sun in the Sixth House, the Taurus ego seeks expression through what he has in terms of health, service, work, pets, and clothing. It is also concerned with money and possessions and love.

The factor that might help to unify the two divergent facets of the identity is that the Sixth House is by nature a practical Earth House, and Taurus can be somewhat comfortable there. Taurus loves sensual pleasures, and that includes both food and clothing, which are Sixth House matters. This combination could produce a fine chef or even a fashion or costume designer.

The challenge for this native is to develop matters of the spirit, to seek his inner Self, and to communicate that Self effectively to others.

Sagittarius Rising with Gemini Sun

"I am because I see; my will/ego finds expression through my ability to think (or have opinions)."

The Sun in this combination will most likely fall into the Seventh House or the Sixth. If it is in the Seventh, the ego expression will find outlet through matters of partnership and associations with others; if in the Sixth, it will be through matters of work, service, health, clothing, and food.

This is an excellent combination, with the Mutable Air of the Gemini Sun feeding the Mutable Fire of the Sagittarius Ascendant, and the fire giving life to the air. However, as with all Seventh House Sun placements, there is a tendency for the native to identify himself through the eyes of other people rather than through his inner nature. With the Gemini Sun in the Seventh House, the ego seeks expression through thoughts and opinions associated with partnership and other people.

But Gemini also brings in matters associated with its native house, the Third, matters of communication, education, writing, and brethren. This individual could work in partnership as a teacher or writer.

His challenge is to develop matters of the spirit, discovering his inner Self, and find a degree of security there as well as in the material world.

Sagittarius Rising with Cancer Sun

"I am because I see; my will/ego finds expression through my feelings."

The Sun in this combination will most likely fall into the Eighth House or the Seventh. If it is in the Eighth, the ego expression will find outlet through matters related to partnership finances, sex, heritage and inheritance, or death; if in the Seventh, it will find outlet through matters of partnership and association with others.

This is not an easy combination, for the Cardinal Water of the Cancer Sun tends to put out the Mutable Fire of the Sagittarius Ascendant, and the fire makes steam of the water. With the Cancer Sun in the Eighth House, the ego seeks expression through feelings related to matters of sex, inheritance, partnership finances, and death.

The Eighth House is almost always a difficult placement for the Sun, and Cancer is no exception. The fact that it brings matters of home, mother, and real estate into the picture does little to help. What Sagittarius perceives and what Cancer feels must find some common ground for unifying the two divergent facets of this native's identity. This is a major challenge, for Sagittarius is much preoccupied with sex and has a tendency toward promiscuity.

To meet this challenge, the native needs to develop mind and body to try to join them to his fire and spirit, acquiring practicality and a sense of the real world.

Sagittarius Rising with Leo Sun

"I am because I see; my will/ego finds expression through my will."

The Sun in this combination will most likely fall into the Ninth House or the Eighth. If it is in the Ninth, the ego expression will find outlet in matters related to higher education, philosophy, travel, or publishing; if it is in the Eighth, it will find outlet through partnership finances, sex, heritage or inheritance, or death.

This is an excellent combination of two Fire signs. The Mutable Fire of the Sagittarius Ascendant is in trine aspect to the Fixed Fire of the Leo Sun. With the Sun in the Ninth House, the ego seeks expression through sheer will related to matters of higher education, philosophy, publishing, and travel. However, Leo also brings Fifth House matters into the picture, matters of entertainment, speculation, romance, and children.

This individual might find a career in education or publishing, being a teacher or writer in the field of drama or film. He could also be an actor or a director. He could also find a profession related to travel, perhaps allied to his tendencies toward risk taking.

His challenge is to become more well rounded, delving into matters of the spirit, discovering his inner Self, and trying to become more practical and financially secure.

Sagittarius Rising with Virgo Sun

"I am because I see; my will/ego finds expression through my ability to analyze."

The Sun in this combination will most likely fall into the Tenth House or the Ninth. If it is in the Tenth, the ego expression will find outlet through public recognition, honors, success, and the father; if it is in the Ninth, it will find outlet through matters related to higher education, philosophy, travel, or publishing.

This is a rather stressful combination of Mutable Fire and Mutable Earth, in square aspect. The Sagittarius Fire tends to scorch the Virgo Earth, and the earth attempts to put out the fire. In the Tenth House, the Virgo sun seeks expression through analysis of matters associated with public opinion, public recognition, business, and politics. It brings in its native Sixth House matters—health, work, service, diet, pets, and clothing.

This individual could find a career as a marketing analyst, or he could be a health inspector or a trend setter in fashion or food. Or he could write on these subjects, since Mercury rules Virgo.

His challenge is to develop spiritually and mentally, to round out his personality. He also needs to acquire some persistence and tenacity to hold onto his success once he achieves it.

Sagittarius Rising with Libra Sun

"I am because I see; my will/ego finds expression through my ability to balance."

The Sun in this combination will most likely fall into the Eleventh House or the Tenth. If it is in the Eleventh, the ego expression will find outlet through friends, group activities, aspirations, or social movements; if it is in the Tenth, it will find outlet through matters related to public recognition, honors, success, and the father.

This is an excellent combination of air and fire, with the Cardinal Air of the Libra Sun feeding the Mutable Fire of the Sagittarius Ascendant, and the fire giving life to the air. With the Sun in the Eleventh House, in sextile aspect, the ego seeks expression through its ability to balance matters related to friends, social concerns, aspirations, and group activities. It also brings in Seventh House matters of partnership.

This individual would be an excellent mediator or judge; he might also be a lawyer concerned with defending the poor or the socially deprived. He would also be a fine politician.

His challenge is to learn to be more practical, to discover truly what others are like, rather than seeing them "pigeon-holed" into social categories.

Sagittarius Rising with Scorpio Sun

"I am because I see; my will/ego finds expression through my desires."

The Sun in this combination will most likely fall into the Twelfth House or the Eleventh. If it is in the Twelfth, the ego expression will find outlet through matters of spiritual regeneration, solitude, institutions, or inhibitions or restrictions he places on himself; if it is in the Eleventh, it will find outlet through friends, group activities, aspirations, or social movements.

This is an extremely difficult combination of fire and water. The Fixed Water of the Scorpio Sun attempts to put out the Mutable Fire of the Sagittarius Ascendant, and the fire turns the water to steam. The Twelfth House Sun placement is almost always difficult, but this can be one of the exceptions, for there is—often secretly—a very spiritual side to Pluto ruled Scorpio.

In the Twelfth House, the Scorpio ego seeks expression through its desires associated with matters of spiritual regeneration, solitude, and service institutions such as hospitals, prisons, and the military. It also brings in matters of its native Eighth House, matters of sex, inheritance, partnership finances, and death.

Of course, there is always the danger that the Twelfth House Scorpio Sun can turn its energy against itself, becoming self-destructive. But directed properly, with the aid of Sagittarius' keen perception, this can be a truly spiritual, giving individual.

The challenge for this native is to find this unity between the two divergent facets of his identity, and to expand his nature to become more practical.

Chapter 15

MUTABLE WATER—PISCES

(February 20–March 20)

Applies to Pisces Sun sign, Pisces Ascendant, and those with Neptune on the Ascendant.

RULER—Neptune
MOTTO—"I believe."
SYMBOL—The Trident
POLARITY—Negative/Feminine
COLOR—Red Violet
KEY WORDS—Compassion, Spirituality, Imagination
MALE IDOLS—Rudolf Nureyev, Christopher Atkins, Robert Conrad
FEMALE IDOLS—Elizabeth Taylor, Liza Minelli, Jean Harlow

THE PISCES LOOK

It's true; Pisces does look rather like a fish—a very sexy, attractive fish, but a water creature nonetheless. It is usually the large, impassive or sleepy eyes and the full mouth that give this impression. Whether the Pisces eyes are pale or dark, there is invariably a "watery" look about them. Pisces complexion is generally rather pale or delicate in appearance, and the shape of the face or head is somehow odd—either extremely thin and narrow or extremely wide. The brows are prominent, and often the eyebrows are thick or large.

Pisces' hair is generally dark, thick, and wavy, contrasting strongly with pale eyes. He is rarely tall, but his shoulders are usually large, contrasting with a narrow or long waist. He has a tendency toward a clumsy gait, walking with a stoop or slumped shoulders. In his stance, he seems to be wanting to pull everything inward.

In his dress, Pisces is always extremely clean—changing clothes several times a day if he feels soiled—but he manages to make his apparel seem sloppy. He wears what is comfortable, usually something loose, and he makes no effort to coordinate colors or styles.

If attending a costume party, Pisces will choose something highly imaginative or creative, too original to predict, or he will select something related to his spiritual nature—such as a religious figure—or his watery base—such as a fish, a sailor, or a sea captain. Because of the connection between Pisces and film, he might also go as some old-time film star or character from the movies.

THE PISCES NATURE

The most mutable of the signs, Pisces sometimes appears to be almost characterless, but those who put down Pisces are missing a great deal, for his can be the most spiritual and the most creative sign of the Zodiac. It can be worth the extra effort it takes to get to know the gay Piscean.

Much hides beneath his surface passivity or aloofness. Pisceans are the poets and dreamers of the Zodiac. In some ways, they are like sponges, soaking up knowledge, understanding, and sensations wherever they go. They miss very little, though they do not react outwardly, and they incorporate every sensation into their very special view of reality.

Despite the fact that gay Pisces loves make believe and fantasy, he does perceive the real world with accuracy. They understand the material, but they value the spiritual more highly, for Pisces is one of the "double" signs—half body, half spirit.

This is one of the reasons Pisces seems so indecisive, unable to make up his mind about the simplest things—making choices on a menu, deciding what to wear, when or where to meet someone. It is also the reason he procrastinates. He sees all of the possibilities, and the "pros" and "cons" of each. He understands too much, and is therefore unable to act.

Pisces is at his best when he devotes his life to helping others; he wants to heal, to relieve suffering, to be of use to humanity; and he can be an excellent doctor or psychiatrist. He is also a good artist or actor. His ruling planet, Neptune, rules films, and he does indeed love the cinematic form.

Pisces likes seclusion, even isolation. If left entirely on his own, he may withdraw completely from the world, preferring to stay at home alone, rather than go out among strangers. But in a relationship, gay Pisces becomes a devoted lover. His selflessness comes to the fore, and he merges his entire being into that of the person he loves. If he cares about someone, he will defend that person to the death, unwilling to see defects in his loved one.

Yet he will not fight for his own rights, but will instead step aside. He does not like competition at all, and for this reason he tends to avoid sports and games.

Because of his passivity, gay Pisces will not be likely to initiate a love relationship; but, so long as his partner takes the lead, he can be a truly passionate lover, for his nature is highly sensual and erotic. His love, however, is not just of the body, but of the spirit as well.

THE PISCES CHALLENGE

The Pisces challenge is a difficult but not impossible one. He must learn to value himself, to stand on his own feet, and to fight for what he wants and what he believes in. Pisces lacks self confidence, a belief in his own worth, and he must endeavor to acquire that in order to be of true value to others.

Pisces tends to retreat when faced with difficulty; this retreat may be into solitude or it may be into things much more dangerous to his deeply spiritual nature—into drugs, alcohol, or a fantasy world. He has a tendency to accept a fatalistic view of his life, rationalizing that what he wants or dreams about is impossible for him, rather than going out and trying, taking the chance of being proven right or wrong.

It is his challenge to overcome all these negative traits, to realize the true talent and creativity he has to offer. The love and approbation he wants so desperately from others will come to him, once he realizes how deeply lovable he is.

PISCES RISING

Pisces Rising with Pisces Sun

> *"I am because I believe; my will/ego finds expression through my beliefs."*

The Sun in this combination will most likely fall into the First House or the Twelfth. If the Sun is in the first, the ego expression finds outlet through matters related to the personality and appearance; if in the Twelfth, through matters of spiritual regeneration, solitude, institutions, or inhibitions or restrictions he places on himself.

The combination of Pisces Ascendant and Pisces Sun can be an excellent one, but as with most double signs, it can produce a rather one-sided individual, with a degree of egocentricity. With the Pisces Sun in the First House, the ego finds expression through its beliefs related to Self, personality, and appearance. It brings its own Twelfth House matters of spiritual regeneration, solitude, and concerns of services to institutions into the picture.

It is this latter that is the saving grace for the double Pisces, for he can be extremely self-deceptive, with Neptune as ruler of both his Sun and his Ascendant. However, he can be extremely creative and artistic as well. The great emphasis for him is on matters of beliefs and spirit, whether this finds outlet through art, religion, or metaphysics.

His challenge is to develop other facets to his identity, to keep from withdrawing too deeply into himself and hiding away from society in a fantasy world. He needs to become more practical, more outgoing, and more interested in matters of the mind.

Pisces Rising with Aries Sun

> *"I am because I believe; my will/ego finds expression through the fact that I am."*

The Sun in this combination will most likely fall into the Second House or the First. If the Sun is in the Second, the ego expression finds outlet through matters related to money, possessions, or the loving, giving nature; if it is in the First, it finds outlet through the personality and the appearance.

This is not an easy combination, but it can be a productive one. The stress derives from the fact that the Mutable Water of the Pisces Ascendant endeavors to put out the Cardinal Fire of the Aries Sun, while the fire turns the water to steam. Indeed, there are no two signs as extreme as Pisces and Aries, and it is quite difficult for the native to unify the two divergent facets into a unified identity, but it is possible.

With the Aries Sun placed in the Second House, the ego seeks expression through Self and personality and appearance in combination with money, possessions, and love. It is the placement of one who must achieve and acquire by sheer drive. If it were not for the Pisces Ascendant, he would be quite ruthless, but his beliefs soften and temper his ego.

His challenge is to unify ambitions and spirit, and to learn to understand others, to become more giving and more loving.

Pisces Rising with Taurus Sun

> *"I am because I believe; my will/ego finds expression through what I have."*

The Sun in this combination will most likely fall into the Third House or the Second. If the Sun is in the Third, the ego expression finds outlet through matters related to communication, education, and brethren; if it is in the Second, it finds outlet through money and possessions, and the loving, giving nature.

This is a very good combination, with the Mutable Water of the Pisces Ascendant nourishing the Fixed Earth of the Taurus Sun, and with the earth giving form and direction to the water. With the Sun placed in the Third House, the ego seeks expression through what it has in matters related to communication, writing, education, and brethren.

This is an excellent mixture for a teacher or writer on subjects of a spiritual or religious nature, especially when directed toward the material world.

The challenge for this individual is to acquire the drive necessary to achieve his goals and to sustain them, and to attempt to develop mentally or intellectually to meet his level of spiritual development.

Pisces Rising with Gemini Sun

> *"I am because I believe; my will/ego finds expression through my ability to think (or have opinions)."*

The Sun in this combination will most likely fall into the Fourth House or the Third. If the Sun is in the Fourth, the ego expression finds outlet through matters related to the home, mother, or real estate; if in the Third, through matters associated with communication, education, and brethren.

This is a rather stressful combination, but one that can be productive. The Mutable Water of the Pisces Ascendant merely coexists with the Mutable Air of the Gemini Sun, unable to mix creatively. With the Gemini Sun in the Fourth House, in square aspect to the Ascendant, the ego seeks expression through its thoughts and opinions in matters of home, mother, and real estate. However, Gemini brings its native Third House concerns of communication, writing, education, and brethren into the mixture, as well.

This individual will likely work out of his home, possibly writing or teaching on matters related to real estate, interior design, landscape design, art, or music. He could write fiction that is of interest to women, such as romance novels.

His challenge is to develop a practical side to his nature, and to come out of his shy seclusion from time to time to experience the world outside.

Pisces Rising with Cancer Sun

"I am because I believe; my will/ego finds expression through my feelings."

The Sun in this combination will most likely fall into the Fifth House or the Fourth. If it is in the Fifth, the ego expression will find outlet through matters related to entertainment, love affairs, romance, speculation, or children; if in the Fourth, it will find outlet through matters connected with the home, mother, or real estate.

This is an excellent combination of two Water signs, the Mutable Pisces on the Ascendant and the Cardinal Cancer for the Sun. With the Sun in the Fifth House, the ego seeks expression through its feelings connected with matters of entertainment, speculation, risk taking, creativity, and children.

This individual has considerable artistic talent, and it could be in a variety of fields. He could be a painter, a musician, a singer, or an actor. Whatever the outlet, he mixes his spiritual beliefs with his feelings and emotions.

His challenge is to develop other facets to his rather one-sided nature, to experience the physical and the intellectual, and to develop a combination of practicality and drive to succeed and sustain success.

Pisces Rising with Leo Sun

"I am because I believe; my will/ego finds expression through my will."

The Sun in this combination will most likely fall into the Sixth House or the Fifth. If it is in the Sixth, the ego expression will find outlet through matters of work, service, health, clothing, and food; if in the Fifth, through matters of entertainment, love affairs, romance, speculation, and children.

This is not an easy combination, but it can be a productive one. The Mutable Water of the Pisces Ascendant tends to put out the Fixed Fire of the Leo Sun, and the fire attempts to turn the water to steam. With the Leo Sun in the Sixth House, the ego seeks expression through its will in matters related to service, work, health, diet, pets, and clothing. It is a placement that is extremely uncomfortable for the strong-willed, ambitious Leo Sun. However, he brings into the mixture matters of his native Fifth House—matters of entertainment, risk taking, speculation, romance, and children.

This individual is challenged to find a creative way of uniting the disparate facets of his identity in his career and in his relationships with others. He is forced to be practical by his Sixth House Sun placement. He must find a way of working and serving others, while serving his own ego and ambition. It is perhaps the spiritual Pisces Ascendant that will show him the way.

Pisces Rising with Virgo Sun

"I am because I believe; my will/ego finds expression through my ability to analyze."

The Sun in this combination will most likely fall into the Seventh House or the Sixth. If it is in the Seventh, the ego expression will find outlet through matters of partnership and associations with others; if in the Sixth, it will be through matters of work, service, health, clothing, and food.

This is an excellent combination, with the Mutable Earth-of the Virgo Sun giving form and direction to the Mutable Water of the Pisces Ascendant, and with the water nourishing the earth. However, as with most Seventh House Sun placements, this individual tends to see himself as reflected through the eyes of partners or other people. With the Sun in the Seventh House, the ego seeks expression through its ability to analyze in matters of partnership and other relationships. However, it also brings in matters connected to its own native Sixth House, matters of work, service, health, diet, pets, and clothing.

This individual combines his spiritual beliefs with his analytical abilities to achieve success in partnerships that may be related to the health services field. He may be a doctor, a dietician, a nurse, or a medical researcher.

His challenge is to develop the will and determination to succeed and to sustain his success once it is achieved, for his double Mutable nature makes him too adaptable and easy going.

Pisces Rising with Libra Sun

"I am because I believe; my will/ego finds expression through my ability to balance."

The Sun in this combination will most likely fall into the Eighth House or the Seventh. If it is in the Eighth, the ego expression will find outlet through matters related to partnership finances, sex, heritage and inheritance, or death; if in the Seventh, it will find outlet through matters of partnership and association with others.

This is not an easy combination, but it is one that can be productive, once the native is able to unify the two disparate facets of his identity in creative ways. The Mutable Water of the Pisces Ascendant merely coexists with the Cardinal Air of the Libra Sun, unable to mix. With the Sun in the Eighth

House, the Libra ego seeks expression through its ability to balance in matters of sex, inheritance, partnership finances, and death.

This individual has a natural talent for financial matters, and can easily work as a bookkeeper or an accountant or an estate lawyer. However, this is rarely enough for him, and he feels compelled to find some way of bringing in his deeply spiritual nature.

His challenge is to find a creative solution for this tug of war, and to acquire pragmatism and the strong will to succeed despite obstacles.

Pisces Rising with Scorpio Sun

"I am because I believe; my will/ego finds expression through my desires."

The Sun in this combination will most likely fall into the Ninth House or the Eighth. If it is in the Ninth, the ego expression will find outlet in matters related to higher education, philosophy, travel, or publishing; if it is in the Eighth, it will find outlet through partnership finances, sex, heritage or inheritance, or death.

This is an excellent combination of two Water signs, with the Fixed Water of the Scorpio Sun giving strength to the Mutable Water of the Pisces Ascendant. With the Scorpio Sun in the Ninth House, in trine aspect to the Ascendant, the ego seeks expression through desires associated with matters of higher education, philosophy, travel, and publishing. It also brings from its native Eighth House matters of sex, partnership finances, inheritance, and death.

This individual could be a teacher or a writer on philosophical subjects related to sexuality or death. He could also be a psychiatrist or a minister.

His challenge is to develop in other spheres beyond the spiritual. He needs to be able to deal with the real, physical world, becoming more practical, and perhaps to acquire greater personal ambition, to insure his success. He has some difficulty in communicating his feelings to those he loves, and he needs to attempt to be more open.

Pisces Rising with Sagittarius Sun

"I am because I believe; my will/ego finds expression through my ability to see or perceive."

The Sun in this combination will most likely fall into the Tenth House or the Ninth. If it is in the Tenth, the ego expression will find outlet through public recognition, honors, success, and the father; if it is in the Ninth, it will find outlet through matters related to higher education, philosophy, travel, or publishing.

This is a stressful combination, but one that can be highly productive. The Mutable Water of the Pisces Ascendant attempts to put out the Mutable Fire of the Sagittarius Sun, while the fire tries to turn the water to steam. With the Sun in the Tenth House, in square aspect to the Ascendant, the Sagittarian ego seeks expression through its ability to see and perceive in matters of public opinion, public recognition, business, and politics.

This individual could be a politician or a political analyst, or he could be a spiritual leader or a teacher, for Sagittarius does bring in Ninth House matters as well. There is the possibility he could be involved in the popular entertainment industry also. Whatever his course, he will achieve attention in the public eye.

His challenge is to unify the two disparate facets of his identity, and to acquire the determination and strength of will to sustain his success. He must also learn to become more practical.

Pisces Rising with Capricorn Sun

> *"I am because I believe; my will/ego finds expression through my ability to use."*

The Sun in this combination will most likely fall into the Eleventh House or the Tenth. If it is in the Eleventh, the ego expression will find outlet through friends, group activities, aspirations, or social movements; if it is in the Tenth, it will find outlet through matters related to public recognition, honors, success, and the father.

This is an excellent combination, with the Cardinal Earth of the Capricorn Sun giving form and direction to the Mutable Water of the Pisces Ascendant, and with the water nourishing the earth. With the Sun in the Eleventh House, in sextile relationship to the Ascendant, the Capricorn ego seeks expression through its ability to use in matters of friends, group activities, aspirations, and social movements. It also brings in matters of public opinion, politics, and business.

This individual could have great success in politics or in high religious office. He could also be a leader in charitable organizations or in philanthropic work, for he combines deep spirituality with one of the most practical of signs.

His challenge is to develop his intellect, and to learn to deal more effectively with intimate personal relationships, for he does have difficulty knowing and expressing deep love.

Pisces Rising with Aquarius Sun

> *"I am because I believe; my will/ego finds expression through who or what I know."*

The Sun in this combination will most likely fall into the Twelfth House or the Eleventh. If it is in the Twelfth, the ego expression will find outlet through matters of spiritual regeneration, solitude, institutions, or inhibitions or restrictions he places on himself; if it is in the Eleventh, it will find outlet through friends, group activities, aspirations, or social movements.

This is an extremely difficult combination, but once unity- is achieved between the two divergent facets of the identity, it can be quite productive. The Fixed Air of the Aquarius Sun merely coexists with the Mutable Water of the Pisces Ascendant, unable to mix. With the Sun in the Twelfth House, the Aquarian ego seeks expression through who or what it knows related to matters of spiritual regeneration, solitude, and service to institutions such as hospitals, prisons, or the military. However, it may also bring in matters of its own native Eleventh House, matters of friends, group activities, aspirations, and social concerns.

It is perhaps the Pisces Ascendant that may point the way to the solution, for the Twelfth House is the natural house of Pisces, and the individual's beliefs may temper the erratic Uranus ruled Aquarian Sun, to keep it from being self-destructive in this placement.

The challenge for this individual is to avoid seclusion, to learn to express his spiritual and social concerns to others, and especially to deal openly and directly with lovers and partners.

PART V

LEARNING FROM YOUR CHART

ACCEPTING AND AFFIRMING YOUR SELF

If there is any value to astrology, it is as a means of stepping aside from the mundane events of everyday life to view the Self with a degree of objectivity, as a means of acknowledging:

- Yes, I am like that.
- Yes, God has made me to be the way I am.
- Yes, I am good and beautiful as I am.
- Yes, I do have room for growth.
- Yes, I recognize my challenges.
- Yes, I can face my challenges and benefit from them.

To be able to do this, it is important for one to be able to see as accurate a picture of himself as possible. The challenges of the Sun signs, the "horoscopes" one reads in the daily papers, are far too generalized to be more than idle entertainment. Yet the specific challenges of each individual cannot be itemized within the pages of a book, for everyone is different.

Utilizing statistics derived from the survey of gay charts, however, it is possible to make further generalizations that a great many gays can relate to, for there are a number of similar astrological aspects that large numbers hold in common.

With a little effort, the reader can add to the astrological picture of himself that has begun with the Sun sign and Ascendant, and perhaps utilize that picture to aid him in his spiritual growth. This requires learning a bit more about how astrology works, including the significance of the Twelve Houses of the horoscope, the aspects of certain planets, and the relationships of planets to houses.

Chapter 16

THE TWELVE HOUSES OF EXPERIENCE

By this time, the concept of the twelve signs of the Zodiac should be clear. The concept of Twelve Houses is something quite different, though related to the signs. In fact, the Twelve universal Houses are synonymous with the twelve signs. However, for individual charts, there are infinite variations on the universal theme.

As indicated earlier, the Ascendant, or Rising sign, sets the pattern for your individual horoscope, giving a specific Zodiacal sign in a specific degree for each of the other Eleven Houses, depending upon the specific place and time of your birth. Unlike the signs, the Twelve Houses may or may not each contain thirty degrees. In fact, in some charts, some signs may govern two consecutive houses, giving these houses much fewer than the standard degrees, while other signs are completely contained within houses of more than thirty degrees, making them weak or ineffective by being "intercepted" between two other signs.

The concept of interceptions is an important one for gay charts, and it will be discussed more fully later (see p. 248). First it is important to understand the nature and function ofthe houses themselves.

THE FIRST HOUSE

The Rising sign determines the First House. At the time of birth, it is just beneath the eastern horizon, rising above the horizon during the two hours after birth. In the universal chart, it corresponds to the sign Aries. In your individual chart, it may be any one of the twelve signs. It states "I am" or "I exist," determining your Self, your identity, your placement in the cosmic scheme, as well as the way you appear to others.

The challenge of the sign governing the First House indicates the sphere of life, or the means by which one becomes aware of his individual nature and relates it to others. To some extent, it may also suggest the means of meeting this challenge. Planets appearing in this house, or conjunct the Ascendant, indicate either obstacles in the way of meeting the challenge or facets of the personality that may be utilized in overcoming it.

In gay charts, the First House is one that is very often emphasized by having important planets or significant astrological points placed within it. Seventy-eight percent of those polled fall within this category, suggesting that identity or individuality or Self is a major concern of gays.

Certain signs and certain planets occurred with a frequency that was considerably higher than chance, indicating that the challenge of Self is similar for a great many.

The First House Sign

The First House sign that appeared most frequently in gay charts was that of LEO. It represented just over eighteen percent of the total. Leo Rising identifies himself as youthful, rather like a child. He is vain, wanting to be the center of attention, and he is manipulative, using others, often purely on whim, simply to prove he can do so. Leo Rising loves soap operas, and tends to gossip maliciously to keep the real-life soap opera around him going.

An important part of the challenge of Leo Rising is to "grow up" and become responsible, to acquire a sensitivity to the needs of others and to become more direct and honest in relationships. He needs to learn to focus his attention into love rather than into love affairs or brief romantic involvements.

Leo is very influential in the gay world. Over 5.6 percent of the poll were double Leos (Sun and Ascendant in Leo), and 2 of the 160 were actually triple Leos (Sun, Ascendant, and Moon in Leo). It is the sign in which Uranus, the gay ruler, is in its detriment, emphasizing its negative rather than its positive qualities. It is the positive qualities of Uranus—the sense of freedom and the creativity of higher mentality—that gay Leo is challenged to acquire. The challenge is extremely difficult, for Leo has the active element of Fire and the stubbornness of being a Fixed sign.

However, he is capable of meeting the challenge, once he realizes it is a matter of pride. Leo cannot bear to think of himself as having any negative qualities; if weaknesses are pointed out to him, he will exert his strong ego toward overcoming them swiftly and thoroughly.

The second most frequently occurring Rising sign among gays, and one that also influences gay life in general, is that of SAGITTARIUS, which had a showing of 13.75 percent in the poll.

Though he and Leo share the action orientation of the Fire element, Sagittarius is Mutable in nature. He possesses the sense of freedom and the higher mentality, as well as the maturity, that Leo lacks, but he uses it in negative ways. He manages to rationalize or justify promiscuity by equating it with freedom in his otherwise excellent mind. In his philosophical approach, love is good, so it is even better the more you spread it around.

Like Leo, he has a great deal of difficulty with responsibility. His mutability makes him easily seduced. A major part of his challenge is to acquire responsibility, to seek the strength and confidence within himself that will enable him to focus his love on just one person.

Gay Sagittarius is not a game player like Leo; he does not manipulate or dissemble simply to display his own powerful ego; in fact, honesty and truth are extremely important to him. Nor is he determined to remain a child. But there is an innocence and a naivete, almost a gullibility, about him that brings about similar results. He trusts others more than he trusts himself, and falls into games inadvertently. He has to be out in the world, not necessarily to have a good time, but to learn and grow.

He is challenged to recognize his inner Self, to trust in it, and to realize that the growth that comes from within is equally as important as that from without.

The third most common Rising sign among gays is SCOR-PIO, representing over thirteen percent of the total. Scorpio Rising uses his sexuality as a means of avoiding facing up to his spiritual identity, afraid of what he might find within himself. Being Fixed Water—or ice—he presents himself as cold and hard on the outside, and generally only he knows how easily he could melt.

The games gay Scorpio plays are invariably sexual ones, and they can be deadly or devastating. He seems always on the make; and, if he is turned down—or if someone doesn't turn him on—he will lash out viciously with his biting wit. As hurtful as he can be to others, it is himself he usually hurts most deeply.

Scorpio's preoccupation with sex is rather a morbid one, sometimes almost clinical in nature. It is not linked closely to love, but more toward his insatiable curiosity and his need to fill an inner void with something tangible and physical.

The challenge of Scorpio is to face his spiritual nature, no matter how fearful it may seem, and to share it with others in love that is as deep as lust. He knows all too well the brevity and the frailty of life, but he must learn that love and sharing spiritually with another is what makes the brief stay on earth of value. And it is the one thing that makes the sexual act deeply meaningful.

These three Rising signs, together, represent 45 percent of the gay population. They are also the three most common Sun signs among gays. For this reason, their overall influence on gay life is very strong. When you consider that almost 67 percent have one of those three signs for either Sun, Ascendant, or Moon, it seems clear that their impact on gay society virtually dominates it.

They are responsible for the commonly held view that gays are children who don't want to grow up—like Peter Pan's "lost boys." It is the game playing of Leo, the promiscuity of Sagittarius, and the bitchiness and morbid sexuality of Scorpio that gives others a bad image of gays. The challenge they give to the gay community is one of responsibility, of accepting the inner Self and learning to love what is there, turning their negative traits into positive ones so that they may give genuine love to another, and receive love in return.

Planets in the First House

Several important planets occur with significant frequency in the First House of gay charts, in numbers far higher than chance. MERCURY occurs in 13.75 percent of the cases, and SATURN occurs almost as often. Mercury in the First House makes communication of great importance, both the spoken and the written word. It may lend a degree of youthfulness to the appearance, and give a quickness to the mind, as well as speech and action. It makes the person adaptable, and gives a fertile imagination.

Saturn's placement in the First House may present more of a challenge, for it has strongly divergent negative and positive attributes. Physically, it may give a slenderness and a serious expression or manner. On the positive side, it tends toward making the individual responsible, with a desire to make it in life on his own. However, this tendency may be carried to the negative pole, causing him to suffer severe guilt or to isolate himself from others, creating a hard outer shell to hide the pain and suffering inside. The challenge here is to strive toward Saturn's positive—toward a deep understanding of responsibility for oneself and for others, sharing burdens and opening up with honesty. Saturn placed here is capable of maturing well, meeting any challenge with time.

The SUN and MARS occur with equal frequency in the First House of gay charts—each represented in just over eleven percent of the cases. The Sun in the First House tends to unify the ego and the personality, which may result in a combination of strong egocentricity and vanity, but this does not have to be. The challenge is toward achieving the positive facets of the Sun—generosity, ambition, and a strong morality. The challenge may also be to learn responsibility, trust, and self-confidence.

Mars in the First House gives the individual a degree of masculine energy, a forcefulness to the personality. It may also make the person rash, headstrong, impulsive, even argumentative at times. This can lead to fights or accidents. (If the person has Mars conjunct the Ascendant, there will usually be a scar on the forehead or the brows.) The challenge is toward using the energy of Mars constructively, toward self-confidence, practicality, and openly giving.

But the one astrological factor occurring most often in the First House of gay charts was not a planet, but something called the PART OF FORTUNE, a specific degree associated with the relationship of the Sun, Moon, and Ascendant. Almost sixteen percent of gay charts had the Part of Fortune in the First House—25 out of 160. This usually signifies the self-made man, the person who sets out on his own and achieves success by his own industry, his personality, his charm, even his appearance. The challenge of Part of Fortune in the First is to unify the emotional nature with the ego and the inner spiritual Self, reconfirming many of the other factors common to gay charts.

THE SECOND HOUSE

Moving roughly thirty degrees below the eastern horizon, we come to the Second House in an individual's astrological chart, the house that corresponds with Taurus in the universal Zodiac, and makes the statement, "I have" or "I own" or "I possess." It is commonly referred to as the house of money and possessions, and the planets placed within it (or the sign that rules it) indicates what one will acquire in the nature of worldly goods.

The Second House though is much more than this. There are connections of a spiritual nature as well. It is the house of life, of living. It indicates one's code of ethics, one's ability to give and to share, even one's ability to love.

Three planets appeared in the Second House of gay charts in numbers significantly higher than chance—SATURN, JUPITER, and the MOON. Appearing alone in the Second, Saturn indicates that money and possessions may be spare or acquired by great effort. It also suggests a degree of stinginess, a very Spartan ethic, and a reluctance to give of one's Self to others. The challenge of such a Saturn is to learn thrift and economy in finances, while giving time and effort toward acquiring what one wants. In spiritual terms, the challenge is toward learning to appreciate what one has and to accept the love of others, however given.

In a great many charts, Saturn was conjunct Jupiter in the Second House, an aspect that can mean the opposite of Saturn placed there alone. The conjunction can signify great wealth, often inherited wealth. Spiritually, it can mean a positive ethic acquired from good family upbringing, and an ability to give and receive love equally.

Jupiter alone in the Second may mean considerable acquired wealth, and a great many possessions. It is the sign of the collector—whether it is stamps, butterflies, paintings, or gold bullion. It also indicates that the person is very giving and very loving, sometimes to his own detriment.

The Moon in the Second generally indicates a heavy influence of the mother on financial affairs and on the person's ability to love. It signifies considerable emotional involvement in giving and sharing of love, but it also makes the individual quite productive.

The Second House challenge for gays, as indicated by these planets, seems to relate to a reluctance to love or a tendency to give too much in love. This is confirmed by the one astrological factor that occurs most frequently in gay charts— a spatial point known as the North Node of the Moon. This is a point in space where the Moon intercepts the ecliptic, or

the earth's orbit. It is the northernmost point where the Moon
does this; the southernmost point is the South Node, which
is always in the opposite sign or house from the North. These
nodal points are the places that cause eclipses. When a New
Moon occurs at one of them, there is a Solar Eclipse; and
when a Full Moon occurs at one, there is a Lunar Eclipse.

Together, the Nodes create a line of balance in an astrological chart, a balance relating to the emotional nature of the individual, his ability to give and receive. Astrologers disagree
as to the precise interpretation of the significance of the
Nodes, but most do agree that the North is the positive and
the South the negative. Those who believe in karma or reincarnation interpret the North as being those qualities that one
must learn or acquire in this lifetime, while the South
represents those that one must divest himself of that come
from a past life.

If this interpretation is an accurate one, placement of the
North in the Second and the South in the Eighth does relate
to the need to love, while divesting oneself of the need for
sexuality unrelated to love, a significant challenge for gays.

THE THIRD HOUSE

Continuing to move beneath the earth, approximately another thirty degrees, toward the Nadir, the point directly beneath the place of birth, we come to the Third House. In the
universal chart, this is the house governed by Gemini, the
house that states, "I think" or "I communicate" or "I convey." It governs the basic learning of an individual, the way
he speaks, writes, and moves out and about in his immediate
neighborhood. It also denotes his relationships with brothers
and sisters.

Interestingly, the planet that occurs most frequently in the
Third House of gay charts is MERCURY, the planet that rules
Third House matters. It is the planet of thought, intellect,
communication, and transportation. But there are several

other planets that occur with a frequency higher than chance—including VENUS, the SUN, and MARS.

These placements tend to confirm the common belief that gays generally are well-equipped mentally and intellectually. Gays do make good writers, teachers, salesmen, and artists. If there is a challenge associated with these positive aspects it is that gays need to avoid relying too heavily on intellect, to reach for abstract faith and belief in a higher power to guide them.

THE FOURTH HOUSE

Beginning at the Nadir, starting the upward climb toward the western horizon, is the Fourth House, the house that, in gay charts, usually signifies the mother, as well as real estate, the home, and the circumstances surrounding death. In the universal chart, it is ruled by the sign Cancer.

In the poll of gay charts, there was less emphasis upon the Fourth through the Eighth Houses. The only planet that appeared in the Fourth House in numbers higher than chance was NEPTUNE. Its placement here is a complex one, with a great many potential interpretations of its meaning. One of the most obvious is that the person will move about a great deal, perhaps having a rather unstable home situation, or the living arrangements may be somewhat unorthodox, odd, or peculiar. These arrangements may be kept secret from the public.

There may also be an emphasis on consumption of alcohol or drugs in the home situation, or the home may be a refuge into which the individual escapes, a fantasy or dream world where he can pretend to be something he is not.

But Neptune is also a spiritual planet, highly imaginative and creative in nature. The challenge of its placement here is to develop spiritually through the home situation. (Neptune in the Fourth also indicates living near water, often by or near a seashore.) Although it relates specifically to the mother in early life, it may be associated with the love partner after maturity. Spiritual growth may be achieved through a close relationship with another.

The NORTH NODE occurs with higher than chance frequency in the Fourth House as well. This means the South Node is placed in the Tenth, which is the house of father, career, and public success. This would indicate a tension between the parents in childhood, in which the mother is perceived as sympathetic and the father as difficult. Its karmic meaning would be that achieving a good home situation or love relationship is one of the objectives of this lifetime.

THE FIFTH HOUSE

One of the least emphasized houses in gay charts surprisingly is the Fifth, the one that is ruled by Leo in the universal Zodiac. It is the house of romance, love affairs, children, gambling, entertainment, and risk-taking. None of the major planets * or astrological points occurred with a frequency significantly higher than chance in the Fifth House.

This suggests that matters of romance and entertainment and risk-taking are not a major challenge for gays as a group. Although at first glance, this appears to run counter to the statistics related to Leo Rising, it merely emphasizes that the concern is truly one of Self, not one of the action itself.

THE SIXTH HOUSE

Approaching the western horizon, we come to the Sixth House, which represents health, work, service, clothes, and food. In the universal chart, it is occupied by the sign Virgo.

---

*One point does appear in the Fifth in 12.5 percent of the cases, and that is the hypothetical placement of Lilith, known as the Dark Moon. See page 253.

In the survey of gay charts, none of the major planets appeared in the Sixth in numbers higher than chance. Only the PART OF FORTUNE occurred in significant frequency, showing 12.5 percent of gays having a Sixth House placement.

This would suggest that gays are more inclined than the general population to achieve success through work and service, especially in matters related to fashion, food, and health or medical care. The challenge of Sixth House matters is not a major one for the larger proportion of gays.

THE SEVENTH HOUSE

We are now moving above the western horizon in our trek through the Twelve astrological Houses. Having completed half, we become concerned with the six that oppose or balance the first six, all of which related to the nature of the individual himself. Those that appear above the horizon are concerned with the relationship of the individual to others, to matters outside himself.

As the house opposing the First of Self, the Seventh(which is represented by Libra in the universal chart) is concerned with other people in general, but more specifically, those persons one joins in partnership or marriage with, those the native associates with on an intimate one-on-one relationship. It is also the house of open enemies.

As Leo, Sagittarius, and Scorpio occur most frequently as the First House signs in gay charts, the Seventh House signs most common to gay charts are Aquarius, Gemini, and Taurus—the Air signs Aquarius and Gemini giving balance to the Fire, and the Earth sign Taurus balancing the Water.

The qualities of these signs contribute much to the ideal nature of gay relationships, for they represent the Seventh House in 45 percent of gay charts. Aquarius is, of course, the most significant, for not only does it represent the highest individual percentage, but it is the natural sign for homosexuality, being ruled by Uranus.

A partner who is free and independent, with a stimulating, creative mind, as well as considerable social concerns would be the gay ideal of the Leo Rising—very Aquarian in nature. (But not necessarily an Aquarian.) For Sagittarius Rising, the ideal would have the characteristics of Gemini—youthful, always on the move and always changing, intellectually stimulating with constant talking, even if it is merely idle chatter.

In both of these cases, the challenge of partnership is not difficult. A great many gays share these ideals, and are capable of providing them. However, with the third sign—Scorpio Rising—the challenge may not be an easy one, for the ideal partnership is of a Taurean nature, and the qualities of Taurus are among the rarest among gays. The Taurean nature is stable, stubborn, and earthy, extremely materialistic, but also very affectionate. He is quite practical, and is probably the most heterosexual of the signs.

The suggestion that Scorpio is actually seeking a partner as stable and down-to-earth as Taurus may seem difficult to believe, but it is true. For all of Scorpio's cynicism and his outrageous, even destructive behavior, he secretly wants the security that comes from the simpler things in life. He may find some of what he seeks in gay partners, but ultimately, his challenge is to find much of it within himself.

In the survey, two of the planets appeared in the Seventh House in higher-than-chance numbers. Both URANUS and PLUTO appeared in 10.6 percent of the cases. Uranus placed there presents the same, or a similar, challenge that the sign Aquarius presents—to achieve high mental and spiritual rapport in partnerships and to strive toward freedom and independence. Unfortunately its presence in the Seventh also indicates a long succession of partnership changes until the native learns to accept and to grant unrestricted freedom in a loving relationship.

Pluto's presence in the Seventh is more complex. Its effect would be similar to having Scorpio occupying the house. Its most obvious challenge is one of sexuality, but Pluto goes deeper than that. There is a need with Pluto in the Seventh to keep matters concerning close partnership, particularly loving sexual partnerships, secret, as well as a dependency on one's partner for spiritual regeneration and growth.

The need for gays to develop loving relationships is confirmed by the significantly high number of occurrences of the NORTH NODE in the Seventh House, with 20 cases out of 160, or 12.5 percent of the total. The karmic balance in these cases is from the Seventh to the First, indicating a need to achieve a good and positive partnership in this lifetime, while divesting the Self of severe self-centeredness, egocentricity, and vanity that stems from a past life.

One other factor that plays an important part in the Seventh Houses of gay charts is one closely related to the Moon's Nodes. It is a point in space known as the Solar Eclipse point. Linked to either of the Nodes, the Solar Eclipse point is the position where a solar eclipse may have occurred within the few months immediately preceding birth. It indicates a specific point in an individual chart that is critical to the development of the ego. There is a Lunar Eclipse point as well, and it indicates an area that is critical to the emotional development.

In the survey, just over eleven percent of gays had the Solar Eclipse point in the Seventh House, indicating that matters of love partnership are of importance in ego development.

THE EIGHTH HOUSE

Moving higher into the western sky, we reach the Eighth House, occupied by the sign Scorpio in the universal chart. It is the house of inheritance, sex, death, partnership finances, and the heritage of the past. It signifies all that results from partnership relationships, as well as that which comes from open enmity.

The Eighth is the opposing force and the balance of the Second House. It is death balanced against life, the receiving of love balanced with the giving of love. The incidence of the SOUTH NODE in the Eighth is equal to the high occurrence of the North Node in the Second, representing those negative qualities the gay individual needs to divest himself of in this lifetime.

Reinforcing this is the high placement of the Solar Eclipse point in the Eighth House of gays (over eleven percent), suggesting that sexuality is a critical factor to the ego.

While these two hypothetical astrological points appeared significantly in the gay charts, none of the major planets occurred in the Eighth House of gay charts in numbers higher than chance.

THE NINTH HOUSE

As we approach the Midheaven, we pass through the Ninth House of higher education, philosophy, religion, long distance travel, and mental expansion. It is the house occupied by Sagittarius in the universal chart. With the Ninth, we return to houses that seem to be significant to the gay challenge, for in the survey, three planets appeared in the Ninth in significantly high numbers. URANUS was placed there most frequently, in just over thirteen percent of the cases, while MERCURY occurred in over ten percent and PLUTO in over eleven percent.

Two of these—Uranus and Mercury—are mental planets, concerned with intelligence and with communication, placed in a mental and spiritual house, while Pluto is concerned with spiritual as well as physical regeneration. It is also involved with the subconscious mind. The challenge of these planets here—the opposing and balancing house of the Third—is for gays to develop educationally and philosophically for deeper understanding of their spiritual and mental natures.

THE TENTH HOUSE

Directly overhead at the time of birth, at the Midheaven, is the beginning of the Tenth House, Capricorn in the universal chart, the house that represents the father, career, public recognition, and success. Based upon the survey, it appears to be a very significant house for gays.

The opposing and balancing house of the Fourth, the Tenth House has a high incidence of SOUTH NODE placement, giving it a degree of karmic challenge, suggesting that ambition for public recognition and success is a desire that has carried over from previous lifetimes.

But four significant planets occur in the Tenth House of gay charts in higher-than-chance numbers. The one planet that appears most often is VENUS, occurring in over thirteen percent of the charts. Venus represents love and beauty and aesthetic values. In the Tenth House and conjunct the Midheaven, it generally bestows extraordinary physical attractiveness, drawing others to the person who has the aspect. The SUN placed in the Tenth reinforces this, but with the addition of a very strong ego; in the survey, 12.5 percent of gays have this aspect as well. Both tend to make the native ambitious and successful.

But they present a considerable challenge. Physical beauty is a difficult burden to bear in the gay world, for it tends to make one superficial, even lazy, getting by on looks alone. The challenge for the gorgeous gay is to develop spiritually, to delve within and discover the beauty of Self, realizing it is far more meaningful than the transitory good looks.

Both MERCURY and the MOON occur in the Tenth House in just over ten percent of gay charts, making the challenge somewhat easier for at least some gays. Mercury grants a communicativeness and a mentality that permits them to understand the need to establish inner values. The Moon contributes a sensitivity of feeling that helps them to transcend the physical.

THE ELEVENTH HOUSE

Moving down toward the eastern horizon, we are nearing the end of the cycle of the Zodiacal houses. The Eleventh House opposes and balances the Fifth. Occupied by Aquarius in the universal chart, it represents group associations, friendship, hopes, dreams, wishes, and aspirations. It is also the house of organizations, political activities, idealism, and social concerns.

Most significantly, it is the house that would most closely represent homosexuality, for it is ruled by Uranus. However, there was very little out of the ordinary in the Eleventh House of gay charts. The only astrological factors that occurred with higher than chance frequency were the presence of URANUS and the SOLAR ECLIPSE POINT. (Both were represented in just over eleven percent of the charts.)

Uranus in the Eleventh was not unexpected. Uranus is the planetary ruler of gays, and it is reasonable for gays to have gay friends and gay group associations. In this era of political activism, it is expected that a good percentage would be active in gay politics. But Uranus in the Eleventh does present some challenge, for it tends to make friendships come and go erratically. The challenge of Uranus is to develop lasting friendships, lasting social and political commitments.

The Solar Eclipse point in the Eleventh is a challenge of ego. Those with this aspect are challenged to establish an identity that is not dependent upon the identities of friends, to discover the Self that is separate and distinctly one's own.

THE TWELFTH HOUSE

The last house in the cycle, just above the eastern horizon, is the Twelfth House, opposing and balancing the Sixth. It is a very important, but also a very complicated and very subtle, house. It is commonly called the house of "self undoing," of institutions and isolation and of secretiveness. But its significance is not entirely negative.

In the universal chart, it is the house occupied by Pisces, and it carries much of the positive nature of that sign. It is a deeply spiritual house, concerned with the imagination, the ability to regenerate and restore faith in life, and the need for creativity. As opposed to and balancing the house of health, it does possess those negative qualities of severe illness and self-destruction, but there are significant positive alternatives.

In the survey of gay charts, the Twelfth House proved to be one of the most significant, with four planets and one Zodiacal point appearing there with a frequency higher than chance. The largest placement was that of the SUN, with fifteen percent of the total surveyed having Sun in the Twelfth.

Gays with Sun in the Twelfth tend to be rather secretive about their true identity, hiding their ego; some even prefer to be alone rather than to go out into social situations. They build a shell or a false front, letting almost no one see what they are really like. The challenge, of course, is for them to learn to share of themselves, to love themselves and to accept love from others; for without it, they will experience deep and profound loneliness.

MERCURY appears in the Twelfth House in almost as many numbers, occurring there in over thirteen percent of the charts. This adds to the secretive nature of the person, making him reluctant to speak of matters that are truly of deep concern to him. The challenge is for him to use his mind and his communicative talents—for he is extremely intelligent and self-perceptive— toward reaching out to share with others and experience spiritual growth.

MARS, PLUTO, and the NORTH NODE all occur in the Twelfth House in over eleven percent of the cases. Mars and Pluto can be difficult in the Twelfth, especially if they are there together and conjunct. Mars and Pluto in the Twelfth can give the native considerable self-destructive tendencies, making him at the very least his own worst enemy. He may use his energy to rationalize inaction rather than to improve himself.

Yet there is considerable potential with this placement, if the native will recognize his challenge and face it honestly.

His energy can be devoted as easily toward spirituality and toward genuine creativity as it can toward self-destruction. If he will let his feelings out, express his deep desires forcefully, he can blossom like a flower in spring.

The placement of the North Node here highlights this possibility, and directs the challenge specifically toward mental and physical health, for its opposite South Node, the karmic one, is placed in the Sixth House.

The Twelfth is truly the house of the spirit and the soul, the deepest nature of the individual, and it can be a house of great personal power if the individual is willing to delve deep within and discover what he possesses inside.

This is the greatest challenge of all for gays—and one that can be met.

INTERCEPTED SIGNS AND HOUSES

Because the division of the horoscope into houses is based upon the twenty-four-hour rotation of the earth, with each two-hour period representing one house, the division of each house into precisely thirty degrees of a sign is rare. Astrological signs occur along the earth's ecliptic, and so their apparent size and strength as seen from the earth may vary according to the time of year and the longitude of birth. The further north a person's place of birth the greater the likelihood of irregularity of house sizes.

In some cases the house division is so irregular that a pair of opposing signs will be completely "intercepted" within the two opposing houses, the signs losing strength because they do not rule the cusps (beginning points) of houses. Two other signs gain strength by governing the cusps of succeeding houses.

An example of this can be seen in Figure 2, page 250. In the chart, the signs Aries and Libra are intercepted in the Twelfth and Sixth Houses.

Because of the latitudes involved in the sampling of 160 homosexual and bisexual charts, it was expected that interceptions would occur in approximately one-third of the total. However, the number was significantly higher.

Fifty-six percent of the gay charts had interceptions. Even more interesting was the fact that the signs most often intercepted were Aries and Libra, while the houses of interception were most often the First and the Seventh. Both by sign and by house, this places a great emphasis on matters related to Self, or identity, and to relationships with others, the same challenge that has shown up with other major significators in gay charts.

This seems to confirm that the major lessons to be learned by a gay lifetime are concerned with the ability to accept the-Self and to understand how to relate to those one loves through trust, honesty, and mutual sharing. These challenges may go so far as to finding definitions of selfless love and selfish love, as well as the causes of jealousy and of possessiveness, which are among the greatest difficulties in many gay relationships.

But it would be a mistake to attempt to generalize too much here, for the specific challenges are dependent upon individual charts.

While the signs intercepted are weakened in nature, the houses intercepted acquire greater significance, because they contain more than thirty degrees (sometimes as many as sixty). Transiting planets take much longer to pass through these houses, emphasizing the matters they govern. If planets or significant astrological points are contained within the intercepted signs, they present special challenges, for there are generally significant delays in establishing the powers they convey. The native must struggle harder than most to deal with matters in these facets of his life. In some cases, a planet may be rendered completely impotent for a time, while challenges are met and faced in other spheres of life.

Of course, it must be understood that one does not have to be gay to have interceptions in his chart. However, it is sig-

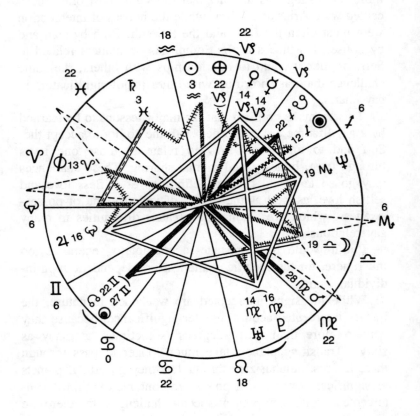

Figure 2

nificant that such a high percentage of gay charts contain interceptions. Gays frequently have to try harder than most people to face the challenges that are thrust upon them, and it often takes them longer to overcome them. At times they seem insurmountable. All of these tendencies are characteristics of interceptions in charts.

This can be seen clearly in the high percentage of charts having interceptions in the First and Seventh Houses, making the difficult challenges related to Self and partnerships, for gays strive—all too often unsuccessfully—to find relationships with each other that are truly loving and understanding.

But one of the most important effects—and perhaps the least understood—of interceptions in charts is the fact that all of the house cusps do not interact harmoniously. The trine is the most harmonious of aspects; it is almost always involved with a single element—Fire, Earth, Air, or Water. Just as the signs are intended to work together, the trining houses should function in harmony—the First, Fifth, and Ninth (the Fire houses); the Second, Sixth, and Tenth (the Earth houses); the Third, Seventh, and Eleventh (the Air houses); and the Fourth, Eighth, and Twelfth (the Water houses).

However, when there are interceptions, the relationships between these "trining" house cusps are no longer trining; they are of differing elements. Again, see Figure 2, page 250. In this example, the First House is an Earth sign, while the Fifth and Ninth are both Fire signs. These three houses, perhaps the most important involved in achieving a truly well-integrated individual, are considered the "personal" houses. They function together as identity, creativity, and higher mind to achieve success.

The person whose chart is represented in Figure 2 is somewhat torn between the earthiness and practicality of his Taurean identity and his fiery approach to pleasure-seeking and to matters of philosophy and higher education. If it were not for the grand trine in Earth signs within these houses, he would find it extremely difficult to achieve the success in life that he desires. Ultimately he will find success, but it is not as easy for him as it would have been if all three house cusps were of the same element.

Often planets are intercepted within the houses; in fact, virtually all of the gay charts with intercepted signs have planets or astrological points within the interceptions. The most frequent occurrence is that of the Moon's Nodes. Twelve percent of all the gay charts analyzed had the nodes intercepted.

The nodes, along with the eclipse points, are considered to be indicators of karma, the North Node representing those qualities that must be acquired in this lifetime, and the South Node indicating qualities brought from a previous lifetime that one must divest himself of in this lifetime. When the nodes are intercepted, the karmic challenge becomes one that is even more difficult to overcome, for there are generally delays in solutions.

Jupiter is intercepted in over ten percent of gay charts, as is Uranus, the Sun, and the Moon. The challenges for these individuals are indeed major ones, especially for those who have either the Sun or the Moon intercepted. While their charts generally provide means for meeting and overcoming their challenges, the frustration at times may seem overwhelming.

The chart in Figure 2 has the Moon intercepted in the Sixth House, opposed by Lilith intercepted in the Twelfth. This individual has had a great difficulty developing emotional and spiritual security. He was separated from his mother (the Moon) at an early age. (Interestingly, Lilith, the destructive Moon, is in Aries, the same sign as his mother's Sun.)

However, in this chart, the challenge presented by these interceptions will be met and overcome, because of the T-square made to the Lilith-Moon opposition by Mercury and Venus in the Ninth House of the higher mind. This individual is blessed with an excellent mental acuity and love of knowledge. Through education, communication, and a loving nature, he will achieve the emotional and spiritual security he wants.

This chart is presented as an example because it is a highly complex one with extraordinary challenges. There are configurations that are generally considered quite negative (squares, oppositions, interceptions), and those that are considered among the most positive (conjunctions, sextiles, trines, and even a grand trine that forms a "kite"). It exemplifies the importance of looking at a chart as a whole, rather than at isolated aspects—either "positive" or "negative"—for the heavens may present solutions to challenges along with the challenges themselves.

THE LILITH CHALLENGE

It may strain the reader's credibility to discuss the subject of Lilith, for this "Dark Moon" of the earth does not really exist in the heavens. And there is no physical proof that it ever did exist; there is only mythology. Supposedly Eve (or the Moon) was not the first woman God created to mate with Adam. Lilith preceded Eve, but she disobeyed God by destroying her own children, and so was cast out into the darkness, making it necessary for God to create Eve from Adam's rib.

Although there is no physical trace of a second Moon around the earth, astrology provides a specific orbit and daily placement for the position that Lilith once occupied.

As strange as it may seem, this point does seem to play a significant role in astrological charts. In the statistics compiled, Lilith appeared to perform its mythological function with some consistency.

Lilith is considered to be the most negative, the most destructive force in astrology, with virtually no redeeming qualities. Supposedly it was for this reason that God destroyed her. Yet, if one believes in God or a Life Force, this destruction must have been effective, and there is some positive value to the negatives her position gives to individual charts. If Lilith's power had been permitted to continue, there would have been no human race on earth, for she was the destroyer of children. Her replacement by Eve (or the Moon) overpowered her negativity.

In individual charts, Lilith's placement appears to present a challenge related to some form of denial or deprivation. Yet it is not an insurmountable challenge. Of course, because Lilith was the destroyer of children, her most powerful position seems to be in the Fifth House of children, creativity, love affairs, and risk-taking.

Interestingly, the Fifth House is one of the two most common placements for Lilith in gay charts. Generally gays are denied children, since they rarely perform heterosexually. Some accept this and find other means of creative fulfillment. However, others have difficulty accepting the lack of physical generation that homosexuality imposes. It appears to be this frustration that Lilith creates in the Fifth House for more than ten percent of gays, giving a challenge to find another outlet for one's creativity.

However, an equal number of gays have Lilith positioned in the First House of identity, selfhood, and personality. Persons with this placement tend to suffer from a lack of self-confidence, an emptiness that seems impossible to fill. The challenge she offers to these individuals is to realize that no one exists without an identity, a Self, and all one has to do is to discover it and to accept it.

Almost as many gays, exactly ten percent, have Lilith placed in the Eighth House of sexuality, partnership finances, and inheritance. Invariably, those with Lilith here have great difficulty achieving full satisfaction from sex. No matter how often they may try, with any number of partners, they seem to ask, "Is that all there is?" Their challenge is to understand that one gets from sexual activity only what he puts into it, that the expression of love is what is truly satisfying, and that happiness derives from happiness given.

The sign placement of Lilith in gay charts seems significant as well. Over thirteen percent have Lilith in Cancer, the sign ruled by the Moon, while over fourteen percent have Lilith in Aquarius, ruled by Uranus, and the "natural" house of homosexuality. In Cancer, Lilith offers a challenge to emotional acceptance, to understanding of women generally and to the mother specifically. In Aquarius, Lilith challenges to accept the spiritual or social function of homosexuality.

Wherever Lilith occurs, it is important to realize that her power is merely illusory, that she only seems to destroy or to deprive, that she can be overpowered by one's own will and commitment. She is powerful only so long as one grants her power.

Chapter 17

FINDING YOUR MATE

It seems clear that a major facet of the gay challenge is learning to love the Self and to accept the love of others—or one other. The need for a partner to share one's life and love is a universal one, whether the person is homosexual or heterosexual. Because of the special spiritual challenges involved with being gay, however, the search for the "ideal" homosexual partnership can be confusing, frustrating, even emotionally painful.

"Mr. Right" seems to appear, an affair or romance blossoms, but within a matter of days or weeks it fades, and "Mr. Right" appears to be just one more "Mr. Wrong" in a long series of disappointments. Inevitably there is the tendency for one to blame himself or the other person because the relationship didn't live up to expectations. The truth is more likely that neither person was to blame, that the individual identities and needs did not meet in the precise form that one or both hoped for.

Astrology can help with relationships, but it would be a mistake to rely too heavily on it to try to predict how two distinctly different individuals might fulfill each other's needs. Formulas for finding a mate should never be followed blindly. The generalizations that many astrologers offer—that Fire and Air signs work best together and Earth and Water signs should be combined—do have some validity; but they are merely generalizations, nothing more. Within each individual's chart, there are so many different forces at work—with a mix of all the elements—that a person could miss out on his ideal partner by blindly following general rules.

Astrologically, what determines the precise relationship of two individuals can only be seen in what is called a "combined chart," utilizing the precise placement by sign and house of each of the planets and significators.

To some extent a generalized formula can be utilized to obtain an approximation of the type of relationship two people might have. It is offered here in the hope the reader will use it more for entertainment than as a means of gauging or weighing specific relationships.

THE COMBINATION FORMULA

A combined chart is arrived at by adding the specific degrees and signs of the charts of two people and dividing in half. The generalized formula is:

$$\text{combined} = \frac{A + B}{2}$$

The combined Ascendant would be the sign and degree halfway between the Ascendants of each at their closest point in the Zodiac. Each of the other Eleven Houses would be determined in the same manner. The Sun, the Moon, and all of the planets and Zodiacal points are combined in the same way, utilizing sign and degree to determine house placement for the relationship. Obviously, the fully accurate combined chart cannot be obtained without fully accurate individual charts.

The ideal is to have specific degrees of specific signs. But it is not expected that the average reader will have this data at his fingertips. Anyone who does have the information can follow the formula, but including degrees as well as signs, and can include all planets to make a complete combined chart.

However, most people will have only the Sun sign and possibly the Rising sign to work with, and this will be adequate to determine the main focus of a relationship, for they are the two most important factors in the combined chart.

Though the details of the interaction between the two people, which are supplied by the other planetary placements, cannot be known, two partners can perceive whether their joining meets with the needs and expectations of each.

Determining the Combined Ascendant

The first step is to obtain a combined Ascendant or Rising sign. From Table III, take the numbers for the Ascendants of the two people involved. (See page 260.) Using the formula above, add them together and divide by 2. The number you obtain should be matched with the table to get the combined Ascendant.

For example, let us say a Sagittarius with Virgo Rising meets an Aquarius with Taurus Rising, and he would like to know what sort of relationship he might have. Figuring the Combined Ascendant, he adds 6 (Virgo) to 2 (Taurus), divides by 2 and obtains 4 (Cancer). He sketches a wheel, such as the one in Figure 3 on page 261, divided into twelve segments, labeling the first as Cancer, and following the second through the twelfth with Leo, Virgo, Libra, Scorpio, Sagittarius, Capricorn, Aquarius, Pisces, Aries, Taurus, and Gemini.

Cancer is the couple's combined Ascendant, and the house where their combined Sun falls will determine the nature of their relationship.

Problems can arise with the formula used in this generalized way, for not all numbers will be divisible by two without a resulting fraction. Unfortunately, there is no way to be absolutely accurate without having the precise degrees of the signs involved in the computation. Generally, however, it will work to round off to the next highest number—i.e., 2.5 would become 3; 4.5 would become 5.

Table III

SIGN NUMBERS

Aries	1
Taurus	2
Gemini	3
Cancer	4
Leo	5
Virgo	6
Libra	7
Scorpio	8
Sagittarius	9
Capricorn	10
Aquarius	11
Pisces	12

The Combined Sun

Use the same table and formula to obtain the sign for the Combined Sun, adding the number representing the Sun sign of one to that of the other and dividing by 2. In the example given of the Sagittarius with Virgo Rising and the Aquarius with Taurus Rising, we add 9 (Sagittarius) to 11 (Aquarius), and dividing the total by 2, we get 10 (Capricorn).

In the wheel we have drawn, Capricorn is the Seventh House, so we place the Combined Sun within that segment. The Seventh House is one of the best possible placements for the Combined Sun, because it is the house of marriage and partnership. These two persons would be likely to have an excellent relationship; they would be partners who each contribute to the other in significant ways, with their identities sharing the common ground of Earth signs, while their egos

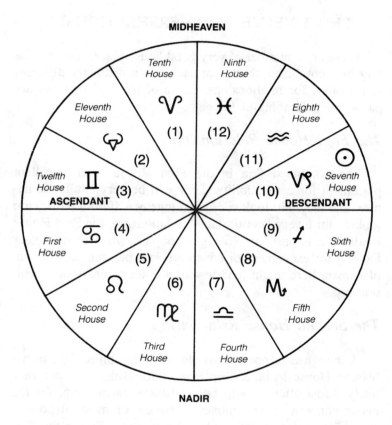

Figure 3

mix fire and air so that there is rarely ever a dull moment in their interchange.

Again, if your calculations result in a fraction, round off upward to the next number.

THE TWELVE PARTNERSHIP HOUSES

There are a number of very good house placements for the Sun in a combined chart, but each has a distinctly different significance for relationships. Some of these placements are particularly meaningful for gays.

The First House Relationship

The combined Sun in the First House is an excellent placement for compatibility. They will be very similar in nature, and they will look very good together. If both parties are looking for a very "comfortable" relationship, the First House is ideal. It is best for older gay couples, who are no longer looking for excitement or adventure in a partner, for the Sun placement here might tend toward a quiet or easy-going relationship.

The Second House Relationship

Although it is not impossible for a combined Sun in the Second House to be a deep love relationship, it is not very likely. Most often, it will be a business partnership, for the major concern is with money, finances, or material possessions. In some cases of combined gay charts, Sun in the Second indicates that one partner is supporting the other financially, or helping him materially in some way.

The Third House Relationship

The combined Sun in the Third House is a good meeting of minds. The two involved will communicate very well with each other. They will find each other intellectually stimulating, but the relationship may be more a "brotherly" or "neighborly" one than a love affair or lifetime partnership.

The Fourth House Relationship

Among gays, the combined Sun in the Fourth House usually indicates "roommates," two people who share living quarters equitably. However, in some cases, one of the two may tend to "mother" the other. Occasionally, however, a Fourth House combined Sun can be an ideal "marriage," for this is a secondary "partnership" house, not as challenging or as exciting as the Seventh House placement, though there can be some stresses involved. This combination can at times indicate two people who will share real estate investment.

The Fifth House Relationship

A combined Sun in the Fifth House can be truly exciting for the two involved. It is the ideal placement for a gay romance or a love affair, and it usually involves passionate sex. However, it is not a good placement for a lasting relationship. The passion burns out too quickly, and often the parting is just as heated as the meeting. Not all Fifth House combinations are love affairs, however; some take the form of a "parent-child" relationship, with an emphasis on entertainment, the older going out with the younger in an attempt to regain youth.

The Sixth House Relationship

The combined Sun in the Sixth House can be a complicated one. It is not necessarily bad, but it is not generally a lasting love partnership, though love may often play a major part. To some extent, the Sixth is a karmic house; the two people are brought together to work out problems through interaction. Their love may be true, but the obstacles they face may be too big to overcome, and so ultimately they part.

Usually, however, they have each performed a service for the other, and both are better for having been together.

The Seventh House Relationship

In most ways, the Seventh is the perfect house for "marriage" or partnership, a relationship in which two people remain distinctly individuals, true to themselves, yet each contribute equally to the other, combining strengths and making up for lacks. However, all combined charts with Sun in the Seventh are not partnership relationships. The Seventh is also the house of open enemies. Other aspects in the combined chart will determine which form the relationship takes. For the purposes here, this is not of great importance, for one recognizes open enemies, and the individuals involved can clearly see the positive or negative interaction. In some cases of gay relationships, the form the enmity takes is a rivalry for the affection of the same person.

The Eighth House Relationship

The Eighth House is a very significant position for a great many combined Suns of gays, for it is the position of a relationship that is primarily sexual in nature, one that is even more brief and transitory than the love affair or romance of the Fifth House. It is the house of the one-night-stand, the passion that is purely physical, quickly spent. In some cases, however, it may be a financial relationship, similar to that of the Second, with the two parties engaged in the handling of inheritance or other people's money. Cases of payment for sex may also fall into this house.

The Ninth House Relationship

When the combined Sun is positioned in the Ninth House, the relationship is similar to that of the Third, but of an even stronger mental nature. To some extent the pairing will be based upon a deep-seated philosophy, even a religion. This may include the teacher-student relationship, the mentor and protege. While it is primarily platonic in nature, it is not devoid of love, or even sex. The two may travel together, or they may grow and expand mentally and spiritually through their association.

The Tenth House Relationship

In most cases, the combined Sun in the Tenth House will be associated with business and career, and the two will be seen in public together a great deal. However, that is only one of several possibilities for this placement. In gay charts, it may be a very successful love relationship, though life together may not always be as easy as it appears on the surface. Both partners will probably have significant careers, which give them little time for each other, and eventually may cause them to drift apart.

The Eleventh House Relationship

This is the significator of truly good friends. Though they may initially be drawn together by sex, the physical quickly wanes, and those who have a combined Sun in the Eleventh House become interested in other pastures. At the same time, however, they continue to share, even the most intimate details of their lives, as close as brothers, or "sisters." There are also cases where combined Sun in the Eleventh is political in nature, where the two individuals meet and become involved through organization or party service.

The Twelfth House Relationship

The combined Sun in the Twelfth House is one of the most difficult, though the ultimate results may be positive. The relationship is not likely to be a lasting one, for it will—sooner or later—self-destruct. However, like the Sixth, it provides for spiritual growth for both of the individuals involved. In most cases, it will not be a sexual linking; and when it is, it is not usually satisfying, for both are searching for something deeper and more meaningful. Some with Sun in the Twelfth will meet through an institution such as a hospital or a prison or the military.

WHEN ONLY THE SUN SIGN IS KNOWN

While the precise nature of the blending of two individuals cannot be known without the Rising sign, it is possible to get some idea of how two egos will interact having only the Sun signs to work with. The formula is the same as that used for the combined charts. However, the reader must realize that this is reducing astrology to its most simplistic form. The formula should not be accepted as an unbreakable rule that must be followed strictly. It would be a mistake to deny oneself the possibility of a relationship or an experience that might be far more complex than the simple meeting of egos.

The Numerology of Astrology

To some extent, astrology can be reduced to mathematics or numerology. Using Table III on page 260 as a guide for the number representing each sign, you can see how your ego will relate to that of another. On the most basic level, one can see immediately that certain numbers can be added together and divided by 2, without resulting in a fraction, while others cannot. Even numbers interact well with even numbers, and odd numbers with odd numbers.

This corresponds to the generally accepted view that Fire and Air Sun signs work well together, and Earth and Water Sun signs make good combinations. Looking at the chart in Figure 4, page 268, you will see that this means that alternating signs—those that are sextile (separated by 60 degrees), trine (120 degrees), opposition (180 degrees), and conjunct

(0 degrees)—work together better than those that are semisextile (30 degrees), square (90 degrees), and quincunx (150 degrees).

This gives only six possible pairings of signs, yet there are Twelve Houses and twelve possible numbers that can be arrived at in combination. What this means is that each combination can work one of two ways, representing each of two opposing houses—the First and Seventh, the Second and Eighth, the Third and Ninth, the Fourth and Tenth, the Fifth and Eleventh, and the Sixth and Twelfth.

If one is attempting to achieve the best possible blending of two egos for a love relationship or a business partnership, the objective is to obtain a 1 or a 7 when the Sun sign numbers are added and divided by 2. The blending for each of the signs is as follows:

- Aries (1) + Aries (1) = 2, divided by 2 = 1
- Taurus (2) + Pisces (12) = 14, divided by 2 = 7
- Gemini (3) + Aquarius (11) = 14, divided by 2 = 7
- Cancer (4) + Capricorn (10) = 14, divided by 2 = 7
- Leo (5) + Sagittarius (9) = 14, divided by 2 = 7
- Virgo (6) + Scorpio (8) = 14, divided by 2 = 7
- Libra (7) + Libra (7) = 14, divided by 2 = 7

The blendings of Sun signs that achieve the numbers 2 and 8 are also excellent, especially for sexual relationships and financial partnerships. The pairings that achieve these numbers are the following:

- Aries (1) + Gemini (3) = 4, divided by 2 = 2
- Taurus (2) + Taurus (2) = 4, divided by 2 = 2
- Cancer (4) + Pisces (12) = 16, divided by 2 = 8
- Leo (5) + Aquarius (11) = 16, divided by 2 = 8
- Virgo (6) + Capricorn (10) = 16, divided by 2 = 8
- Libra (7) + Sagittarius (9) = 16, divided by 2 = 8
- Scorpio (8) + Scorpio (8) = 16, divided by 2 = 8

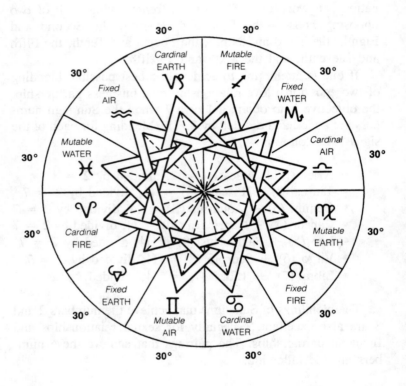

Figure 4

The 3 and 9 combinations indicate relationships that are good meetings of minds. Intellectually and philosophically, the two partners are very compatible. They may be either like brothers (or sisters), or they may grow and expand their horizons together. The pairings that achieve 3 and 9 are:

- Aries (1) + Leo (5) = 6, divided by 2 = 3
- Taurus (2) + Cancer (4) = 6, divided by 2 = 3
- Gemini (3) + Gemini (3) = 6, divided by 2 = 3
- Virgo (6) + Pisces (12) = 18, divided by 2 = 9
- Libra (7) + Aquarius (11) = 18, divided by 2 = 9
- Scorpio (8) + Capricorn (10) = 18, divided by 2 = 9
- Sagittarius (9) + Sagittarius (9) = 18, divided by 2 =9

One looks for a 4 or a 10 when seeking a good roommate situation or a career partnership that will be beneficial to both. In some cases the 4 and 10, however, can indicate a good love relationship, but usually one of the two is stronger or more dominant. The breakdown for achieving a 4 or 10 is as follows:

- Aries (1) + Libra (7) = 8, divided by 2 = 4
- Taurus (2) + Virgo (6) = 8, divided by 2 = 4
- Gemini (3) + Leo (5) = 8, divided by 2 = 4
- Cancer (4) + Cancer (4) = 8, divided by 2 = 4
- Scorpio (8) + Pisces (12) = 20, divided by 2 = 10
- Sagittarius (9) + Aquarius (11) = 20, divided by 2 = 10
- Capricorn (10) + Capricorn (10) = 20, divided by 2 = 10

The 5 and 11 relationships are also very good, but they are best for romances and love affairs, or for good and lasting friendships. They emphasize companionship and pleasurable entertainment together. The pairings that achieve 5 and 11 are:

- Aries (1) + Sagittarius (9) = 10, divided by 2 = 5
- Taurus (2) + Scorpio (8) = 10, divided by 2 = 5
- Gemini (3) + Libra (7) = 10, divided by 2 = 5
- Cancer (4) + Virgo (6) = 10, divided by 2 = 5
- Leo (5) + Leo (5) = 10, divided by 2 = 5
- Capricorn (10) + Pisces (12) = 22, divided by 2 = 11
- Aquarius (11) + Aquarius (11) = 22, divided by 2 = 11

Of the possible relationships, the 6 and 12 combinations are considered the least satisfactory, but there are positive benefits to such pairings. The two come together to work out mutual problems for spiritual and emotional growth. The combinations that produce 6 and 12 are as follows:

- Aries (1) + Aquarius (11) = 12, divided by 2 = 6
- Taurus (2) + Capricorn (10) = 12, divided by 2 = 6
- Gemini (3) + Sagittarius (9) = 12, divided by 2 = 6
- Cancer (4) + Scorpio (8) = 12, divided by 2 = 6
- Leo (5) + Libra (7) = 12, divided by 2 = 6
- Virgo (6) + Virgo (6) = 12, divided by 2 = 6
- Pisces (12) + Pisces (12) = 24, divided by 2 = 12

The Incompatible Elements

The problem with this system of determining relationships is that it denies the possibility of air mixing with water, fire with earth, fire with water, and air with earth. Obviously, these signs must relate to each other in some way, for there are many successful and long-lasting relationships involving incompatible signs.

To some extent there is truth in the belief that water and earth put out fire, while air merely coexists with earth and water. As was indicated earlier, each individual chart is such a mix of planets in various signs that there are many factors involved in relationships. The meeting of egos is merely one facet of combining charts.

To see what kind of relationship you might have with one of the elements incompatible with your sign, use the formula above and simply add 1 to the total before dividing by 2. But be aware of the quality of the two elements involved, and know that they will causes stresses or difficulties between the two egos.

Of all the possible incompatible pairings, the sign preceding your own is generally considered to be the most difficult for you, because it brings out your own self-destructive potential. For example, the three Fire signs are all preceded by Water signs—Aries by Pisces, Leo by Cancer, and Sagittarius by Scorpio.

Not only do the Water signs put out the Fire of each of these, but the conflicting natures affect the individuals' egos. Aries' Cardinal nature becomes confused by Pisces' mutability; Leo's Fixed ego is frustrated by Cancer's Cardinal quality; and Sagittarius' Mutable nature is overpowered by Scorpio's Fixed quality.

The Earth signs are all preceded by Fire—Taurus by Aries, Virgo by Leo, and Capricorn by Sagittarius. Fire scorches the earth, tending to make it barren. Also, the Cardinal nature of Aries is too impulsive and action oriented for placid, Fixed Taurus, while the stubborn, Fixed nature of Leo overpowers Virgo's mutability, and the expansive mutability of Sagittarius confuses the Cardinal nature of Capricorn.

The Air signs are preceded by Earth—Gemini by Taurus, Libra by Virgo, and Aquarius by Capricorn. Earth tries to pull the Air signs down from the clouds to be more practical and less idealistic. With Mutable Gemini, the materialism and the preoccupation with money that is typical of Fixed Taurus becomes extremely frustrating. Cardinal Libra seeks to achieve balance and sharing of ideas, but has difficulty with Mutable Virgo's preoccupation with mundane details. And socially concerned, Fixed Aquarius, whose need is to achieve absolute freedom, can be devastated by Cardinal Capricorn's demands for limitations and responsibility.

And finally, the Water signs are troubled by the Air signs that precede them—Cancer by Gemini, Scorpio by Libra, and Pisces by Aquarius. Cardinal Cancer's need to act to achieve a stable home has great difficulty with Mutable Gemini's flightiness and need to be out in the world. Fixed Scorpio's stubborn sexuality is plagued by Cardinal Libra's desire to achieve fairness and equality. And Mutable, spiritual Pisces is trodden beneath the heels of Fixed, free-wheeling Aquarius.

These are, of course, generalizations. They should be used as nothing more than a basic framework from which to depart in getting to know and understand the nature of a partner or a friend. The real adventure in love is in getting to know all of the intimate details of what makes another distinctly individual. What astrology tells us can be only a small part of that adventure, but a part that helps us step aside from reality, if only briefly, to see things from a different perspective.

Chapter 18

THE LIBRA-SCORPIO CONNECTION

This generation of gays faces a great many special challenges that generations before have not had to deal with. The times have never been easy for one who is a homosexual, but what was a promise of better times a few years ago has faded, and the future seems even more difficult than the past.

However, it is important that the gay community not look upon the current crisis with fear. It is a challenge, and one that can be met.

Perhaps astrology can help to view the situation with objectivity, and therefore aid toward achieving a positive solution.

During the last forty years, the heavy, slow-moving planets—Uranus, Neptune, and Pluto—have been passing through the same set of signs and houses of the universal chart, functioning more closely together than they have in centuries. During the mid- to late-1980s, they have been joined by Jupiter and Saturn, along with frequent visits from Mars on its year-and-a-half cycle.

The focus of much of the activity of these planets has been on two signs—Libra and Scorpio, the signs of loving partnership and sexuality—though its origins reach back to Leo and its resolutions can be expected in Aquarius, its effects spanning a complete half-cycle of the Zodiac, from the house of romance and love affairs to the house of friendship, group efforts, and social causes.

The house also of homosexuality.

When it is all over with—all of the media hype about the sexual revolution of the 1960s and 1970s, the "me" generation of the 1970s and 1980s, the drug explosion, the preppies and the yuppies—it will be seen that the true crisis of the post-World War II era has been a search for the meaning of love in relationship to Self and others—an understanding of the nature of the sign Libra, whose challenge is the need to balance, to give and receive equally and honestly, to be fair to oneself and to those one loves and cares about. It is a challenge of partnership and marriage, the union of souls or spirits, a need to find new definitions.

It is a challenge of coexistence, as important on the personal level as it is in international affairs.

Gradually, the transits of each of the heavy planets through Libra have sought to teach lessons of love. Some have been heeded; some have not. Ultimately the consequences of the transits of one house must fall into the following house, as the planets move on.

The consequences of the lessons of Libra—learned or unlearned—and their challenges—met or unmet—have fallen into Scorpio, the universal sign of legacies, the tangible or material results of partnership, sexuality, and death. And Scorpio has given new lessons, new challenges, now being faced in that sign and the two following—Sagittarius and Capricorn—for the planets do not turn back, except for brief retrograde periods, to allow humanity to reassess its mistakes. They then move on through the cycles of human experience.

Scorpio's challenge to face the nature of sexuality, the need for physical sharing, and the meaning of death is a difficult one. Pluto, the ruler of Scorpio, is now in his own sign for the first time since his discovery, having entered in 1983, after eleven years in Libra. But two other planets paved the way for his arrival. Neptune moved through Scorpio from 1955 to 1970, and Uranus passed through between 1974 and 1981. Saturn has made two passages through the sign in this era, the first between 1953 and 1956, and the most recent between 1982 and 1985.

Each of these planets have contributed its own special challenge to the nature of love, sex, and understanding as they have moved through Libra, Scorpio, and Sagittarius. Even Jupiter contributed as it spent one year in each sign in the early 1980s.

Two of these planets—Saturn and Neptune—along with the Lunar Nodes are considered significators of karma, very serious spiritual challenges that individuals must face in this lifetime because of failings from the past.

This has made the overall challenge a highly complex one. To understand the full impact, it is necessary to look at each one individually and in combination, relating them to their placements in the birth charts of the generation facing their challenges.

THE NEPTUNE CHALLENGE

Of all the planets, Neptune is the most difficult to define. By its very nature, it is all things that are vague, without boundaries, indefinable. It is water, oil, chemicals, gases, fantasy, imagination, creativity, fears, anxieties, infections, illness, viruses, medicine, drugs, alcohol, even the spirit and the soul. It has negative qualities that are terrifying; at the same time it has positive values that we could not live without. As with all of the planets, we are faced with the challenge to seek the positive side and divest ourselves of the negatives.

But with Neptune, because it is so nebulous and indefinable, we have difficulty seeing the difference. In fact, Neptune is sight or vision itself, as well as the inability to see or perceive. So wily is he that he deliberately tries to prevent us from recognizing the truth, daring us to uncover it by our own ingenuity and perception (both Neptunian qualities).

Before we attempt to unravel the mysteries of Neptune's activities in this century, it might be helpful for the reader to glance at the Table of Neptune's transits (Table IV, page 276), to see where the planet was placed at the time of his birth, in order to relate the generational trends to his own life. For Neptune will contribute to the individual some of the qualities

Table IV

SIGN PLACEMENT OF NEPTUNE

September 23, 1914 to November 5, 1970

DATES	SIGN
9/23/1914–12/21/1914	Leo
12/22/1914–7/24/1915	Cancer
7/25/1915–9/20/1928	Leo
9/21/1928–2/18/1929	Virgo
2/19/1928–7/23/1929	Leo
7/24/1929–10/2/1942	Virgo
10/3/1942–4/18/1943	Libra
4/19/1943–8/2/1943	Virgo
8/3/1943–12/23/1955	Libra
12/24/1955–3/11/1956	Scorpio
3/12/1956–10/18/1956	Libra
10/19/1956–6/16/1957	Scorpio
6/17/1957–8/4/1957	Libra
8/5/1957–1/4/1970	Scorpio
1/5/1970–5/2/1970	Sagittarius
5/3/1970–11/5/1970	Scorpio

of its sign placement (though its full impact is dependent upon house placement).

Neptune in Leo

Since the transits of each house or sign are linked inextricably to those that precede and follow, it is important to begin some years before the present challenge began—in 1914, when Neptune entered Leo for its fourteen year stay.

Significant Neptunian changes took place between 1914 and 1928. The automobile came into common usage, utilizing gas and oil (Neptune) to propel it. It became a leisure time activity or entertainment (Leo). Immediately people took risks (Leo) with it, resulting in accidents.

Motion pictures (Neptune) became a staple of public entertainment (Leo), and Hollywood quickly took on the role of fantasy-maker (Neptune), with a loose sexual morality (Leo). It was a romantic era (Leo) filled with creativity (Neptune).

Because it was a time of Prohibition, alcohol (Neptune) was romanticized (Leo). As Leo is the sign of love affairs, sexual fantasy (Neptune) became an important part of relationships, especially extra-marital and secret ones (Neptune). This began the significant spread of sexually transmitted diseases (Neptune).

The combination of Neptune and Leo was a challenge for humanity to perceive the distinction between reality and fantasy, to take chances, but guarded ones. We did not heed the challenge, and so we were headed for a fall. It was to be an economic one, for Leo also rules the stock market and investments.

Neptune in Virgo

Between 1928 and 1943, Neptune passed through Virgo, the sign of its detriment (opposing its own sign of Pisces). Although this weakened Neptune's power somewhat, it still had a significant impact, part of it negative, part positive. Since the world had not heeded the Leo challenge, the Virgo challenge became one people could not avoid facing.

Not long after Neptune's entry into Virgo, the stock market fell, and the world entered an era of economic depression and food shortage. The Mutable Earth sign Virgo governs work, health, medicine, food, clothing, and service to others. The world was forced to become more practical (Virgo), paying for the foolish risks it had taken in Leo.

Motion pictures (Neptune) began to speak (Mercury, ruler of Virgo), and they began to attack social issues, becoming an art that performed a service (Virgo) and communicating a message (Mercury).

Because Neptune was in its detriment in the Earth sign Virgo, there were water shortages in some areas, resulting in famine. Many farmers had to move (Neptune) out of the dustbowl seeking work (Virgo). All of the old definitions of work (Virgo) dissolved (Neptune) and had to be reformulated, including the concept of worker's insurance or Social Security (Neptune).

Virgo is the growing or raising of food; during this period, chemical fertilizers (Neptune) were devised to attempt to reclaim the land and increase productivity.

As Virgo is the sign of medicine, health care came in for some steps forward, with the creation of new drugs (Neptune), such as tranquilizers and antibiotics.

The challenge of Neptune in Mutable Virgo was to use restraint in the reformulating of old customs and the development of new chemicals and techniques—to be practical and to understand the negatives associated with the positives of Neptune's new contributions. It was not met entirely, for Neptune inevitably misleads and confuses, even deceives.

Neptune in Libra

From 1943 to 1956, Neptune passed through Libra, the first of the two signs we are most concerned with here. In the sign of love and harmony, of equality and fairness in partnership and marriage, Neptune's activities were less obvious, more hidden beneath the surface—more devious and deceptive—for Libra is also the sign of open enemies.

After the end of World War II, there was hope for peace and justice and democracy in the world, for understanding between peoples, for respect for differences (Libra), and Neptune encouraged that fantasy for a time, working beneath the surface to create fear (Neptune) that it ultimately was impossible to achieve. In the United States, fear-mongering and distrust of partners and open enemies (Libra) reached a peak with the McCarthy era. Paranoia (Neptune) was rampant.

The world became divided between East and West, and there were efforts toward a "balance of power" and "peaceful coexistence." But, throughout it all, there was fear.

In Hollywood, the beauty (Libra) of the stars had become even more important, color (Libra) came into widespread use, and romances and love stories (Libra) became a major focus. The Hollywood hype and gossip mill (Neptune) reached a peak during this time. "Love" became everyone's fantasy (Neptune), especially young love, often with beach settings (also Neptune).

(Interestingly, some of the films to win Academy Awards during this period were *The Lost Weekend*—about alcoholism—*On the Waterfront, Three Coins in the Fountain*, and *From Here to Eternity*, with its famous love scene on the beach.)

One of the most serious changes brought about by Neptune in Libra, though, was an emphasis on chemicals added to food and to cosmetics. (While Virgo rules the growing of food, Libra rules the sensual pleasure of dining.) Food processing became a major industry, with an increasing number of additives, and there were new soaps, deodorants, and beauty preparations (also Libra) utilizing new chemical miracles and dyes. This reached a point where one major corporation advertised, "Better things for better living through chemistry."

Vitamins and drugs (both ruled by Neptune) came into common use, and sleeping pills became very popular. (Sleep and dreams are both ruled by Neptune.)

The challenge of Neptune in Libra was to avoid overdoing the new chemicals that had come into use, accepting them as purely beneficial, and to beware of the fantasy of expecting life to be a constant romance, filled with beautiful people like in the movies, and on that new entertainment form that had entered the living room—the television set. The challenge was not met.

Neptune in Scorpio

Though Neptune worked silently and insidiously in Libra, its power became blatantly obvious in the period that followed. Between 1956 and 1970, it passed through Scorpio, a Water sign, trine its home, and many of its effects made the headlines. Scorpio rules the subconscious mind and the primitive animalistic instincts, and the drugs developed during the preceding years began to be used for recreational purposes, along with newly developed "mind altering" drugs. Hallucinogens were extremely popular during this period.

Scorpio's rule of sexuality was also greatly affected by Neptunian influences. Not only did sex, drugs, and Rock and Roll become inextricably linked in people's minds, but sexual fantasies gradually crept into magazines and films as pornography became a big business. (Still photography as well as film is ruled by Neptune, as is fantasy itself.)

The deep love and romance of Libra was quickly forgotten, and the emphasis turned to sex, the physical act itself. Nudity became shockingly commonplace onstage and in films, graphically showing the sexual act. Popular songs praised drugs and sex.

Venereal disease (Neptune) was getting out of hand, and more drugs were developed to cope with the different strains of viruses that were causing virtually a new and different influenza every year. There were scandals involving some chemicals added to soaps and foods, but as soon as the villains were taken off the market, new chemical additives were created to take their place, many of them even more dangerous to health. Air pollution (Neptune) reached crisis proportions in the major cities of the world.

Death, another of Scorpio's facets, was constantly in the headlines, and much of it was related to Neptune. Many of the biggest stars of Hollywood, some of them considered "sex symbols," died of drug overdoses or under mysterious circumstances. (In some cases, there were questions in the public mind, of covert operations by the Mafia or C.I.A. being responsible for the death of stars such as Marilyn Monroe. Pluto, ruler of Scorpio, governs both the Mafia and the C.I.A.—in fact, all things hidden or "undercover.")

By the end of the period, there were attempts to meet at least some of the challenges of Neptune in Scorpio. There were efforts to curb the recreational use of drugs, without much success, and people began to demand a reduction in air pollution as well as some of the chemical additives to food, cosmetics, and even fabrics. Still much of the challenge remained unresolved.

Neptune in Sagittarius

From 1970 to 1984, Neptune passed through Sagittarius, the sign ruling higher education, higher mentality, long distance travel, philosophy, religion, and expansion and growth. Neptune was uncomfortable in the Mutable sign that is square its home, and again it worked subtly. There were efforts to undo much of what it had done while in Virgo—threats made against the concept of social security, subsidies to farmers, union guarantees of work.

At the same time, Neptune's lack of boundaries combined with the expansiveness of Sagittarius (ruled by Jupiter) to make this the era of the megacorporation, with businesses spreading their offices and factories around the globe. International trafficking in drugs became commonplace, as drug use continued to expand, with an emphasis on "altered states of mind."

Neptune had its effect on higher education; curriculums changed drastically, with new experimental methods of teaching and courses that were far from traditional. Similar things happened to organized religions, as they altered their rituals and "liberalized" dogmas. New religions surfaced, some returning to old formats, such as "born again Christianity," others following hypnotic leaders such as Sun Myung Moon. There were many new "philosophies" for meeting the needs of new lifestyles—such as est, transcendental meditation, rebirthing, and so on.

There was a resurgence of sea travel, as one-week and two-week cruises came into vogue. One television series that became one of the biggest hits of this period was *Love Boat*. And films took on an international flavor, not only being filmed in foreign locales, but often involving cooperative efforts of several countries. Many films used travel as their subject, such as the series of *Airport* pictures. Science fiction came back to the screen in a big way, beginning with *Star Wars*. And international drug trafficking became a familiar theme, beginning with *The French Connection*.

The challenge of Neptune in Sagittarius was to understand and to deal with the negative aspects of Neptune—the drugs, the fantasy and deception, the pornography, the pollution of the air and of food, and the chemical effects on the human body and mind. Much of the challenge was not met, and we are beginning to be forced to face it now, with Neptune in Capricorn.

Neptune in Capricorn

In 1984, Neptune entered Capricorn, where it will remain until 1998. We are only beginning to see the effects it will have, with efforts at placing restrictions on drinking, smoking, and drug use, especially in public places. The scandals involving some of the new television evangelists are also a part of the new wave, and so are the attempts to restrict pornography.

As time passes, there will also be efforts to control chemical additives to food. As Capricorn is an Earth sign, there should be a definite move toward pure, unprocessed foods, as well as control of chemical fertilizers and water and soil pollutants.

Many of the efforts to control Neptune's activities may not be successful; it will be more likely to drive them underground.

Capricorn is the ruler of all matters involving public life, fatherhood, careers, leaders of nations, famous and successful people, older people in responsible positions, and time itself. There will probably be many more cases involving drugs and famous people, perhaps even cases revealing involvement of responsible figures in drug trafficking. Some may even be governmental leaders or heads of nations.

Chemistry and medicine, ruled by Neptune (which always dissolves structures), have already begun to break down the definition of "fatherhood," with the development of a birth control pill for men, test tube babies, and artificial insemination of women.

There will be much more focus on older people and on aging in the media, and there should be medical advances related to aging.

Motion pictures will probably begin to focus on themes involving older people and on stories of success. There has already been a move in this direction with films such as *On Golden Pond, Cocoon,* and *The Whales of August.* The historical epic may return, and there may be more films with stories involving time travel.

Precisely how Neptune will affect our concept of time itself cannot be accurately determined at this stage. However, there might be some alteration in the way we now think of this "fourth dimension."

Perhaps most importantly, there should be significant advances in medicine, with an emphasis on limiting the spread of communicable diseases, infections, and viruses.

The challenge of Neptune in Capricorn will be to learn to structure and control many of Neptune's negative qualities while taking advantage of its positive ones. Whether we can do this successfully, only time (Capricorn) will tell.

THE PLUTO CHALLENGE

Since shortly after World War II, Pluto has been moving at approximately the same speed as Neptune, keeping up a continuing sextile (sixty degree) relationship between the two.

This began as Neptune was in the first half of Libra, while Pluto was in the first half of Leo. Normally Pluto moves much more slowly than Neptune, but because of its erratic orbit it is currently moving at about the same speed. As it moves through its own sign between 1984 and 1995, it will actually be moving faster than Neptune.

To determine where Pluto was at the time you were born, refer to Table V on page 285.

Pluto's main concerns are with sexuality, death, the subconscious mind, human regeneration, destroying and rebuilding, criminal or underworld activities, banking, insurance, legacies, and taxes.

For our purposes here, we will trace only Pluto's movement from Leo through Scorpio.

Pluto in Leo

Pluto first entered Leo in 1937, staying there only a month before returning to Cancer for almost a year. It moved in for its lengthy stay in August 1938, not leaving until 1956-57. As mentioned earlier, Leo is the sign of love affairs, romance, movies, entertainment, gambling, risk-taking, children, investments, and the stock market.

Pluto's passage through Leo had a wide variety of effects. It destroyed and rebuilt virtually all of the Leo factors during that time, working hand in hand with Neptune in Libra from about 1946 onward. Pluto created the era of the "baby boom," and it completely revolutionized concepts of child-rearing. It took gambling from strictly an underworld activity (though it did not remove the underworld's influence entirely) and made it respectable through the creation of Las Vegas.

After the end of the Great Depression, it created new methods and techniques for both banking and Wall Street, and during its long stay it altered motion picture entertainment completely, taking it away from the "family entertainment" it had been before and transmitting it into the living rooms of the world by way of Neptune.

Table V

SIGN PLACEMENT OF PLUTO

September 23, 1912 to August 27, 1984

DATES	SIGN
9/23/1912–10/23/1912	Cancer
10/24/1912–7/9/1913	Gemini
7/10/1913–12/28/1913	Cancer
12/29/1913–5/26/1914	Gemini
5/27/1914–10/8/1937	Cancer
10/9/1937–11/25/1937	Leo
11/6/1937–8/3/1938	Cancer
8/4/1938–10/21/1956	Leo
10/22/1956–1/15/1957	Virgo
1/16/1957–8/18/1957	Leo
8/19/1957–10/4/1971	Virgo
10/5/1971–4/17/1972	Libra
4/18/1972–7/29/1972	Virgo
7/30/1972–11/5/1983	Libra
11/6/1983–5/18/1984	Scorpio
5/19/1984–8/27/1984	Libra

Its effect on our concepts of romance and love affairs also went hand in hand with Neptune in Libra, making a subliminal sexuality much more important than love for a human soul. From this time onward, the physical would always be of much more important in "love" than the spiritual.

Pluto in Virgo

From 1956-57 through 1971-72, Pluto moved through the sign Virgo, the sign representing work, health, service, the raising of food, medical care, clothing and fashion, and pets.

During this entire time, it was moving fully in unison with Neptune in Scorpio, the sign Pluto rules. Their actions were closely linked. Pluto was a part of the sex and drugs revolution, wreaking its destruction on old concepts of employment, worker-management relations, health and medical care, and food-growing, so that it could build up new concepts for each, new approaches.

The communication of its new ideas was very important in Virgo, which is ruled by Mercury, but much of the communication was complaints that "Things aren't what they used to be."

Things weren't what they used to be. Health care did become less personal. An animosity had arisen between workers and employers, in which each felt the other owed more than they were giving. Food didn't taste anything like it had before, and after this period, concepts of fashion would never be the same.

Pluto in Libra

Pluto made its passage through Libra as Neptune was moving through Sagittarius, between 1971-72 and 1983-84. Its objective was to destroy old concepts of marriage and partnership, toward fairness and equal respect between people, and to establish a new approach by the time it left.

The divorce rate soared during this period, and the singles scene became the standard of male and female relationships. Among gays, the concept of "dating" came in, patterning themselves on the old concepts of straights. This was the era of "me," a time in which selfishness and self-centeredness was the approved norm, with little regard for the needs or feelings of others. With relationships breaking down constantly, almost everyone shrugged shoulders and commented, "There are other fish in the sea." (Neptune in Sagittarius.)

By the end of this period, people began to question what they were doing, wondering if they would ever again be able to establish lasting relationships. The answers would wait until they experienced Pluto's transit of its own sign Scorpio.

Pluto in Scorpio

The questioning of sexuality began slowly in 1983-84, as Pluto entered its own sign. Sex became more closely linked with death than it had been in centuries, because of the threat of new sexual diseases. Before it leaves its home in 1995, all of the Scorpio/Pluto factors will pass through a period of destruction and rebuilding on a new basis. Not only will old concepts of sexuality and death undergo change, but also organized crime and underworld activities in general, our understanding of the subconscious mind and human motivations.

Since Pluto is still linked with Neptune, now in Capricorn, much of this will involve changes related to drugs, films, oil and gas, and chemicals in general. There should be connections between Pluto's destructiveness and the limitations, restrictions, and restructuring of Capricorn which is imposing responsibility on all things Neptunian.

The precise manner in which this will take place will be dependent upon the actions of the faster moving planets, as they relate to Pluto, Neptune, and Uranus.

THE URANUS CHALLENGE

Although it is a heavy planet with generational aspects to its nature, Uranus moves much faster than either Pluto or Neptune, passing through one sign in approximately seven to eight years. The effect of Uranus is to free the mind for creative solutions to social problems, at the same time uniting people for its revolutionary approaches. It does appear to create upheaval and turmoil, and there are stops and starts to its activities, but its ultimate effects are generally good.

To see where Uranus was at the time of your birth, refer to Table VI, page 288.

For our purposes here, we will consider only the movement of Uranus from Leo through Scorpio, the period in which it has been interacting closely with Neptune and Pluto.

Table VI

SIGN PLACEMENT OF URANUS

January 31, 1912 to November 15, 1981

DATES	SIGN
1/31/1912–9/4/1912	Aquarius
9/5/1912–11/18/1912	Capricorn
11/19/1912–1/22/1920	Aquarius
1/23/1920–3/30/1927	Pisces
3/31/1927–11/4/1927	Aries
11/5/1927–1/12/1928	Pisces
1/13/1928–6/5/1934	Aries
6/6/1934–10/9/1934	Taurus
10/10/1934–3/27/1935	Aries
3/28/1935–8/7/1941	Taurus
8/8/1941–10/5/1941	Gemini
10/6/1941–5/14/1942	Taurus
5/15/1942–8/29/1948	Gemini
8/30/1948–11/11/1948	Cancer
11/12/1948–6/9/1949	Gemini
6/10/1949–8/24/1955	Cancer
8/25/1955–1/27/1956	Leo
1/28/1956–6/8/1956	Cancer
6/9/1956–10/31/1961	Leo
11/1/1961–1/7/1962	Virgo
1/8/1962–8/9/1962	Leo
8/10/1962–9/28/1968	Virgo
9/29/1968–5/20/1969	Libra
5/21/1969–6/24/1969	Virgo
6/25/1969–11/19/1974	Libra
11/20/1974–5/1/1975	Scorpio
5/2/1975–9/7/1975	Libra
9/8/1975–2/16/1981	Scorpio
2/17/1981–3/21/1981	Sagittarius
3/22/1981–11/15/1981	Scorpio

Uranus in Leo

Uranus entered Leo in 1956, at about the same time that Pluto left that sign and entered Virgo and Neptune made its move from Libra into Scorpio. Uranus was gaining on the two slower moving planets, being only thirty degrees from catching up to Pluto and being square (ninety degrees) to Neptune.

Uranus was in its detriment in Leo, made somewhat weak by being opposition its own sign of Aquarius, but it had its effect nonetheless.

In the sign of entertainment, love affairs, romance, gambling, risk taking, and children, Uranus brought a degree of intellectualism and objectivity to those aspects of society. "Movies" became "films," more intellectually stimulating than entertaining. One of the factors of romance became the exchange of ideas; a man and a woman had to appreciate each other for their minds as well as their bodies.

And homosexuality, ruled by Uranus, played a great part in this, as homosexuals slowly, cautiously took the first steps out of the closet.

With all three of the heavy planets changing signs during 1955-56, the change in society was more noticeable than usual. Music changed drastically with the advent of Rock and Roll. Television became the norm in people's living rooms, no longer just a curiosity. And there was a new sense of freedom and adventure, even a new hope in the air. For decades afterward, the years between 1955 and 1962 would be looked upon as romantic ones, with the difficulties and challenges forgotten.

Uranus in Virgo

Between 1962 and 1968-69, Uranus passed through Virgo, catching up to Pluto and then moving on ahead. While they were in the same sign—and particularly between 1963 and 1967, when they were conjunct—they joined their separate energies toward the same aspects of society. (During much of the period when they were conjunct, they were also both sextile Neptune in Scorpio, so that all three heavy planets were working jointly, but in different facets of life.)

Pluto's actions in Virgo have already been noted. Uranus directed its energy toward greater freedom in employment and more intellectual stimulation in the workplace. The whole concept of work came up for intellectual scrutiny and revision. Employers used ingenuity in changing the roles of employees for greater productivity, offering services other than higher wages to effect compensation for greater effort expended. In this period, computers (ruled by Uranus) came into use in "service" to humanity, though in some cases there were questions of whether machine was serving man or vice versa. Whatever the case, computers did revolutionize the workplace.

There were numerous medical breakthroughs during this time, with a greater understanding of diet and nutrition and its effect on illness or wellness. Vitamins became almost a fad; the consumption of Vitamin C especially burgeoned. People began to talk about preventive medicine.

Acting together, Uranus and Pluto are truly revolutionary. Though their efforts may have been subtle, the changes they effected were drastic, as later years would prove.

Uranus in Libra

Uranus moved on to our focal sign of Libra in 1968-69, remaining there until 1975. Now ahead of Pluto, it was moving swiftly to attempt to catch up with Neptune (which it will not do until 1991-92). While Uranus was in Libra, everyone focused attention on love and partnership. Because Uranus strives for freedom and independence, this was the era of Woodstock, of flower children, of "free" love. People were shedding their clothes in order to be more free. "Streakers" showed up in unorthodox places, running naked except for sneakers, expressing their need to be free of all encumbrances, displaying the beauty of their bodies rather than of the clothes they wore.

But Uranus' need to set free and his determination to see everything through the light of intellectualism was also focused on concepts of marriage and love relationships. The institution of marriage was scrutinized intellectually and found wanting. A great many people chose simply to live together without a legal or formal bond. Others who were more traditional tried living together for a time before making the ultimate commitment.

(The way for this had been paved by Neptune, with the development of contraceptive devices that would make planned parenthood possible. However, many of these devices would later come into question themselves.)

For gays there were positive factors associated with Uranus in Libra. With the new freedom in love relationships, it was possible to come out of the closet completely and be accepted as no different from other people. What two men or two women shared together could be looked upon truly as love.

In fact, the revolutionary facet of Uranus permitted gays to demand that society recognize the love they had been sharing secretly before. Interestingly, while Uranus had made its first tentative move into Libra in September of 1968, it did not actually leave Virgo behind completely until June 25, 1969. Two days later, two of the most significant events of the Gay Movement occurred. Early on that Friday of June 27, gays had wept openly in the street at the funeral of Judy Garland, who had represented their "Earth Mother" (Virgo). She had died the previous Sunday in London, and several days had been allowed for mourners to pay tribute before the funeral. That evening, or more precisely, at 3:00 A.M. on Saturday, the New York police raided the Stonewall bar, arresting gays, and for the first time in history homosexuals fought back as a group against repression. The "riots" continued for days afterward, resulting in gays being granted the right to congregate in bars. That event is recognized as the official beginning of the Gay Liberation Movement. It occurred when Uranus was at zero degrees and two minutes into Libra.

But one of the legacies of intellectual Uranus in Libra was that "love" became something one thought about more than felt or responded to intuitively. Freedom-loving and independent Uranus caused lovers to be concerned about their individuality and separateness within their relationship. And the erratic nature of Uranus disrupted the delicate balance of Libra's scales, the balance that before had permitted two loving partners to coexist with an acceptance of each other's failings, as well as an appreciation of each other's positive attributes. When two people had a problem, the solution was often to sever the relationship rather than to face the problem and deal with it. It would be left to Pluto to correct this problem as it followed into Libra.

Uranus in Scorpio

From 1975 to 1981, Uranus passed through Scorpio, bringing its intellectualism and its demand for freedom to concerns of sexuality. The techniques, the purpose, and the need for sex were dissected and analyzed and discussed and written about. "Free love" was a thing of the past, of the Libra era; "sexual freedom" became the new focus, as if there really had been no difference all along.

For gays this became a period of activism, of growing gay pride. In Libra, they had been proud to express their love openly, but as with everyone else, love was dropped in preference for sex. Scorpio rules hidden or secret places, such as bars and baths, and freedom (Uranus) reigned there for gays.

We must remember, though, that Scorpio also rules matters connected with death, and ultimately Uranus would have to deal with the subject. On an intellectual level, there were discussions of euthanasia and the right to die, because of the number of people who were kept alive in hospitals as "living vegetables." The development of "life support" machines, rather than prolonging life, really prolong death, which is ruled by Scorpio. There were a number of cases of persons being prosecuted for "pulling the plug" on loved ones. However, this was not dealing with the association between sex and death. That would be seen much later, as an after-effect of the activities of this period.

1978

Midway through its transit of Scorpio, Uranus reached a position halfway between the position of Pluto in Libra and that of Neptune in Sagittarius. Throughout most of the year 1978, the three planets were lined up in consecutive signs, exactly thirty degrees apart. Uranus, the planet of freedom, intellectual stimulation, social concerns, group activities, and homosexuality, seemed to hold the other two in balance. Pluto, planet of sexuality and death, was in the sign of love and partnership; while Neptune, planet of all things nebulous and unsure (such as fantasies, infections, viruses, drugs, alcohol, films, as well as the human soul and spirit), was in Sagittarius, the sign of growth and expansion, of the higher mind and philosophy.

The heavy planets—one ruling sexuality, another of the intellectual capacity, and the third ruling the spirit—were working together in separate spheres—in love, sex, and growth. It was a peak of sorts for gays; and it was also insidiously attacking the newfound freedom. That was the year that it was most likely the disease of AIDS was introduced to the gay community, giving the ultimate challenge for the reassessment and understanding of love and sex and personal relationships, the challenge that each planet had begun with its transit of Libra.

It is a challenge that will continue for homosexuals—as well as heterosexuals—for some time to come.

THE MEETING IN CAPRICORN

During 1988, Uranus makes its gradual entry into Capricorn, but it will take several years for it to reach and to pass Neptune. That will finally happen in 1993, while Jupiter—planet of generosity and beneficence—is in Libra, and Saturn—planet of repayments for effort expended, keeper of time—is in Aquarius. At this point, Uranus and Saturn will be in "mutual reception," which means that each are in the sign ruled by the other. They become virtually interchangeable, taking on each other's qualities. The two old "enemies" will become "friends" for a period. All of the heavy planets are lined up to make a concerted effort to face the challenges they began in Libra.

Before 1993 is over, the challenges should be met, the obstacles overcome, and people can move forward, united, with a new understanding of love of Self and of others, with sexuality placed in its proper perspective.

As 1994 begins, the sextile between Pluto and Neptune that has lasted for almost fifty years will end. The following year, Pluto will leave the sign that is its home, having built a new basis for the understanding of human sexuality. And, as 1996 begins, Uranus, the gay ruler will enter his own sign of Aquarius at home and secure, bringing freedom and understanding to the nature of friendship and social concern.

GLOSSARY

Air Signs—Gemini, Libra, and Aquarius constitute the Air triplicity. Of the Twelve Houses, they form a trine, 120 degrees apart from each other. Air signs are considered to be primarily mental or intellectual in nature. While they are all of the same element, each is of a different nature. Gemini is Mutable; Libra is Cardinal; and Aquarius is Fixed.

Aquarius—The eleventh sign of the Zodiac, Fixed in nature, it occurs during the period when winter is at its peak. It is an Air sign, though it is called "The Water Bearer," and—to some extent—it does partake of the Water nature, though its water is cold and impersonal. It is ruled by Uranus.

Aries—The first sign of the Zodiac, Cardinal in nature, it is the sign that begins with the Spring Equinox, signalling the advent of spring. It is a Fire sign, and is the most ambitious of the signs. It is ruled by Mars.

Ascendant—The specific degree of the sign that is rising above the horizon at the time of one's birth. It sets the pattern for the division of the Twelve Houses of the individual horoscope, and it is determined by the specific time and location of the person's birth. It is the cusp that begins the First House.

Aspect—Two or more planets or astrological points can join their energies when they are considered in aspect; i.e., appearing in approximately the same degree of the same or different signs. The aspects are (1) conjunction, 0 degrees; (2) semi-sextile, 30 degrees; (3) sextile, 60 degrees; (4) square, 90 degrees; (5) trine, 120 degrees; (6) quincunx, 150 degrees; and (7) opposition, 180 degrees. To be in aspect, the planets do not have to be in the precise degree. Most astrologers allow at least five degrees. The way the energies of the planets combine depend upon the nature of the planets, the precise aspect they are in, and the sign and house they occupy.

Autumn Equinox—The position of the Sun that signals the beginning of autumn and the beginning of the sign Libra. It is the time when the position of the Sun is such that the nights and days are of equal duration, but after which the days grow shorter.

Cancer—The fourth sign of the Zodiac, Cardinal in nature, beginning with the Summer Solstice, when the days are longest and the nights are shortest, Cancer signals the beginning of summer. It is a Water sign and represents the feeling or emotional nature of the spiritual side of the native. It is ruled by the Moon.

Capricorn—The tenth sign of the Zodiac, Cardinal in nature, beginning with the Winter Solstice, when the days are shortest and the nights are longest, Capricorn signals the beginning of winter. It is an Earth sign, and represents the utilitarian facets of the material side of the native. It is ruled by the planet Saturn.

Cardinal Signs—Aries, Cancer, Libra, and Capricorn are the four Cardinal signs. They occur ninety degrees apart and so are in square or opposition to each other. Each signals the beginning of a season—Aries, the spring; Cancer, the summer; Libra, the autumn; and Capricorn, the winter. For this reason, the Cardinal signs are considered ambitious in nature, very much concerned with initiating things. However, they are also known for not being able to sustain their efforts.

Combined Chart—A chart that is derived entirely from mathematical calculations in order to see how two individuals will relate to each other. It is determined by figuring the median points of the house cusps of the two individual charts, then figuring the median points of each of the planetary placements. The position of the luminaries—the Sun and the Moon—in any of the Twelve Houses are considered to divine precisely what form the relationship will take.

Combust—When a planet appears in a chart in close conjunction with the Sun, it is considered to be combust, with the Sun overpowering and depleting the energy of the other. The planet that is most often in this aspect with the Sun is Mercury. However, when Mercury is at precisely the same degree as the center of the Sun, it is considered to be cazimi, which is a positive aspect.

Conjunction—Two or more planets are considered to be in conjunction with each other when they occur in the same sign, within five degrees of each other. (Some astrologers allow more than five degrees, some as many as ten, especially with the Moon, which travels swiftly.)

Cusp—The term "cusp" may be used in either of two ways, one referring to astrological signs and the other to the houses of the horoscope. Sign cusps are the points of division between adjoining signs. For example, the cusp between Libra and Scorpio occurs when the Sun passes from 29 degrees 59 minutes of Libra to 0 degrees of Scorpio. A number of people are born "on the cusp," and therefore are considered to partake of qualities of both signs. This may be true to some extent, but generally the person is more heavily one sign or the other. House cusps are the dividing points of each of the Twelve Houses in an individual chart, and they may occur at any degree of the signs governing these houses, which are determined by the precise time and place of one's birth. Each house may or may not occupy precisely thirty degrees. In fact, some charts have two opposing signs "intercepted" within two opposing houses that are therefore well over thirty degrees in size. Since these intercepted signs do not govern houses, two other signs will each govern two consecutive houses. A high percentage of gay charts contain interceptions.

Descendant—In an individual chart, the precise degree of the sign that is falling over the western horizon at the time of one's birth is called the Descendant. It is the opposite sign and degree of the Ascendant, and it forms the cusp of the Seventh House of the horoscope.

Earth Signs—Taurus, Virgo, and Capricorn form the Earth triplicity. Of the twelve signs, they form a trine, 120 degrees apart from each other. Earth signs are considered to be primarily practical or materialistic in nature. While they are all of the same element, each is of a different nature. Taurus is Fixed; Virgo is Mutable; and Capricorn is Cardinal.

Eclipse Points—(See Lunar Eclipse Point, Solar Eclipse Point)

Ecliptic—The apparent path of the Sun around the earth, which passes through the twelve signs of the Zodiac. It is along this path that solar and lunar eclipses occur.

Eighth House—In a horoscope, the Eighth House rules sex, partnership finances, inheritance, and death. In the standard chart, the Eighth House is ruled by Scorpio.

Eleventh House—In a horoscope, the Eleventh House rules friends, aspirations, group associations, social concerns, and political activities. In the standard chart, the Eleventh House is ruled by Aquarius.

Equinoxes—(See Autumn Equinox, Spring Equinox)

Fifth House—In a horoscope, the Fifth House rules entertainment, speculation, gambling, risk taking, creativity, and children. In the standard chart, the Fifth House is ruled by Leo.

Fire Signs—Aries, Leo, and Sagittarius form the Fire triplicity. Of the twelve signs, they form a trine, 120 degrees apart from each other. Fire signs are considered be primarily ambitious and action oriented. While they are all of the same element, each is different in nature. Aries is Cardinal, Leo is Fixed, and Sagittarius is Mutable.

First House—In a horoscope, the First House rules the Self, the personality, and the appearance. In the standard chart, the First House is ruled by Aries.

Fixed Signs—Taurus, Leo, Scorpio, and Aquarius are the four Fixed signs. They occur ninety degrees apart and so are in square or opposition to each other. Each occurs at the peak of a season—Taurus, in the spring; Leo, in the summer;

Scorpio, in the autumn; and Aquarius, in the winter. For this reason, the Fixed signs are considered resistant to change, very determined, and capable of persevering until their goals are achieved.

Fourth House—In a horoscope, the Fourth House rules the home, mother, real estate, and the circumstances surrounding death. In the standard chart, the Fourth House is occupied by Cancer.

Gemini—The third sign of the Zodiac, Mutable in nature, Gemini is the sign that appears at the end of spring, just before the beginning of summer. It is an Air sign, and is very concerned with communication. It is ruled by Mercury.

Grand Cross—When an individual horoscope has a configuration of at least four planets forming oppositions and squares in all four houses of a specific nature—Cardinal, Fixed, or Mutable—it is called a Grand Cross. It is a relatively rare configuration, and considered to represent great difficulties the native must overcome.

Grand Trine—When an individual horoscope has a configuration of at least three planets trining each other from the three signs of the same element—Fire, Earth, Air, Water— the native is said to have a Grand Trine. It is generally considered to be a very beneficial configuration, and it appears in a relatively small percentage of charts.

Intercepted Houses—In some horoscopes, a pair of opposing signs may fall entirely within two opposing houses without ruling the cusps, so that two other signs occupy two houses each. The signs and the planets that fall within these interceptions are considered to be weakened, causing delays in the development of matters ruled by these houses.

Jupiter—The largest planet in the solar system, Jupiter's energy is considered to be beneficent, generous, and expansive. It rules the sign Sagittarius.

Kite—When one of the three points of a Grand Trine has a fourth planet in opposition, so that it is in sextile to the other two points, it is called a Kite, a configuration that is more rare than a Grand Trine and considered to be much more beneficial because it focusses the energies of the entire configuration toward the planet being opposed by the fourth planet.

Leo—The fifth sign of the Zodiac, Fixed in nature, it is the sign that appears when the summer is at its peak. It is a Fire sign, and is the most willful, egocentric of the signs. It is ruled by the Sun.

Libra—The seventh sign of the Zodiac, Cardinal in nature, it is the sign that appears at the Autumn Equinox, signalling the beginning of fall. It is an Air sign, and seeks to balance between Self and others. It is ruled by Venus.

Lilith—According to legend, the earth had another satellite before the Moon, just as Adam had another wife before Eve. Both were named Lilith. Supposedly God cast Lilith out into the darkness because she destroyed her children. A specific orbit around the earth is assigned to Lilith, and the position it would have occupied is known for each day, so positions within individual charts can be calculated. Wherever Lilith occurs in a chart, she has a tendency to deprive or deny.

Lunar Eclipse Point—When a Lunar Eclipse occurs in the nine months preceding birth, the point (degree and sign) where the eclipse occurred is noted in the individual natal chart. It is linked to either the North or the South Node of the Moon, and therefore is involved in one's karma, representing emotional matters that one must develop or rid oneself of during this lifetime.

Mars—The fourth planet in order from the Sun, with its orbit just beyond that of the earth. In astrology, it is considered to represent the masculine principle, energy, the sex drive, and anger or hurtfulness. It rules the sign Aries.

Mercury—The smallest planet in our solar system, and the closest to the Sun. In astrology, it is considered to represent the mind, communication, travel, and manual dexterity. It rules two signs, Gemini and Virgo.

Midheaven—The degree of the sign directly overhead at the time of one's birth. In the individual chart it represents the cusp of the Tenth House, which governs public recognition, success, and the father.

Moon—One of the two luminaries, the other being the Sun. In astrology, it is considered to rule the emotions, the Mother and women in general, and productivity. It rules the sign Cancer.

Mutable Signs—Gemini, Virgo, Sagittarius, and Pisces are the four Mutable signs. They occur ninety degrees apart and so are in square or opposition to each other. Each occurs at the end of a season, as the season begins to change—Gemini at the end of spring, Virgo at the end of summer, Sagittarius at the end of autumn, and Pisces at the end of winter. For this reason the Mutable signs are considered changeable and adaptable in nature, very much concerned with adjusting to the needs of the moment and to the pressures from others.

Nadir—The degree and sign exactly opposed to the Midheaven, and considered to be the weakest point in an individual's chart. It is the cusp of the Fourth House, which represents home, mother, real estate, and the circumstances surrounding death.

Neptune—The third largest planet in our solar system, and one of the two furthest from the Sun, Neptune is considered to govern imagination, creativity, fantasy, alcohol, drugs, oil, gases, and water. It rules the sign Pisces.

Ninth House—In a horoscope, the Ninth House rules higher education, philosophy, travel, and publishing. In the standard chart, the Ninth House is ruled by Sagittarius.

Nodes—(See North Node, South Node)

North Node—On the ecliptic the point furthest north that the Moon reaches in its orbit is considered the North Node. When the Moon reaches this point, there is generally an eclipse, either lunar or solar, depending upon whether it occurs at the New Moon or the Full Moon.

Opposition—When two planets are positioned roughly 180 degrees apart — in opposing signs and houses — they are considered to be in opposition. This is usually a stressful aspect, though ultimately there can be benefits.

Part of Fortune—In Arabic astrology, there are a number of mathematical points that are calculated to signify special facets of one's fate. Some of these are the Part of Spirit, the Part of Love, the Part of Marriage, the Part of Friends, the Part of Commerce. The only one that is utilized in western astrology is the Part of Fortune, which is calculated by adding the degree and sign of the Ascendant to the degree and sign of the Moon and subtracting the degree and sign of the Sun. In one's chart, it is to the Moon what the Ascendant is to the Sun.

Pisces—The twelfth sign of the Zodiac, Mutable in nature, it is the sign that occurs at the end of winter, just as the season is about to change to spring. It is a Water sign, and the most spiritual of the signs. It is ruled by Neptune.

Pluto—One of the two planets furthest from the Sun, Pluto in astrology governs sexuality, the subconscious mind, death, organized crime, and all things that are hidden. It rules the sign Scorpio, and its purpose in a sign or house is often to destroy the status quo in order to rebuild on a better basis.

Quincunx—When two planets appear roughly 150 degrees apart, they are considered to be in quincunx aspect. Thirty degrees away from an opposition, but also thirty degrees away from a trine, the effect of a quincunx is considered to be a somewhat odd combination of energies.

Retrograde—Because the Sun and the planets do not in fact revolve around the earth, but the earth revolves around the Sun along with the other planets, at some times of the year certain planets appear to stop and turn backward in their course through the Zodiac. At such times they are considered retrograde.

Rising Sign—(See Ascendant)

Rulership—(See the specific signs for the specific planetary ruler of each)

Sagittarius—The ninth sign of the Zodiac, Mutable in nature, it is the sign that occurs at the end of autumn, just before the change to winter. It is a Fire sign, and is considered expansive (also excessive), liberal, and generous. It is ruled by Jupiter.

Saturn—The sixth planet in order from the Sun, it is famous for its rings. In astrology, Saturn is responsible, restrictive, concerned with time and the past. It rules the sign Capricorn.

Scorpio—The eighth sign of the Zodiac, Fixed in nature, it occurs at the peak of autumn, when the season seems most unchanging. As such, it is stubborn and resistant to change. It is a Water sign, and it governs matters of sex, partnership finances, inheritance, and death. It is ruled by Pluto.

Second House—In a horoscope, the Second House rules one's income, money, possessions, and capacity for love. In the standard chart, the Second House is ruled by Taurus.

Semi-sextile—When two or more planets appear in consecutive houses, roughly thirty degrees apart, they are considered to be in semi-sextile relationship. This is considered to be one of the least important aspects, but truly no aspect is unimportant.

Sextile—When two or more planets appear roughly sixty degrees apart, they are considered to be in sextile relationship. Because this is a combination of compatible elements (Fire and Air, Earth and Water), this is one of the most compatible of aspects.

Seventh House—In a horoscope, the Seventh House rules partnership, open enemies, legal activities, and other people in general. In the standard chart, the Seventh House is ruled by Libra.

Sixth House—In a horoscope, the Sixth House rules work, service, health, employers, employees, diet, pets, clothing, and medicine. In the standard chart, the Sixth House is ruled by Virgo.

Solar Chart—When the date of birth is unknown, but the precise time is not, the only kind of chart that can be erected is called a Solar Chart. It places the Sun at the Ascendant, with the houses divided accordingly.

Solar Eclipse Point—When a Solar Eclipse occurs in the nine
months preceding birth, the point (degree and sign) where
the eclipse occurred is noted in the individual natal chart.
It is linked to either the North or the South Node of the
Moon, and therefore is involved in one's karma, representing ego concerns that one must develop or rid oneself of
during this lifetime.

Solstices—(See Summer Solstice, Winter Solstice)

South Node—On the ecliptic, the point furthest south that the
Moon reaches in its orbit is considered the South Node.
When the Moon reaches this point, there is generally an
eclipse, either lunar or solar, depending upon whether it occurs at the New Moon or the Full Moon.

Spring Equinox—The position of the Sun that signals the beginning of spring and the beginning of the sign Aries. It is
the time when the position of the Sun is such that the nights
and days are of equal duration, but after which the days
grow longer.

Square—When two or more planets appear ninety degrees
apart in signs of the same nature (Cardinal, Fixed, Mutable), they are said to be square. It is considered to be a
stressful relationship, but a productive one, for the native
must strive to overcome the difficulty it presents.

Summer Solstice—The position of the Sun that signals the
beginning of summer and the beginning of the sign Cancer.
It is the time when the position of the Sun is such that the
days are at their longest and the nights at their shortest.

Sun—One of the two luminaries in astrology, the other being
the Moon. It is considered to represent the individual's
will and ego, and of course is beneficent. The Sun rules the
sign Leo.

Sun Sign—The astrological sign the Sun appears in at the
time one is born. It is the sign that defines one's ego and
how one expresses his will, while the Ascendant, or Rising
sign, defines one's Self, appearance, and personality.

T-Square—When two planets are in opposition to each other
(180 degrees apart) and a third planet is halfway in between

(90 degrees from each of the other two), they are said to
form a T-square. This is considered to be far more beneficial than having a Grand Cross, for the planet in the middle
mediates the stressful connection between the other two opposing planets.

Taurus—The second sign of the Zodiac, Fixed in nature, Taurus occurs when spring is at its peak, when it seems unchanging. It is an Earth sign and represents the materialistic
possessions of the individual, as well as a loving and giving
nature. It is ruled by Venus.

Tenth House—In a horoscope, the Tenth House rules, public
opinion, public recognition, success, politics, business, career, and the father. In the standard chart, the Tenth House
is ruled by Capricorn.

Third House—In a horoscope, the Third House rules communication, writing, education, short distance travel, the
neighborhood, and brethren. In the standard chart, the
Third House is ruled by Gemini.

Transiting Planets—In their course through the heavens, the
planets move through the signs of the Zodiac. Their movement through a sign is called a transit. The way one's daily
horoscope is calculated is to relate the transits for that day
to the natal chart.

Trine—When two or more planets are in aspect roughly
ninety degrees apart, in signs of the same element (Fire,
Earth, Air, Water), they are said to be trine. The trine is
considered to be a beneficial aspect because the planets are
working through the same nature.

Twelfth House—In a horoscope, the Twelfth House rules
spiritual regeneration, isolation, solitude, self-destruction,
restraints, and service in or to institutions such as hospitals,
prisons, or the military. In the standard chart, the Twelfth
House is ruled by Pisces.

Uranus—The seventh planet from the Sun, Uranus represents
freedom, upheaval, abrupt changes, violence, genius, scientific advancement, and homosexuality. It rules the sign
Aquarius.

Venus—The second planet from the Sun, Venus is considered to govern love, beauty, art, aesthetics, and the womanly feminine nature. It rules two signs, Taurus and Libra.

Virgo—The sixth sign of the Zodiac, Mutable in nature, Virgo is the sign that signals the end of summer, as the change to autumn is about to take place. As such it is quite adaptable, and represents the need of the individual to serve others. It is ruled by Mercury.

Water Signs—Cancer, Scorpio, and Pisces constitute the Water triplicity. Of the twelve signs, they form a trine, 120 degrees apart from each other. Water signs are considered to be primarily spiritual or sensual in nature. While they are all of the same element, each is of a different nature. Cancer is Cardinal, Scorpio is Fixed, and Pisces is Mutable.

Winter Solstice—The position of the Sun that signals the beginning of winter and the beginning of the sign Capricorn. It is the time when the position of the Sun is such that the days are at their shortest and the nights at their longest.

BIBLIOGRAPHY

General Sources

Bartolet, Sam, *Eclipses and Lunations in Astrology*
(American Federation of Astrologers, no date).

Brau, Jean-Louis, Helen Weaver, and Allan Edmands,
Larousse Encyclopedia of Astrology (McGraw-Hill,
1977).

Davison, Ronald, *Synastry: Understanding Human
Relations Through Astrology* (Aurora, 1983).

Elenbaas, Virginia, *Focus on Neptune* (American
Federation of Astrologers, 1977).

Elenbaas, Virginia, *Focus on Pluto* (American Federation
of Astrologers, 1974).

Eshelman, James A., *Interpreting Solar Returns* (Astro-
Analytics, 1979).

George, Llewellyn, *A to Z Horoscope Maker and
Delineator* (Llewellyn, 1977).

Goodman, Linda, *Love Signs: A New Approach to the
Human Heart (2 vols)* (Harper & Row, 1978).

Grebner, Bernice Pill, *Lunar Nodes: New Concepts*
(American Federation of Astrologers, 1980).

Green, Jeff, *Pluto: The Evolutionary Journey of the Soul,
vol. 1* (Llewellyn, 1986).

Greene, Liz, *Saturn: A New Look at An Old Devil*
(Weiser, 1976).

Goldstein-Jacobson, Ivy M., *The Dark Moon Lilith in
Astrology* (Frank Severy, 1961).

Heimsoth, Karl Guenter, M.D., *Homosexuality in the
Horoscope* (American Federation of Astrologers, 1978).

Hickey, Isabel M., *Pluto or Minerva: The Choice is Yours*
(Fellowship House, 1977).

Jansky, Robert Carl, *Interpreting the Aspects* (Astro-Analytics, 1978).

Jansky, Robert Carl, *Interpreting the Eclipses* (Astro Computing Services, 1977).

Jay, Michael, *Gay Love Signs* (Ballantine, 1980).

King, Dr. Chancey D., *Sexual Behavior in the Zodiac: Choosing the Mate Happily* (American Federation of Astrologers, 1969).

Leo, Alan, *Jupiter: The Preserver* (Weiser, 1972).

Lowell, Laurel, *Pluto* (American Federation of Astrologers, 1979).

McCormick, John, *The Book of Retrogrades* (American Federation of Astrologers, 1975).

Mann, A.T., *The Round Art: The Astrology of Time and Space* (Galley Press, 1979).

Marks, Tracy, *The 12th House* (Sagittarius Rising, 1977, 1978).

Mason, Sophia, *Forecasting with New, Full, & Quarter Moons through the Houses* (Aquarian-Cancerian, 1980).

Paul, Helen, and Bridget Mary O'Toole, *Interpreting the Houses* (Astro-Analytics, 1976).

Roberts, Press and Ima, *Transits in Plain English* (Vulcan, 1975).

Robertson, Marc, *Using the Birth Chart to Determine Sex, Mind, & Habit Compatibility* (American Federation of Astrologers, 1975).

Rudhyar, Dane, *The Astrological Houses: The Spectrum of Individual Experience* (Doubleday, 1972).

Rudhyar, Dane, *The Lunation Cycle: A Key to the Understanding of Personality* (Shambhala, 1971).

Sakoian, Frances, and Louis S. Acker, *The Astrologer's Handbook* (Harper & Row, 1973).

Sakoian, Frances, and Louis Acker, *Transits of Saturn* (Sakoian, 1972).

Schulman, Martin, *Venus: The Gift of Love* (Golden Light, 1981).

Sepharial, *Eclipses* (Symbols & Signs, 1973).

Townley, John, *The Composite Chart: The Horoscope of a Relationship* (Weiser, 1974).

Townley, John, *Uranus* (Weiser, 1978).

Van Dam, Wim, *Astrology & Homosexuality* (Weiser, 1983).

Van Norstrand, Frederic, *Jupiter through the Signs* (Clancy, 1979, 1980, 1983).

Watters, Barbara H., *Sex & the Outer Planets* (Valhalla, 1971).

White, George, *The Moon's Nodes and the Importance in Natal Astrology* (American Federation of Astrologers, 1927).

Wilson-Ludlam, Mae R., *Lilith Insight: New Light on the Dark Moon* (Macoy, 1979).

Yott, Donald H., *Intercepted Signs & Reincarnation* (Weiser, 1977).

Sources Used in Calculating Horoscopes

Doane, Doris Chase, *Time Changes in the USA (revised edition)* (Quarto, 1973).

Dalton's Tables of Houses: Spherical Basis of Astrology (Macoy, 1975).

Longitudes and Latitudes in the U.S. (American Federation of Astrologers, 1945).

Pluto Ephemeris, 1773-2000 (Omega, 1969).

Simplified Scientific Ephemeris, 1910-1919 (Rosicrucian, 1918).

Simplified Scientific Ephemeris, 1920-1929 (Rosicrucian, 1920).

Simplified Scientific Ephemeris, 1930-1939 (Rosicrucian, 1930).

Simplified Scientific Ephemeris, 1940-1949 (Rosicrucian, 1939).

Simplified Scientific Ephemeris, 1950-1959 (Rosicrucian, 1940).

Simplified Scientific Ephemeris, 1960-1969 (Rosicrucian, 1959).

Simplified Scientific Ephemeris, 1970-1979 (Rosicrucian, 1976).

Index